CHANGE MANAGEMENT

A Guide to Effective Implementation

Biographies

James McCalman

Dr. James McCalman is Lecturer in Organization Design and Development at the Glasgow University Business School. He is the author of four books and several book chapters on change in organizations. Dr. McCalman has also taught and consulted widely in the areas of organization development, change management and teamwork training, including projects with several multinational organizations such as British Petroleum, Digital Equipment Corporation, Compaq Computers, and Guinness.

Dr. McCalman's current work at Glasgow includes MBA and undergraduate classes in International Management and Inter Personal Skills as well as training programmes for management educators. He has also had spells of teaching and consulting in the United States and Europe. His current research work concerns management behaviour in global organizations.

Robert A. Paton

Robert Paton is Director of Undergraduate Studies at Glasgow University Business School. He is also Lecturer in Management Studies specialising in Change and Operations Management. He is author of several book chapters and journal articles and has taught and consulted widely in the field of change management and its impact on small and medium-sized firms.

His current work at Glasgow involves the design and delivery of management development programmes for several UK-wide organizations. These include British Gas, Scottish Power, and the Post Office. He is also involved in developing new learning mechanisms and assessment procedures for teaching management at undergraduate level.

CHANGE MANAGEMENT

A Guide to Effective Implementation

James McCalman and Robert A. Paton
Glasgow Business School

P·C·P
Paul Chapman
Publishing Ltd

*The authors and publishers wish to acknowledge their debt to the Open University for permission to make extensive use of its course **P679** Managing Change, particularly in parts 1 and 2 of this book, and to Bill Mayon-White and Lewis Watson who wrote the original material.*

First published 1992

Paul Chapman Publishing Ltd
144 Liverpool Road
London N1 1LA

British Library Cataloguing in Publication Data

McCalman, J.
  Change Management: Guide to Effective
  Implementation
  I. Title II. Paton, R. A.
  658.4

ISBN 1-85396-155-8

Typeset by Setrite Typesetters Ltd, Hong Kong
Printed and bound by Athenaeum Press Ltd., Newcastle Upon Tyne, England.

This book is dedicated to recent additions to our clans:

Robert Stephen Paton
James Thomas Buchanan
Rachel Lynn Buchanan

Contents

PART 4   PRACTICAL CASES IN CHANGE MANAGEMENT

Acknowledgements

The ability to get on well with people is a distinct benefit in both teaching and writing about the management of change. We therefore need to thank a host of friends, colleagues and acquaintances who got on with us so well that they more or less wrote this book for us!

In particular, we wish to express our sincere gratitude to Sylvia Kerrigan for turning three or four disks into a manuscript. We would also like to thank Janet Gowans, Kirsteen Daly and Sylvia, again, for the production of tables and figures.

We would like to thank Dave Buchanan, Professor of Human Resource Management at Loughborough University Business School, who shared the research work for the Digital VLSI case study in Chapter 11. In a similar vein, we were asked a couple of years ago to write the study guide for the Open University Business School's course on Planning and Managing Change. This acted as a catalyst for the production of this book and we would like to thank the course development team, in particular, Lewis Watson and Bill Mayon-White, for providing us with this opportunity.

From a professional point of view we would like to thank the following for both their assistance and access to case study material:

Laurence V. C. Megson, Pat Kennedy, Charlie Docherty and Alan Russell of Digital Equipment Corporation.
Dough Riach, Keith Ellice, Steve Elms, and Jane Roberts at BP in Aberdeen.
Jim MacDonald, MTC Limited, Glasgow.
Argyll and Clyde Health Board, in particular Rosemary I. Jamieson, Information Manager.
British Gas (Scotland) plc, in particular James Kelly, Purchasing Manager.
Caledonian Airmotive Ltd, in particular David J. Crews.
Froud Consine Ltd and Babcock Industries plc, in particular Brian A. Wilson of Babcock Industries.
McGrigor Donald Solicitors, in particular Carole Thomson, Director of Administration.
John R. Agar.
Texstyle World Ltd, in particular John Gilchrist.
Vitafoam and Kay Metzler Ltd, in particular George Cook of British Vita plc.

We would also like to thank the staff of the Department of Management Studies, University of Glasgow, for their help during Jim McCalman's period of study leave which made the production of this book a more straightforward task than originally envisaged, in particular, Janet Gowans, David Boddy, Sheena Dobbie and Nan Gray.

James McCalman
Robert Paton
University of Glasgow
September 1991

Part 1

The Imperative and Definition of Change

1
Introduction: Change Management

A slightly irate MBA student came up to us at the end of a joint teaching session on Managing the Process of Change. The conversation was short because it was 9.30 p.m. on a Monday evening and she had a desire to return home after having spent a full day in her office and three and a half hours on our management of change course. The conversation went something like this:

MBA Student: 'You know, this management of change course isn't really teaching us anything we didn't know already. It's just putting it into a context that I never thought of. All this stuff about "hard" and "soft" change and technical, organizational and people change is really just common sense, isn't it?'

Jim McCalman: 'Yes, but we never claimed that it was anything else.'

MBA Student: 'So what's the point? I mean, what you're teaching us here is what management does on a day-to-day basis. We know that there are technical aspects to change and that there are people aspects as well. Sometimes you play on one and sometimes on the other.'

Robert Paton: 'I don't think it's as easy as saying there is a trade-off between one and the other. For example, how do you go about managing the bit in the middle, where the question of change is one of striking a balance between the two, as well as trying to reconcile this with how the organization as a whole responds to change?'

MBA Student: 'Oh yeah, your grey area. That's what we're paid for, isn't it? I mean, the problem parts in the middle create the biggest headaches. I know that, but what I don't understand is, if it's so easy to realize that a lot of the change that occurs in companies is going to be in the middle of this spectrum between "hard", technology issues and "soft", people issues, you know grey, indefinable, why is it such a problem to apply?'

Jim McCalman: 'Well, that's what this course is supposedly about, making you aware that solutions to change problems aren't always so clear-cut as you like to think they are.'

MBA Student: 'That's easy for you to say, you're not at the butt-end of the problems all the time. It's okay for me to come along here for three and a half hours each week and look at it from a viewpoint of 'here's the concept and here are some ways of tackling it', but when push comes to shove my manager wants results. A lot of the time he's not interested in how I get the result, he doesn't have to manage the mess of some of the board's decisions. That's the side I've got to deal with.'

Jim McCalman: 'Maybe you should suggest he does an MBA course.'

MBA Student: 'Ha! You're joking, he's already got all the answers.'

Jim McCalman: 'Yeah, but I never can resist touting for more business.'

To the extent that the conversation ended there, the situation remained unresolved. That is our purpose in writing this book; to try and begin to resolve some of the questions that MBA and undergraduate students ask when faced with the concept of the management of change. We have deliberately set this book out in a framework which offers models for tackling the different change scenarios facing organizations. However, we have also set out to provide examples of where the models are used, for the sake of reality. What we wanted from this book, for ourselves and for the reader, were four things:

(1) *Valid and defined models* for the effective management of change.
(2) *Proactive approaches* to change that relate to internal and external business performance.
(3) *Practical, step-by-step means* of handling change.
(4) *Illustrations* of the use and validity of the models through current, real-life case studies.

If we are successful, the reader will leave this book with the sense that the management of change is about the grey area; with the belief that solutions to change are never a *choice* between technological, organizational or people-oriented solutions, but involve combinations for best fit. In this sense, the management of change adopts the contingency approach to organizations: It all depends. However, recognition of what it depends on is the subject of this book.

THE IMPERATIVE OF CHANGE

Any organization which ignores the concept of change does so at its own peril. One might suggest that the peril will come sooner rather than later. The issues which face modern organizations in terms of internal and external criteria are such that business has to deal with what Schwartz (1986) terms 'visible evolution'. If we take an external perspective for a moment, the average modern organization has to come to terms with a number of issues which will create a need for internal change. At the point of writing, we can identify six major external changes that organizations are currently addressing, will have to come to terms with in the next two years, or will need to resolve before the end of the decade:

(1) *A bigger global market-place made smaller by increasing competition from abroad*. The liberalization of Eastern European states, the creation of a single European community market by the end of 1992, the establishment

of a unified Germany, the increasing spread of Japanese multinational enterprises, the rise in newly industrialized countries such as Korea, and reductions in transport and communication costs mean that the world is a different place from what it was. How does the individual organization respond to the bigger picture?

(2) *A world-wide recognition of the environment as an influencing variable.* The legal, cultural and socio-economic implications of realizing that resource use and allocation is a finite issue and that global solutions to ozone depletion, toxic waste dumping, raw material depletion, and other environmental concerns will force change on organizations, sooner rather than later. How does the individual organization respond to the bigger picture?

(3) *Health consciousness as a permanent trend amongst all age groups throughout the developed world.* The growing awareness and concern with the content of food and beverage products has created a movement away from synthetic towards natural products. Concerns have been expressed about salmonella in eggs and poultry, listeria in chilled foods, 'mad cow disease', aluminium in soya-based baby milk, lead levels in petroleum, and bleaching agents in cleaning and hygiene products. How does the individual organization deal with a health-conscious market?

(4) *The demographic slump means there are fewer 16−19 year-olds to go round.* In 1971 there were 900,000 births in the United Kingdom. Since then the figure has failed to reach 800,000 in any subsequent year. By 1994 there will be half a million fewer youngsters in the 16−19 age group. How does the individual organization cope with a smaller consumer market or restricted labour force?

(5) *The changing workplace and skills shortages create a need for non-traditional employees.* Estimates are that by the year 2000 70 per cent of jobs will be brain ones and only 30 per cent will be manual. There is a lack of graduates going into higher education. By 1992 European-wide competition will be heightened. In order to make up the shortfall, organizations currently resort to poaching staff from other companies. However, a greater proportion of the population who have not been traditional employees (e.g. women with school-aged children) will need to be attracted into the labour force. Equal opportunity in pay *and* non-pecuniary rewards will be issues in the future. How will the individual organization cope with these pressures?

(6) *Women in management will be the trend in the 1990s.* The current shortage of graduates is leading to a greater recruitment of female management trainees. In less than ten years' time these managers will occupy posts of increased responsibility. The general shortage of graduates will accelerate the trend towards breaking the male monopoly of management positions. How does the 'macho' organization cope?

To the extent that we could have picked half a dozen other issues for discussion indicates the imperative for change in organizations. What is important, however, is recognition that change occurs continuously, has numerous causes, and needs to be addressed all the time. Lawler (1986, p. 232) sums this up quite effectively by noting that, 'Overall, planned change is not impossible, but it is often difficult. The key point is that change is an ongoing process, and it is incorrect to think that *visionary end state* can be reached in a highly programmed way.'

The difficulty is that most organizations view the concept of change as a highly programmed process which takes as its starting point the problem that needs to be rectified, breaks it down to constituent parts, analyses possible alternatives, selects the preferred solution, and applies this relentlessly — problem recognition, diagnosis and resolution. Simple, straightforward, and relatively painless. But what if the change problem is part of a bigger picture? For example, how does recognition, diagnosis and resolution address the problem of global warming; 'It's not our problem, we'll leave it for the politicians to sort out.' A simple and effective response, until the point in time when the political solution begins to have an organizational impact.

We are not suggesting here that all organizations need to come up with an answer that solves the problem of ozone depletion. This is a problem that nations will have difficulties trying to address. However, what we are trying to point out is that, as an issue, it creates an imperative for change in organizations. There are two ways of responding to that imperative. The individual organization can wait for legislation to hit the statute book and react to the legislation, or it can anticipate and institute proactive change. Most organizations will not. That's because they are geared and managed to run on traditional, analytical lines of decision making, 'If it ain't broke, why fix it?' What we would like to suggest here is that before it even gets to the point where a slight stress fracture appears, organizations should be addressing the potential implications of change scenarios, and dealing with them accordingly.

THE CAUSES OF CHANGE

What makes an organization want to change? There are a number of specific, even obvious, factors which will necessitate movement from the status quo. The most obvious of these relate to changes in the external environment which drive alteration. An example of this, in the last couple of years, is the move by car manufacturers and petroleum organizations towards the provision of more environmentally friendly forms of produce. Pettigrew's (1985) analysis of change at ICI attempted to identify what precipitates change. He pointed out that there were no clear beginnings and ends to strategic change. Environmental disturbances were seen as the main precipitating factor, but he also believed that these were not the sole causes of, or explanations of, change.

To attribute change entirely to the environment would be a denial of extreme magnitude. This would imply that organizations were merely 'bobbing about' on a turbulent sea of change, unable to influence or exercise direction. This is clearly not the case. Pettigrew (1985) went on to argue that changes within an organization take place both in response to business and economic events and to processes of management perception, choice and action. Managers in this sense, see events taking place that, to them, signal the need for change. They also perceive the internal context of change as it relates to structure, culture, the system of power, and control. This gives them further clues about whether it is worth trying to introduce change. But what causes change? What factors need to be considered when we look for the causal effects which run from A to B in an organization? We have already hinted at one cause of change — external, environmental trigger mechanisms which mean that the organization has to reposition itself to remain effective.

We would like you to think of changes that have occurred in your organization over the last year. How often were these changes the reaction to events that occurred outside your organization? For example, can you cite examples linked to your company's response to

- Changes in the level of technology used?
- Changes in customer expectations or tastes?
- Changes as a result of competitors' activities?
- Changes as a result of government legislation?
- Changes as a result of alterations in the economy?

(Huczynski and Buchanan, 1991, p. 527).

Internal changes can be caused as responses or reactions to the outside world and are regarded as external triggers.

There are also a large number of factors which lead to what are termed internal triggers for change. Organization redesign to fit a new product line or new marketing strategy are typical examples, as are changes in job responsibilities to fit new organizational structures.

The final cause of change in organizations is where the organization itself tries to be ahead of change itself by being proactive. For example, where the organization tries to anticipate problems in the market-place or negate the impact of world-wide recession on its own business, proactive change is taking place (Huczynski and Buchanan, 1991, p. 528).

THE ROLE OF TRANSITION MANAGEMENT

If the concept of change can be examined from an internal, external or proactive set of viewpoints, then the response of managers has to be equally widespread. Buchanan and McCalman (1989) suggest that this requires a framework of Perpetual Transition Management. Following from Lawler's (1986) concept of the lack of a visonary end state, what appears to be required is the ability within managers to deal with constant change. This transition management model, although specifically related to large-scale organization change, has some interesting insights into what triggers change in organizations, and how they respond. It suggests that four interlocking management processes must take place both to implement and sustain major organizational changes. These processes operate at different levels, and may involve different actors in the organizational hierarchy. The four layers are:

(1) *The trigger layer* concerning the identification of needs and openings for major change deliberately formulated in the form of opportunities rather than threats or crises.

(2) *The vision layer* establishing the future development of the organization by articulating a vision and communicating this effectively in terms of where the organization is heading.
(3) *The conversion layer* setting out to mobilize support in the organization for the new vision as the most appropriate method for dealing with the triggers of change.
(4) *The maintenance and renewal layer* identifying ways in which changes are sustained and enhanced through alterations in attitudes, values, and behaviours, and ensuring regression back to tradition is avoided.

The suggestion that transition management has to plan, divert resources to, and implement four sets of interlocking processes designed to implement, to sustain, and to build on change and its achievements is an attempt to address the issues associated with change over time. The argument here is that these layers – trigger, vision, conversion, and maintenance and renewal – are necessary processes that occur in change management. The respective emphasis and priority attached to each of them will alter over time, but recognition of their existence goes a long way in determining the management action needed.

The model of perpetual transition management starts out with a number of questions. How do we explain successful change? How do we explain attempts at change in organizations that were doomed from the start? How do we explain change that is initially successful but wanes or fizzles out half-way through? Effective large-scale change demands a series of management actions linked to the four interlocking layers or processes. See Figure 1.1.

In terms of the trigger layer, it is necessary to understand what is causing a need for change in the organization. These triggers need to be expressed in a clear way and communicated throughout the organization. For example, unsuccessful trigger identification and communication processes are best seen when the first that employees know of the difficulties facing the organization is when they are called in to discuss redundancy terms. People are generally willing and able to deal with change but many managers do not understand this. They are afraid that change is associated with some form of failure and they need to hide the changes that are needed in some form. People will accept change when they know it is necessary and accept the explanation for the need for change.

It is necessary for these triggers to be expressed and communicated throughout the organization in clear and identifiable terms. This may appear as simple logic but it is important to recognize elements such as language during this process. For example, the trigger in many organizations is often á crisis, but it does not necessarily have to be a threat. People will respond to the challenge of a crisis but may react negatively to a threat. Expressing any potential crisis as an opportunity for change may assist the process itself. In this sense, the language in which the triggering mechanism is transmitted to the internal organization has to be clearly expressed as opportunity, and communicated widely. The chances of successfully implementing change are significantly increased when everyone concerned has a shared understanding of what may happen and why.

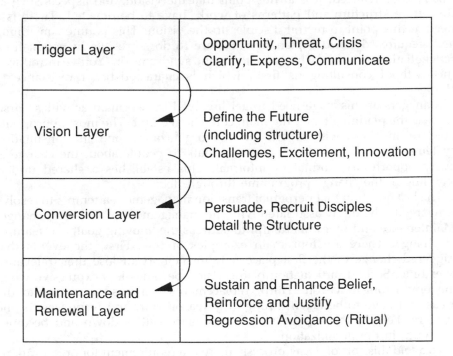

Figure 1.1 Buchanan and McCalman's model of perpetual transition management (Buchanan and McCalman, 1989, *High Performance Work Systems: The Digital Experience*, Routledge, London, p. 198).

If the trigger for change has been clearly recognized and expressed, it is also a requirement for management within the organization to define the future. This does not call for crystal ball gazing but for the establishment of a vision layer. The requirement here is for definition and expression of where the organization intends to go. Just as shared understanding and awareness of the triggers for change helps smooth the process, so does shared awareness and understanding of the new vision and the desired organizational goals. Management must visualize the future in terms of three criteria. The first is that change is seen to provide an effective response to the events triggering change. Second, there is identification of the desired future condition of the organization in terms of its design, its products and its goals. Finally, it must provide challenges and stimulation. Change is assisted by a climate of enthusiasm and participation. Resistance is a result of fear, prejudice, anxiety and ignorance.

The third layer of perpetual transition management is related to gaining recruits for the change. By this it is meant that those likely to have to work through the change process need to be converted to the ideas and concepts and own them as their own. Defining a future that no one can 'buy into' will slow or hinder the change itself. Everyone involved in making change work has to feel part of it and accept the reasoning for the vision and how this is to be realized. It is at this point that the vision, and aspects such as the future structure and patterns of work, have to be detailed. There is a need at this point to recruit disciples to the vision. This is time consuming as it requires detailed explanation. Failure to do so results in negotiation, renegotiation, or decay. This is related to the syndrome of, 'You've introduced this without consulting us first', which is characteristic of resistance to change.

Managers at this stage need to get involved in two main activities. First, there is the planning team, the main core-change unit. The most appropriate mechanisms here will depend on the organization and its consultation systems. Second, it is also necessary to talk to people about the change at every opportunity, formal or informal. This establishes a shared under-standing of the change programme through debate.

The last question that perpetual transition management attempts to resolve is related to the decay associated with the management of mid-term change. Maintenance and renewal attempt to address the 'moving goalpost' features of change. There are four main examples of this. First, the events that triggered change in the first place fade in memory or lose their relevance over time. Second, articulation of the vision becomes less expressive when the originators move on. Third, replacements feel less committed to the ideas and have to be taken through the reasons for, and responses to, the triggers. Fourth, the change which took place settles down and becomes the norm in the organization.

To avoid this sort of decay process, there is a requirement for organizations to allocate resources to maintaining and renewing the original visions in an evolutionary framework. In this sense, management takes part in a process which is described as one of permanent transition. It is this point that can be regarded as the crucial concept. Getting managers to recognize that change is a constant feature in modern organizations, and one which they have to deal with, goes a long way towards addressing some of the factors which lead to resistance to change.

OUTLINE OF THE BOOK

What we intend doing in the remainder of this book is to look at examples of change management from two different perspectives. The first analyses how management can deal with the 'hard' change issues from a systems design viewpoint. The second looks at 'soft' change issues from an organ-ization development outlook. Somewhere in the middle, the grey area, is where we try to balance the two.

In Chapter 2, the need to address the nature of change is introduced. All organizations, from both an external and internal basis, operate within dynamic environments. Prior to entering a change situation the manager must classify the nature of the change facing the organization. It is the 'nature' which will determine the initial approaches to the management process.

A number of tests and/or techniques are both introduced and demonstrated which permit the manager to place the particular change situation on a scale. This scale, termed the change spectrum, gives an initial indication of the nature of the transition. Is it technical and systems oriented? Is it 'soft' and people oriented? Depending upon the results of the classification the manager can determine the best route forward. Part 1 of the text explores systems-based solutions and Part 2 the 'softer', organizational development, approaches.

Chapter 2 also identifies key issues which must be addressed in any transition process and discusses the importance of the problem owner to the change event. The problem owner is the manager, or group, deemed to be responsible for the change process. They may operate and control the process of change through change agents, who are key players in the change environment. In Chapter 3, the means of identifying change agents and defining the change environment are fully discussed and illustrated.

A systems-based analytical approach, involving the use of diagramming techniques, is suggested in Chapter 3 as being one of the optimal ways to define a change environment. The diagramming tools covered within Chapter 3 may be employed to define an environment no matter what the classification of the change. Each diagram introduced is illustrated with a practical example of its application. The value of the diagrammatic approach to change definition cannot be overstated. It offers a communications vehicle, analytical processes, planning and control aids, and a means of defining complex organizational environments.

In Part 2 of the book, we deal with systems intervention strategies and additional systems-based models and practical applications. In Chapter 4, the systems-based approach to change is discussed. The Intervention Strategy Model (ISM) is introduced and its processes discussed. This model is designed to tackle change from the 'hard', technical, end of the change spectrum, although, as we will see, it may be employed to deal with 'softer', people-related issues to quite some effect. The origins and justification of the model are discussed and this is followed by a sequential review of the model's component parts. Application issues, along with 'dos and don'ts', round off this chapter.

Chapter 5 is dedicated to the exploration of practical issues which illustrate each stage of the ISM. The key implementation issues and management processes associated with the model are illustrated by a number of mini-cases, which are topical from both change and business perspectives.

The model, along with a number of project management techniques, is developed within Chapter 6 to address project-specific issues. To a greater or lesser extent all managers are in fact project managers. Chapter 6 introduces a management process entitled Total Project Management, a product of the Glasgow Business School, which addresses the whole issue of project management. This chapter describes the process, and outlines its rationale. Total project management develops the technical, mechanistic elements associated with network analysis to incorporate the 'softer', people-oriented issues which are present in most major projects. Very often it is poor people management, not the degree of technical competence, which leads to less than effective project implementations.

In Chapter 7, we examine the need for an organization development model for change. In many Western organizations, the concept of management is so restrictive that control and decision-making operates as a hindering device on performance. The belief is that management and workforce are separate entities that sometimes come together to manufacture product or deliver services, but often act as polar opposites in some form of industrial struggle for superiority. Chapter 7 puts forward the proposition that it does not have to be like this. By examining some of the basic concepts of design and development, organizations can begin to combine the needs of the individual worker with those of business to find a mission which results in effective performance. This effective performance is reflected in results which are categories in terms of numbers – profits, sales revenue, etc. – but also in terms of the quality of working life. However, to achieve this, managers have to suspend some of their inherent assumptions about work organization, the nature of work and how they attain commitment from the work force. The basis of design is couched in the organization and its mission. As Matsushita (1984) comments, there has to be more to life than profit:

> Every company no matter how small, ought to have clear-cut goals apart from the pursuit of profit, purposes that justify its existence among us. To me, such goals are an avocation, a secular mission to the world. If the chief executive officer has this sense of mission, he can tell his employees what it is that the company seeks to accomplish, and explain its *raison d'être* and ideals. And if his employees understand that they are not working for bread alone, they will be motivated to work harder together toward the realization of their common goals.
>
> (Matsushita, 1984, p. 83)

To be able to manage change effectively, organizations need to be able to go through a process of identifying possible faults, looking at alternatives to the current situation, weighing up the pros and cons of these alternatives, reaching decisions on the future state of the organization, and implementing the necessary changes. This clear-cut and simplistic summation belies the pain and suffering that is often caused by the instigation of change. The resentment that is often felt during the management of change is not resentment to change *per se* but to the processes by which it is managed. Where people are involved, the potential for pain and the likelihood of resistance are increased tenfold. Peters and Waterman (1982), sum this up quite succinctly in their inimitable fashion. 'The central problem with the rationalist view of organizing people is that people are not very rational. To fit Taylor's model, or today's organizational charts, man is simply designed wrong (or, of course, vice versa, according to our argument here).'

In Chapter 8, we examine the Organization Development Model (ODM) for managing change. In this, we look at how organization development can assist the move from a situation which is regarded as undesirable to a new state which, hopefully, is more effective. The key to the ODM is looking at what change is required, what level the change takes place at, who is likely to be involved, and the processes by which change is instigated. Chapter 8 outlines the techniques of organization development and the steps that the change agent is likely to be involved in.

The concept of a change agent is similar to that of the problem owner, identified in Part 2 of the book. We change the name, not to protect the innocent but to imply significance to the role. In Chapter 9 we examine the role of the objective outsider. The ODM suggests the need for individuals from outwith the area of change in the organization who display a number of unique characteristics. Chief amongst these are their ability to remain impartial or neutral and their ability to facilitate the process of change needed within that organization. Chapter 9 sets out the need for a change agent in terms of what managers, and organizations as a whole, can and cannot do.

In Part 4 of the text we move on to deal with in-depth practical issues illustrating the application of both the intervention strategy and organizational development approaches. Chapter 10 develops three cases which were first introduced in Chapters 3 and 5, namely, the Argyll and Clyde Health Board, Caledonian Airmotive and British Gas plc. Each case illustrates a different aspect of the ISM and they are concluded by a review of the key learning experiences.

The organization development case studies look at the management of change from three different criteria. Case 4 cites a specific work organization change process at Digital Equipment Corporation. Case 5 looks at the environmental impact of change on MTC Ltd. Case 6 provides the reader with an opportunity to put forward a proposal for managing an organization development process.

2
The Nature of Change

INTRODUCTION

A manager, or individual, whether at work, home or play, when faced with a change situation must firstly, no matter how informally, analyse the nature of the change. Only by considering the nature of the change can we determine its likely magnitude and potential impact. Successful determination of the nature of the change, at an early stage of the change cycle, should indicate the most appropriate means of managing the change and therefore allow the pre-emptive marshalling of forces.

One must be aware that a full definition of the change environment is required prior to the final selection of a change management methodology. Defining a change environment is the subject of Chapter 3. It would be foolhardy for the manager responsible for the effective planning and control of a transition process to base their approach only on consideration of the generic nature of the change. There are many factors and considerations which must be taken into account prior to selecting a solution methodology.

The aim of this chapter is to provide a means of evaluating the nature of an impending change situation so as to facilitate the marshalling of management expertise in readiness for the transition process. This will be accomplished by examining five areas of management analysis and significance associated with successful change classification. They will be considered under the following headings:

(1) The selection and role of the problem owner. The right person for the job in terms of their managerial skills, involvement and commitment to the problem or project.
(2) Locating change on the change spectrum. Determining the nature of the change with regard to both its physical and organizational impact. Is it, for example, a purely technical or a more complex people-related change?
(3) The TROPICS test. A quick, yet effective, means of addressing the following key factors affecting the classification of a change situation: Time scales, Resources, Objectives, Perceptions, Interest, Control and Source. By considering the change in relation to the above factors the manager responsible may determine, through an enhanced knowledge of the nature of the change, the optimal route forward.
(4) Force field analysis: a positioning tool. A diagramming technique which assists in answering questions such as: What forces are at play and what are their likely magnitude? Who is for the change and who is against? Can a proactive stance be adopted? The aim is to determine the nature and magnitude of the forces acting upon the change environment.

(5) Success guarantors: commitment, involvement and the shared perception. Successful change management requires an understanding of the likely impact of the change on those systems most affected by it, and thereafter the development of a means of establishing a shared perception of the problem amongst all concerned. The commitment and involvement of those charged with managing the change and those affected by it are crucial to achieving effective transition management.

THE ROLE AND SELECTION OF THE PROBLEM OWNER

How does one become a problem owner? There are essentially two routes. The first is the most straightforward and will positively influence the managers' evaluation of the change situation. Effective managers monitor their environment. By doing so, they may identify change situations developing on the horizon, and as identifiers of the change they, at least initially, become the change owners. Such ownership of the change will lead to a more positive evaluation of its nature in relation to the degree of 'threat' associated with its arrival. Early identification and ownership tends to increase the probability of a change being seen in an opportunistic manner and therefore possibly being considered to be less threatening.

It must be noted that ownership of the change by a single change agent as outlined above does not ensure that all those ultimately affected by the change will identify with the owner's positive evaluation. Later chapters investigate the important role which organizational culture plays in the management of change. In organizations, be they industrial, commercial or social, where an effort has been successfully made to secure a culture which exhibits both enterprising and democratic characteristics, along with a shared view of both the internal and external environment, one may expect to find an almost automatic sharing of the problem owner's initial view of the change.

The other route to problem ownership is the traditional one of delegation. The need for change is identified elsewhere and the problem owner is appointed by more senior management. 'Ownership' does not belong to the individual or group charged with the management of the change and they simply become change minders rather than change agents. Such situations are unlikely to produce positive opportunistic evaluations of the nature of the change, as it is difficult to be proactive and positive when you have been 'left holding the baby', possibly without a clear understanding of what is required. This can lead to rather messy situations developing!

For delegation to be effective in a change context, or for that matter in management in general, it must be accompanied by both an educational process and a selling exercise designed to pass over the ownership, responsibility and capability for the task at hand. Again, organizational culture plays a crucial role in determining the success of devolved ownership. When one feels part of a team working towards common goals then delegated problems will be viewed as common to all; if alienation and confrontation exist within the work place then achieving devolved ownership may be a long process.

Problem ownership affects our perception of a change situation. Positive feelings of ownership will result in a more opportunistic evaluation of the nature of the change whereas delegated ownership, which has been managed poorly, will highlight the threats and disrupt existing positions. The problem owner plays a pivotal role in the successful management of change. Given the obvious advantages of securing a proactive stance towards the change situation it is essential to identify the most effective problem owner. They must possess both the skills to manage the transition process and the determination to see the change through.

All too often the problem owner is selected for their proven management skills in the general field of project management. It must be noted that this does not guarantee that they possess ownership of the problem at hand and are therefore motivated towards achieving the change objectives. An additional difficulty may arise if their 'skill' is of a technical or process nature. Successful change management requires far more than the understanding of network analysis and budgetary control. Alternatively the selection decision may be based on who is least busy, resource constraints rather than logic determining the problem owner. The problem owner must be directly involved in the change process and must see clear linkages between their future success and the effective implementation of the change.

A positive problem ownership is clearly an important factor associated with successful change management. As ownership need not be directly linked to management ability and position, then it may on occasion, other factors permitting, be advisable to invest resources in developing the necessary management skills and providing additional support to the most appropriate problem owner(s). One volunteer is worth a hundred conscripts.

Often problem owners identify themselves, since they have initiated the change process. No matter what their position within the hierarchy, in an ideal world, the initiator should own the process. In circumstances where the individual or individuals at the core of the change do not have necessary skills, authority or resources to manage the change process, then management must facilitate the change in such a way as to ensure their continued commitment and involvement. Initiators, although not directly involved in the actual management of the change, are generally still the problem owners and as such make committed and useful advocates of the change. When the pivotal role of problem owner has to be delegated and/or assigned, then every care must be taken to select according to a detailed examination of the systems affected and the nature of the change. Such a key role should not be assigned solely to an individual or group from without the affected system.

The manager responsible for the change has to this point been termed the 'problem owner'. Similar terms in common usage would include 'change agent', 'project manager' and 'transition manager'. The terminology is relatively unimportant, their role is not. The previous paragraphs have hinted at the fact that the original problem owner may, for a number of reasons, not be the actual manager appointed to handle the change process. The remainder of this text, unless otherwise stated, will refer to the manager of the change process as the 'problem owner'. When, as is generally the case, the owner acts as part of a management team then the individuals concerned and the team as a whole will be termed 'change agents'.

LOCATING CHANGE ON THE CHANGE SPECTRUM

The nature of change influences our reaction to it; when a change is of a purely technical nature, such as a machine or component upgrade, then the expectation would be that existing systems-based knowledge would be applied in a mechanistic manner to implement the change.

Change which requires the problem owner to apply their existing knowledge base in a systematic manner to problems requiring technical solutions, with minimal inputs from other quarters, may be regarded as the management of change in a static and isolated environment. The management process is simplified as the impact is limited to a clearly identifiable and semi-autonomous component of a technical system. Systems-based technical problems which call upon the application of knowledge of a highly structured and mechanistic nature do not create major managerial difficulties. Solution methodologies are based firmly in the systems school of managerial decision making and analysis:

Definition:	(a) Objective clarification
	(b) Data capture and performance indicators
	(c) Systems diagnostics
	(d) Systems analysis
Design:	(e) Determination of solution options
	(f) Solution evaluation
Implementation:	(g) Solution implementation
	(h) Appraisal and monitoring

The basic building blocks of definition, design and implementation are applied to the problem by like-minded technocrats who measure success against quantifiable and well-defined performance indicators. A technical change requires a systematic analysis and a mechanistic solution. That is not to say the solution will be easily arrived at, as the degree of intellectual input and technical expertise is likely to be significant, but rather that the methodology employed will be well tried and tested.

Obviously, not all technical change situations are of the pure, totally systems-oriented variety described above. The mechanistic solution methodologies of the systems school of management can be applied to a wide range of systems-related problems and provide optimal solutions to system interventions. A truly technical problem would be placed at the extreme 'hard' end of the change spectrum as shown in Figure 2.1.

Purely technical change, 100% 'hard' or mechanistic change, exists towards the left hand side of the spectrum. It will be characterized by a reasonably static change environment, clear, quantifiable objectives and constraints, immediate implications, short time scales and minimal man−machine interfaces: in short, a purely scientific or engineering problem. Such problems are reasonably uncommon as some form of human interface, even if it is only an operative who lubricates and checks a machine periodically, can generally be found if one digs deep enough.

At the extreme 'soft' end of the spectrum, one finds change situations which have a 100% people orientation. Objectives and time scales will be

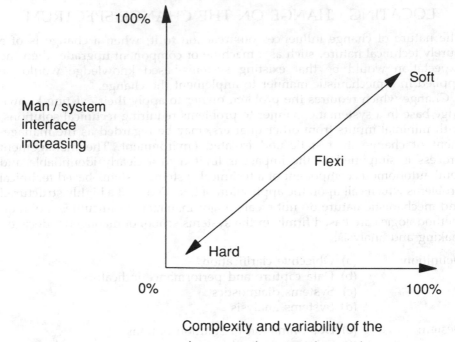

Figure 2.1 The change spectrum.

unclear, the affected environment will be highly dynamic and difficult to specify, with exceptionally subjective performance measures. Typical of the kind of problems found towards the 'soft' end of the spectrum would be ones in which personal relationships and emotional responses are predominant. As in the case of purely technical change, 100% people change is also uncommon, as most individuals and groups interface with systems of a physical nature.

Solution methodologies applied to the 'softer' end of the spectrum must reflect the highly volatile and dynamic nature of the change environment; they will originate in the organizational development school of thought. The systematic and mechanistic solution methodologies associated with scientific management will not provide answers to predominantly soft change situations. In fact they are more likely to create greater instability if applied.

By far the majority of change situations which managers are called upon to address fall within the 'flexi' region of the spectrum. A tendency towards either end of the spectrum indicates the appropriate solution methodologies which should be adopted. Part 2 of this book deals with systems-based approaches designed to deal with situations which tend towards the harder end of the change spectrum, and Part 3, entitled the Organization Development Model, tackles 'soft' change exhibiting characteristics associated with situations requiring a significant people-management input.

Table 2.1 'Hard' and 'soft' problem attributes

'Hard' problems	'Soft' problems
Quantifiable objectives, constraints and performance indicators.	Subjective and at best semi-quantifiable objectives, constraints and performance indicators.
Systems/technical orientation.	People orientation.
Limited number of potential solutions.	A wide range of potential solutions.
Clear problem definition.	Unclear problem definition.
Clear resource requirements.	Unclear resource requirements.
Structural solution methodology.	Variable solution methodology.
Reasonably static environment.	Dynamic environment.
Known time scales.	Fuzzy time scales.
Bounded problem with minimal external interactions.	Unbounded problem with many complex external interactions.

As often is the case in management, a contingency model or theory is required to cover all the *ad hoc* situations which may arise. Within the final sections of this book a contingency approach to change management will be argued. No single school of thought holds the answer to change management. One must not be afraid to adopt a systematic methodology when faced with a people-oriented, messy situation. It must of course be flexible enough to incorporate organizational development techniques and concepts, as and when appropriate, and if necessary abandon all pretexts of systems methodology in the face of an increasingly dynamic environment. Similarly the management of change centred on organization development practices can be enhanced through the adoption of systems-based solution techniques when more static environmental circumstances are encountered.

Table 2.1 highlights the attributes associated with change situations from both ends of the spectrum. It should help clarify the position regarding the classification of change.

A brief review of the factors associated with a pending change, conducted as seen fit by the problem owner, would be sufficient to classify the change position on the spectrum. Exact positioning is not required. The more complex the change, the greater the probability that the problem owner will have insufficient knowledge to conduct the investigation on an individual basis. The final topic of this chapter, Force Field Analysis, may assist in determining the appropriate management team to tackle the problem. This analysis may have to be augmented by the application of the diagrammatic techniques outlined in Chapter 3.

THE TROPICS TEST

The TROPICS test may be applied as an early warning device to access both the impact and magnitude of the impending change. It is capable of determining the most appropriate solution methodology for entering the change management process. This may have to be altered as the problem unfolds, by examining certain key factors associated with the transition process. It requires a minimal expenditure of management time and resources as it does not require detailed quantifiable information as input.

The factors which should be considered at as early a stage as possible by both the problem owner and any associated management team are as follows:

> Time scales,
> Resources,
> Objectives,
> Perceptions,
> Interest,
> Control,
> Source.

By considering TROPICS the manager, or the appropriately identified management team, will get a feel for the nature of the change and thus be able to establish the optimal route forward. Table 2.2 illustrates the use of TROPICS.

Table 2.2 The Tropics test

Tropics factor			Solution methodology (tendency towards.)
Time scales	Clearly defined/ short to medium term A	Ill defined/ medium to long term B	A = Hard B = Soft
Resources	Clearly defined/ reasonably fixed A	Unclear and variable B	A = Hard B = Soft
Objectives	Objective and quantifiable A	Subjective and mission orientated B	A = Hard B = Soft
Perceptions	Shared by those affected A	Creates conflict of interest B	A = Hard B = Soft
Interest	Limited and well defined A	Widespread and ill defined B	A = Hard B = Soft
Control	Within the managing group A	Shared outwith the managing group B	A = Hard B = Soft
Source	Originates internally A	Originates externally B	A = Hard B = Soft

Note: "Hard" refers to a systems-based solution methodology.
"Soft" refers to an organizational development methodology.

Managements faced with straight 'As' or 'Bs' are shown a clear path to a solution methodology of which they can be reasonably certain. TROPICS can only provide a starting point and a tentative indication of the generic type of methodology to follow. Difficulties arise when the output is garbled in some way, with the user facing a combination of 'As and Bs'. The examples below provide illustrations of combination outputs and suggest possible user interpretations:

Case A: time scale 'A', with all other factors 'B'

This scenario would indicate an emergency situation, a time of crisis. Organizational development models and concepts are called for but the time scale indicates a need for an 'immediate' solution. This would be a hard-hitting dictatorial solution to overcome the short-term difficulties, to be followed by a longer period of education and cultural change to gain acceptance of the new state.

Case B: source 'B', with all other factors 'A'

This could represent an external technical change to a system, possibly as a result of a manufacturer's technical update. A systems approach to implement the change along with a limited education programme for operatives and maintenance may be required.

Case C: control 'B', with all other factors 'A'

This may represent an internally driven change which requires external permission to proceed. A satellite plant may wish to diversify into product design rather than act as an assembly plant. A systems-based methodology may provide the answers to the internal systems' changes but it is unlikely to convince the parent organization of the need to change.

TROPICS offers the manager an efficient and effective means of entering the change situation. Inputs need not be based on hard factual evidence; all that is needed is an educated assessment of the likely impact of change and its general characteristics.

FORCE FIELD ANALYSIS: A POSITIONING TOOL

As we have seen in the previous sections it is important that the nature of the change facing the organization, department and/or problem owner is defined according to its position on the change spectrum. Force field analysis is a positioning tool which assists the management of change by examining and evaluating, in a basic yet useful manner, the forces for and against the change. Such analysis can then be incorporated in the spectrum positioning or the TROPICS test. It is also of use when considering the position of the problem owner and/or management team with reference to the power sources, both internal to and external to the change, which may influence their ability to effectively manage the situation.

The organization's, or individual's, view of a change situation will be strongly influenced by the source of the change and their position relative

Table 2.3 Features and attributes associated with the source of a change

Internally generated change	Externally generated change
Pro-active stance	Re-active response
Positive feelings	Negative feelings
Greater driving forces	Greater restraining forces
Viewed from an opportunity-exploitation position	Viewed from a problem-solving position
Greater certainty	Greater uncertainty
Greater control	Reduced control
Less disruption	Greater disruption
Closed boundaries and fixed-time scales	Vague boundaries and variable/unclear time scales

to it. Ownership of the problem or project is the key element in establishing our reaction to change. When an individual or group has initiated certain actions, which in turn have to be managed, then they are more likely to display positive attitudes towards the situation and view the whole transition process as an opportunity to be exploited.

When the feeling of ownership is combined with the knowledge that one controls the surrounding environment, then the driving forces for the change will be significant. However, one must be aware (the TROPICS test can be of assistance here) of the degree of control within the managing group. Control shared with others, especially those above in the hierarchy, when they exhibit greater restraining forces will lead to conflict and potential blockages.

Table 2.3 illustrates the attitudinal responses and key features which can be attributed to the source of a change.

Externally generated change generally produces the greatest degree of negative feedback from those affected. External change need not solely relate to change generated outwith the organization. A department, section or individual will regard external change as being any development forced upon them from outwith their own environment.

Proactive attitudes and actions permit the management of a situation in an opportunistic and progressive manner. A proactive management team identifies and exploits opportunities associated with a transition between two states well in advance of the environment impinging on them and forcing them into a negative, reactive stance.

A generic representation of a Force Field Diagram is illustrated by Figure 2.2. Please note that the format of the diagram is of little interest. The value of such a diagram is in its power to force the problem owner into considering the position of other power sources with regard to the change at hand.

By producing a force field diagram for each individual, group or function affected by the change, the problem owner can analyse the relative magnitude of the conflicting forces, as well as develop an understanding of the under-lying arguments, fears, and influencing factors associated with the change situation. The systems diagramming tools introduced in Chapter 3 will assist the identification of interested parties.

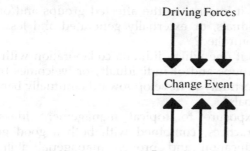

Figure 2.2 A force field diagram.

Generally speaking, change which has been generated by the 'system' most affected by the change is likely to produce driving forces which outweigh any restraining forces, the opposite being true for externally generated change.

SUCCESS GUARANTORS: COMMITMENT, INVOLVEMENT AND THE SHARED PERCEPTION

Possibly one of the most fundamental steps in achieving the successful implementation of change, is that of obtaining a shared perception amongst those affected, concerning their view of the issues and implications associated with the change. If the problem owner can reach a point at which all those parties with a vested interest in influencing and possibly determining the outcome of the proposed change view it in such a way as to see common objectives and mutual benefits, as well as understand or at least recognize the conflicting views and arguments, then a great deal of progress will have been made towards the successful conclusion of the change event.

One major obstacle to the formation of at least a partially shared perspective is the 'common sense' approach to both change management in particular and decision making in general. All too often individuals and groups attempt to sell their own particular brand of 'common sense' as if they are the only possible providers of wisdom and truth. Unfortunately, all individuals or groupings affected by a changing environment are bound to possess their own particular brand. All that can result from such an approach is a mini brand war, with no clear winners and a confused market.

There are a number of influential factors which will come together in such a way as to mould the way in which individuals, groups and organizations view particular change situations. The main factors are as follows and may be applied to all who are concerned and/or affected by the impending change.

(1) Organizational culture: Is it open or closed, enterprising or mechanistic, democratic or autocratic, progressive or entrenched, conducive to group work and common goals or oppressive?

(2) Source of change: Is it internal to the affected groups and/or individuals, or externally generated and less easily controlled?

(3) Social background: Is it one which inhibits collaboration with other groups and/or individuals, or welcomes the opportunity to develop towards mutually beneficial goals?

(4) Education history: Exposure to topical management ideas and practices, combined with both a good general education and proven managerial ability, or internally focused development reinforcing traditional practices and customs, working against prior educational understanding and external ideas.

(5) Employment history: Has historical experience coloured the way in which change will be viewed? Will the 'them and us' mentality interfere with the attainment of a shared perception?

(6) Style of management: The style of management exhibited by those directly involved in the change situation will obviously influence those whose co-operation and assistance they require. They may mirror the global organizational style of management, or possibly be at odds with it, but to be successful they must achieve general commitment and involvement within their terms of reference.

(7) Problem ownership: The importance of this problem owner, and where appropriate the management group, has been emphasized throughout this chapter. The involvement and commitment of the problem owner is essential, as is the managerial suitability of the problem owner to the task at hand.

(8) Experience: The track records identified with those individuals, groups and the organization affected by the change, judged in terms of their past ability to cope with change, will influence the expectations of all concerned. If experience of a particular situation is lacking then, culture and style permitting, external sources of expertise must be approached and engaged.

A crucial factor associated with successful implementation of change is the ability of the problem owner to overcome any personal prejudices regarding the change, while at the same time ensuring that the views and indeed prejudices exhibited by all other affected parties are taken on board, understood, countered or incorporated where appropriate, throughout the transition process in the solution.

To summarize, the problem owner must:

(1) Recognize that not all the suggestions offered and views expressed can be totally wrong, just as the problem owners are unlikely to be totally correct at all times.
(2) Ensure that they are seen to be actively encouraging collaboration. Change management of all but the simplest projects is a multi-disciplinary group activity; everyone must be pulling in the same direction.
(3) Be seen to have as much support and authority as possible. Senior management must be clearly identified with the project.

A change management consultant, while making a company presentation, provided the following quote which he attributed to Bertrand Russell, to emphasize the dangers of adopting a commonsense approach: 'When an intelligent man expresses a view which seems to us obviously absurd, we should not attempt to prove that it is somehow not true but we should try to understand how it ever came to seem true.' By following this advice the problem owner can begin the process of modifying perspectives through both education and understanding, moving along with those involved towards a shared perception of the situation and the ultimate solution of the problem.

3
Defining Change

INTRODUCTION

As we have seen in the previous chapter it is important that the nature of the change facing the organization, group or individual is defined according to its position on the change spectrum. The use of techniques such as the TROPICS test and Force Field Analysis, along with the need to consider the role and position of the problem owner and any other associated change agents, have been discussed in relation to the initial evaluation of a change situation. Physical or mechanistic change, exhibiting both systematized technical attributes and a low degree of man—machine/systems interface, should be addressed by adopting a systems-based solution model from the scientific management school. On the other hand, more complex and generally messy change, involving complex personalized relationships and organizational cultures, warrants the adoption of a more people-based model from the organizational development stable.

The solution methodology associated with both ends of the change spectrum is therefore identifiable through a relatively limited examination of the change environment. Unfortunately most change occurs within what has been referred to as the 'flexi' area of the spectrum. The application and consideration of the change factors and techniques discussed in Chapter 2 are insufficient to accurately determine the position of a situation where the environment exhibits multiple characteristics of both a 'hard' and 'soft' nature.

Messy change situations, those which may be classified as 'flexi', present management with a multitude of complex, interrelated and conflicting problems and issues. The 'mess' resembles, in its complexity of relationships, the structure of a spider's web. The spider builds a complex structure, which if the imagination is stretched, may be regarded as its organization. The structure of interdependent threads has the primary objective of satisfying the beast's appetite. The structure is organized in such a manner that it provides a collective strength which may be brought to bear against intruders, be they a potential lunch or an aggressive predator. An organization is built on a foundation of systems which, just like those of the spider, have a common primary role of some description and their systems should respond as one when faced by an intruder or indeed by change.

When a predator begins to snip away the threads of the web, its strength weakens. Initially the problem for the spider will be a structural one, classified as a 'hard' change; as the threads continue to be destroyed, the change moves along the spectrum to the 'soft' end. As the web disintegrates the primary objective becomes threatened and the spider will have to reappraise the situation. Once the destruction is almost complete, all that can be done with the remaining components of the system is to use them as a means of escape. For the primary objective to succeed, all the systems must be pulling effectively in the one direction.

The systems which constitute the organization in the 1990s are complex in their own right. They each have their own formal and informal objectives which, when managed effectively, collectively achieve the primary objective. Change of a significant nature in any one system, or in its relationship with others, may therefore impact on the total structure and eventually on organizational performance.

To understand the nature of a change situation which falls between the two extremities of the change spectrum, the systems and their relationships must be examined as a whole. When the interaction between the human resource and the system undergoing the change becomes significant in relation to the effective achievement of objectives, then the need to fully define the change in terms of its interactions with existing systems, individuals, groups, departments and the organization as a whole, becomes a necessity. How can management begin to cope with this complexity: to define, understand, and analyse complex change situations with the view to implementation? The answer, in part, is to represent complex change situations in diagrammatic form and view the whole process of change in systems terms.

This chapter examines a number of tools which facilitate the thorough definition, analysis and communication of the impact of messy change. The management tools covered may be applied to either 'hard' or 'soft' change situations and in so doing further the problem owners' understanding of the affected environment. They are often associated with systems change, due to their origins in systems analysis and design. It would be foolish to limit their use to systems change alone for they can be profitably employed as a precursor, providing valuable diagnostic information, to the adoption of an organizational development approach.

The change problem may be viewed in terms of the systems, and associated components and elements which it affects. Management can then represent the systems in terms of their physical and attitudinal characteristics, alongside the principal relationships, in diagrammatic forms. Thus the inherent complexity of the problem is reduced to manageable dimensions through diagrammatic systems representation. Diagramming conventions, such as those used by systems analysts and programmers, need not feature in change diagramming. What is required is consistency within studies and subsequently standardization within the management unit. If a standard format exists and is widely used by management then it should be adopted, possibly with modifications, within the planning and managing change process. What is important is that the diagrams assist in the definition, analysis and communication of the change event. Do not let preconceived notions of the complex nature of systems diagramming prevent you from employing such a powerful communication medium and analytical tool. The diagrams described and demonstrated in the pages which follow have been selected for their simplistic, yet powerful, analytical characteristics.

The principal construction and application rules which govern their usage remain more or less unchanged, no matter what the complexity of the problem. Formal conventions and terminology from the systems analysts' vocabulary have been intentionally ignored in an effort to reduce the entry barrier to non-systems readers.

No matter what your background or future career path, your analytical and communicative competence will be enhanced through effective utilization of diagramming skills. These simple techniques described in this section should be the starting point for experimentation in diagramming as an investigative tool and a communication medium.

If you followed the previous paragraphs, having had no need to pause for a while to deliberate the meaning of a passage and/or re-read to ensure understanding, then the written word has done its job. If, on the other hand, you had difficulty grasping the 'message' on first reading then the written word, or at least the author's usage of it, has failed. Diagrams can be used to simplify the written word, and they assist in definition, understanding and communication.

Figure 3.1 attempts to communicate, in a logical and concise manner, the major points raised in the last few paragraphs. The diagram simply and concisely explains that forces act upon a change situation, which is in turn integrated with the dynamic environment. This amalgamation must be defined. By viewing the amalgamation as a system and using diagrams to assist definition then we have a tool to facilitate definition, analysis and communication. Diagrams are useful tools. Let us now consider their role in systems investigations more fully.

THE ROLE OF DIAGRAMMING IN SYSTEMS INVESTIGATIONS

There are essentially four reasons why a problem owner, with or without an associated management team, should adopt certain diagramming techniques in their pursuit of effective change management:

(1) Diagramming, along with the systems approach, can bring a much needed sense of logic and structure to messy change problems.
(2) By adopting standardized diagramming techniques, the problem owner will develop a clear and concise view of change environments and at the same time introduce a change handling methodology. This will simplify and standardize future change investigations, as well as provide the basis of a systems specification and relationships library.
(3) Unfortunately, verbal or long-winded descriptions of messy change tend to be messy in their own right. They are often ineffective in terms of their ability to provide the listener or reader with a clear understanding and are generally limited in their use as analysis platforms for future deliberations. Diagrams assist the process of understanding by providing a clear and structured map of the problem and assist analysis and implementation by effectively illustrating potential developments and options.

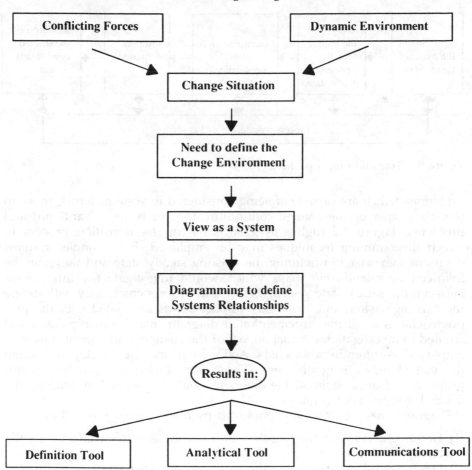

Figure 3.1 The need for diagramming.

(4) The communication of ideas/options is an essential component of the
    change management process. Diagrams can assist the communications
    process by providing a standardized, impersonal and credible interface
    between concerned parties.

In any problem-solving or systems analysis exercise one may find an
effective role for diagrammatically based analysis. It is in a manager's
interest to develop both a practical understanding of the available techniques
and a level of expertise in applying and exploiting them. A range of diagramming tools are available for use by the change management practitioner,
and they may be employed throughout the change management process.

Diagrams may be employed throughout the transition as Figure 3.2,
illustrates.

Diagrams may be employed to define fully the whole change process and
are particularly effective when applied to the solution of complex messy

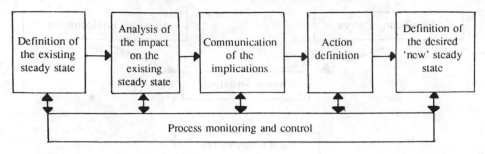

Figure 3.2 Transition process chart.

problems, which are capable of being considered in systems terms, those in the 'flexi' area of the change continuum and, of course, 'hard' physical problems. Figure 3.2 highlights each stage of the transition process in which diagramming techniques may be employed. For example, systems diagrams may assist in defining the existing steady state and they may be followed by relationship maps which would investigate the interactions between the steady state systems. Flow and process charts may both define the existing system and emphasize impact points associated with the proposed changes. All the aforementioned diagrams may be manipulated and studied to investigate the actual impact of the change, and they also may be employed as communications aids. Action steps may be developed through the use of networking diagrams. These would also be used to monitor progress and once again all the diagrams could be utilized in defining the desired systems configuration.

Diagrams may be profitably employed by management when they are:

(1) Defining and understanding the nature of those systems affected by the change (Before).
(2) Defining and understanding the nature of the desired solution/situation (After).
(3) Illustrating the means and stages associated with progress from the present to the desired situation (During).

In other words, diagrammatic representations may be used to assist the problem owner when they are engaged in:

- specification/definition;
- understanding;
- manipulation/modelling/analysis;
- communication;
- implementation;
- standardization.

The remainder of this chapter will deal with the most common and useful diagramming techniques. We will commence with those which are both simplistic, but reasonably powerful, with a wide range of general management applications, and conclude with more advanced and complex techniques associated, in the main, with systems investigations.

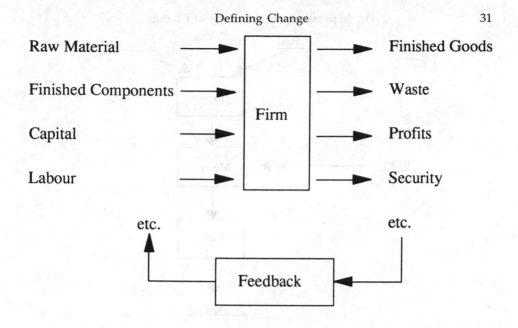

Figure 3.3 An input/output diagram with feedback.

A REVIEW OF BASIC FLOW DIAGRAMMING TECHNIQUES

Three of the most common and revealing techniques employed by change management practitioners deal with 'flow' analysis. First is the input/output diagram which provides an easy to follow means of investigating the input and output flows of physical materials and/or information with reference to any given system. The feedback mechanisms facilitating both control and performance measurement may also be included. Such a diagram is illustrated in Figure 3.3.

The second technique within this diagramming category is the traditional flow diagram, which permits the investigator to study the process steps and related activities, including interdependencies, associated with a particular system. Once again a pictorial representation provides a useful insight into a system at work as the example contained in Figure 3.4 illustrates.

Both the input/output and flow diagrams may be further developed to incorporate such information as:

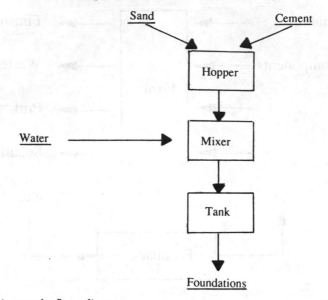

Figure 3.4 A sample flow diagram.

- Who does what and why?
- What information do they require and why?
- Where does the information come from − channels, formats, etc.?
- What factors influence systems/individual performance?

The last diagram of this section addresses the 'softer' issues associated with systems investigation through the medium of 'flow' analysis. Activity sequence diagrams consider issues and stages of a process or elements of a system which are of a non-physical/technological nature. For example, let us consider the purchase of a car depicted in Figure 3.5.

In such diagrams the activities associated with key decision points relating to a particular sequence of events are emphasized for subsequent study.

All three diagrams described in this section may be employed throughout the transition management process, to assist in the definition of the existing system, or to indicate the steps which must be taken in achieving the goal and finally that may be used to help specify the desired outcome.

Practical case: Argyll and Clyde Health Board

The Argyll and Clyde Health Board, due to their statutory obligations resulting from the introduction of the Government White Paper entitled *Working for Patients*, were required to ensure that the processing of their Scottish Morbidity Records (SMRs) was enhanced in line with the new performance targets specified within the White Paper.

The SMR is the document which records the details of each episode of care for a patient treated within a National Health Service hospital. The aggregated data for all patient transactions are used as the basis for research,

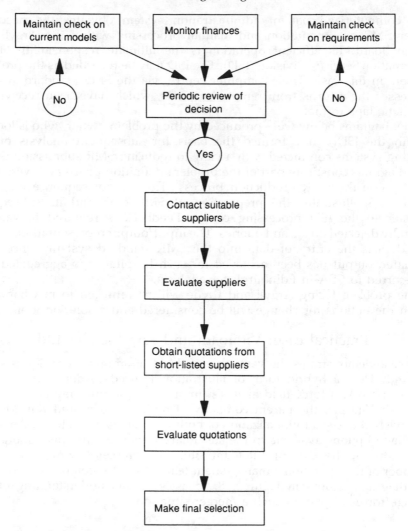

Figure 3.5 An activity sequence diagram.

epidemiological study and, possibly most importantly, as the basis for the planning and funding decisions taken by the centre for each individual Health Board.

From 1991 onwards, completed SMR data for each Scottish Board must be lodged with the Common Services Agency (CSA) of the Health Service in Edinburgh within two months from the completed collation of any given month's SMRs. The CSA collates the data for the 15 Scottish Boards and funding is subsequently allocated according to the number and types of patient treated. Prior to 1991 the performance target was somewhat more liberal, with SMR data for one year having to be submitted to the CSA by the mid-summer of the following year.

A computerized patient administration system obviates the need for paper SMR documentation and manual processing within the Argyll and Clyde Board. Its efficient operation is the ultimate responsibility of the Information Services Division (ISD). The ISD may be regarded as the problem owners in this case. Their computer centre, via the SMR standard system, processes the returns from remote hospitals, which have been received in magnetic tape format.

The diagrams below were produced by the problem owner, who is located within the ISD. They formed the basis for subsequent analysis of the existing systems conducted with a view to reducing SMR submission times. The diagrams constitute part of the problem definition phase and were used to illustrate the SMR production process. The activity sequence diagram, Figure 3.6, illustrates the preparation of SMR data and its subsequent transfer to the ISD processing centre. Feedback is required to validate centrally detected errors and queries. The input/output representation, Figure 3.7, depicts the entry of data into the SMR standard system. Once fully validated output has been achieved for each hospital, it is aggregated and transferred to CSA in Edinburgh for analysis.

The problem facing Argyll and Clyde will be returned to in Chapter 9, when the options for change will be considered and a solution identified.

Practical case: Vitafoam and Kay Metzler Ltd

This case demonstrates the versatility of the diagramming techniques so far covered. Here a hybrid form of illustration is used to depict the change forces at work, a force field analysis, in an input/output graphic.

British Vita plc, the parent company of both Vitafoam and Kay Metzler Ltd, wished to see a rationalization of both companies' operations. Amongst the many options available to the subsidiary organizations was a merger of operations at the current Vitafoam site. The problem owner, in 1990 a member of the operational management team at the Vitafoam site, produced the diagram, shown in Figure 3.8, to assist in his understanding of the change forces at play in such a merger situation.

SYSTEMS RELATIONSHIPS: THE KEY TO SUCCESS

To understand fully the nature of a particular change situation, a problem owner must consider the relationships which exist between those affected by the change. By developing a relationship map the problem owner may begin to appreciate the systems interfaces and complexities which are at work in the change environment.

By way of an example let us consider the relationship map in Figure 3.9, which may have applied in the recent privatization of steel (it is not intended to be comprehensive).

Practical case: Caledonian Airmotive Ltd

Caledonian Airmotive Limited (CAL), based at Prestwick Airport in Scotland, is a well-established company operating in the highly competitive inter-

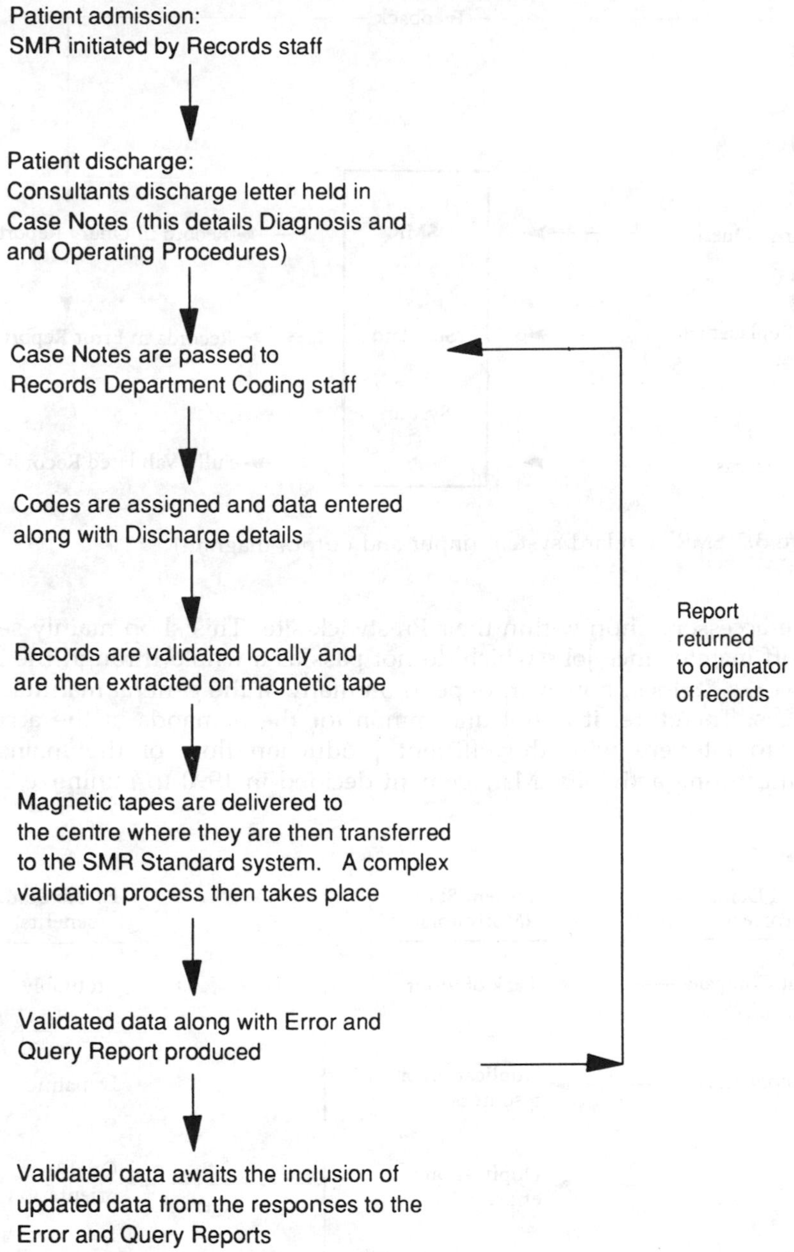

Patient admission:
SMR initiated by Records staff

Patient discharge:
Consultants discharge letter held in
Case Notes (this details Diagnosis and
and Operating Procedures)

Case Notes are passed to
Records Department Coding staff

Codes are assigned and data entered
along with Discharge details

Records are validated locally and
are then extracted on magnetic tape

Report
returned
to originator
of records

Magnetic tapes are delivered to
the centre where they are then transferred
to the SMR Standard system.   A complex
validation process then takes place

Validated data along with Error and
Query Report produced

Validated data awaits the inclusion of
updated data from the responses to the
Error and Query Reports

Figure 3.6 SMR production (activity sequence).

national business of aero-engine overhaul. The company is the subject of
one of the detailed system-related changes in Chapter 9.

As CAL will be dealt with in more depth in later chapters all we require
to know at this point is that the change deals with the total reorganization

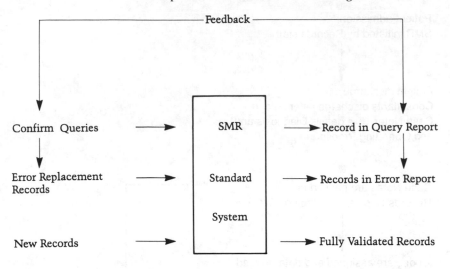

Figure 3.7 SMR standard system (input and output diagram).

of the accessory shop within their Prestwick site. This shop mainly services one-off maintenance jobs which do not pass as a whole through the rest of the works. It does, however, depend on many of the general manufacturing services. Therefore, it is not uncommon for the demands of the accessory shop to interfere with the efficient production flow of the mainstream manufacturing activities. Management decided in 1990 to minimize disrup-

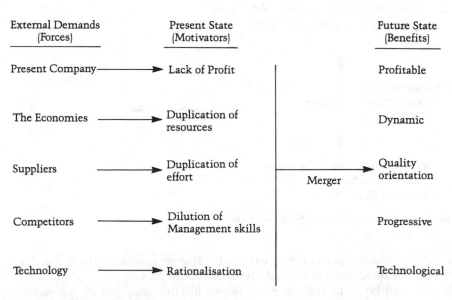

Figure 3.8 Change analysis diagram.

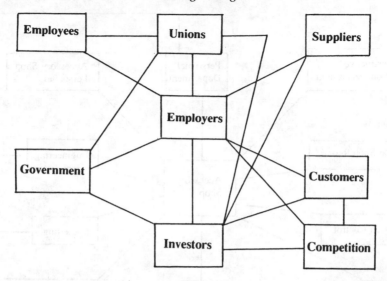

Figure 3.9 A sample relationship map.

tion to mainstream engine overhaul by creating an autonomous accessory shop, which would be totally self-contained and no longer a source of disruption to other service groups.

The relationship map, Figure 3.10, was produced at an early stage in the change process to assist in determining the key players and establishing linkages between them.

The complex change situation which emerged from the diagram indicated that although at the core of the problem was a significant system change there was also likely to be a major organizational change. The identification of the need to integrate both schools of thought, systems and organizational, to provide a solution is a very common outcome of the diagnostic diagramming phase.

SYSTEMS DIAGRAMMING

Having considered the problem of defining and understanding the basic influences associated with change, the next step is to investigate in more depth the actual systems affected by the change. Systems diagramming is an essential component of the Intervention Strategy. The systems approach, through diagramming, brings a degree of sanity to messy change situations.

The principal diagramming techniques which will be employed within the Intervention Strategy section are as follows:

(1) systems mapping,
(2) influence charts,
(3) multiple cause diagrams.

Each will be treated in turn and will be presented along with a practical case to illustrate their usage.

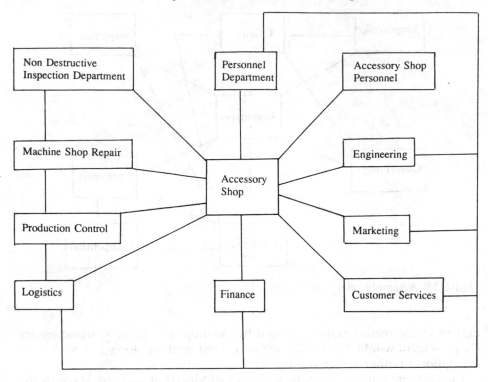

Figure 3.10 Relationship map for the accessory shop change.

SYSTEMS MAPPING

Systems maps need not be complex nor difficult to construct. Their basic function is to present a pictorial representation of the system undergoing the change and they can if necessary incorporate systems interrelationships. The systems map is often employed in conjunction with the relationships map discussed in the previous section. The systems map identifies the systems and any sub-systems associated with the problem, and the relationship map analyses the nature of the linkages between the systems, their components and their elements.

A system consists of component parts, or indeed sub-systems, which in turn may be further broken down. Sub-division ceases once the element level has been reached, an element being incapable of further division. The systems approach is examined in more detail in the next chapter. System maps can therefore be produced for all levels of the change environment. For example a map may be produced for the Glasgow Business School, a sub-system of the University of Glasgow's system, such as the one shown in Figure 3.11.

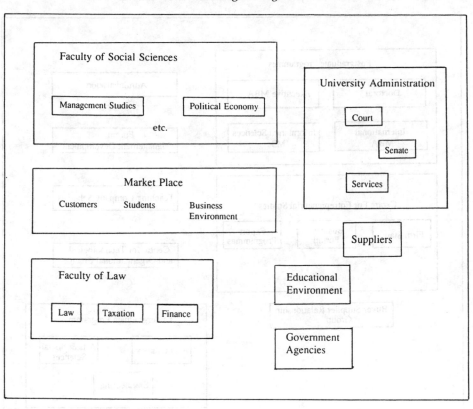

Figure 3.11 The Glasgow Business School systems map.

This map could be further divided to show the component parts of the Department of Management Studies, which could then be in turn further analysed. This is represented in the sub-division shown in Figure 3.12.

The problem owner and/or the management team concerned with the handling of the change must decide at which level of analysis the process should cease. Not only does mapping highlight the systems involved but it also gives a clear indication of the parties who should be involved in the management process and also at which point in the process they should be brought in.

Practical case: Texstyle World Ltd

This company, while involved in a review of its existing stock-holding procedures, constructed the systems map, Figure 3.13, to highlight the systems likely to be affected by any changes in their warehousing and computerized stock control system. This problem will be revisited when considering cause and effect diagrams, and when the reasons for the alteration to the systems are examined.

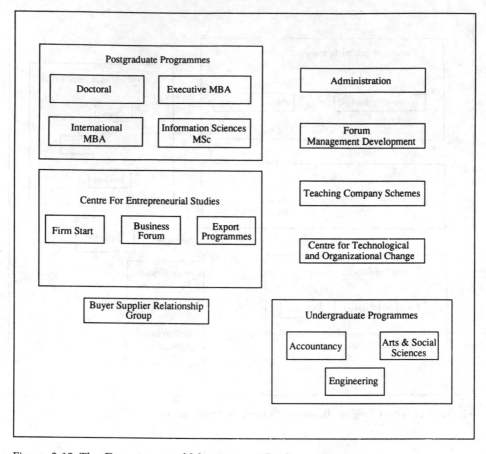

Figure 3.12 The Department of Management Studies systems map.

INFLUENCE CHARTS

The systems map is, in many ways, only of use when it is followed up by the production of influence charts. Such charts illustrate, for the prime systems components, those factors, groups and systems which influence the way in which they work and relate to their environment. For example, what influencing factors or groups could act upon a typical manufacturing firm? Figure 3.14 depicts the influences at play.

Influence diagrams connect the systems associated with the change and indicate lines of influence. Often, depending on their complexity, both systems and influence diagrams can be shown as one.

Practical case: Caledonian Airmotive Ltd

The change facing the accessory shop of Caledonian Airmotive has already been introduced. Figure 3.15 illustrates certain of the systems and factors which influence this sub-system of the manufacturing establishment.

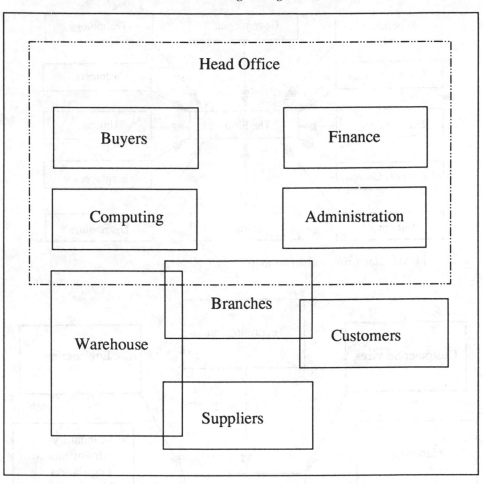

Figure 3.13 Texstyle World systems map.

MULTIPLE CAUSE DIAGRAMS

A means of further developing the influence chart is to consider the causes associated with a change situation or problem. Multiple cause diagrams examine the causes behind particular events or activities and express them diagrammatically.

For example one may depict, as in Figure 3.16, the factors which accumulatively build up to create the energy costs within the home. From this figure the demand factors could be examined as shown in Figure 3.17.

Multiple cause diagrams may be presented in a number of ways as illustrated by the following practical cases. Such diagrams are of great value in determining the various factors which are behind a particular event. They identify 'cause chains' and assist in identifying the key elements.

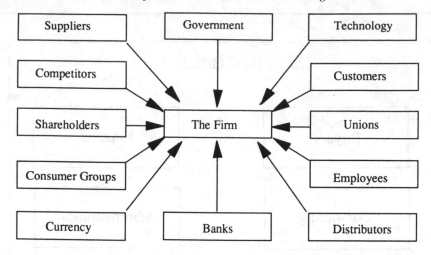

Figure 3.14 Manufacturing influence map.

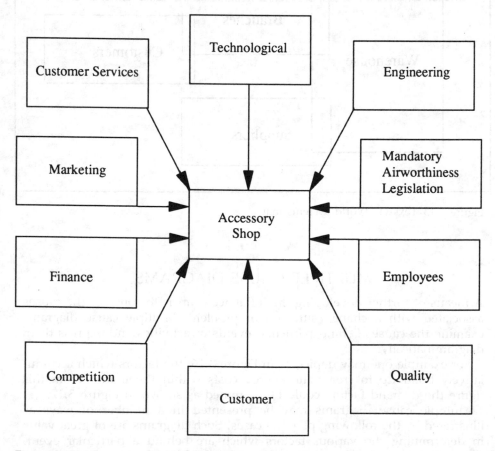

Figure 3.15 Accessory shop influence map.

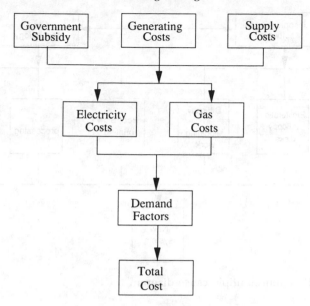

Figure 3.16 Energy costs multiple cause diagram.

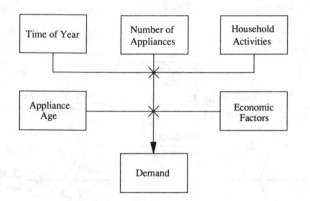

Figure 3.17 Demand factors multiple cause diagram.

Practical case: McGrigor Donald (solicitors)

When McGrigor Donald, a large law firm, upgraded its word processing services in 1989, the problem owner was the Director of Administration and she produced the multiple cause diagram in Figure 3.18.

Although rather simplistic, it does quite clearly indicate the reasons for the upgrade and in so doing point the way forward with respect to the

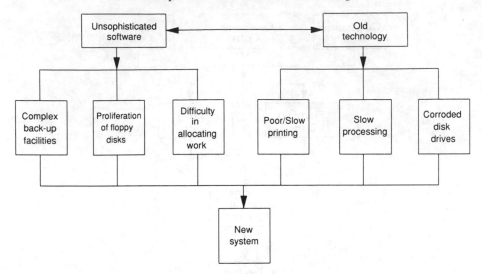

Figure 3.18 WP system multiple cause diagram.

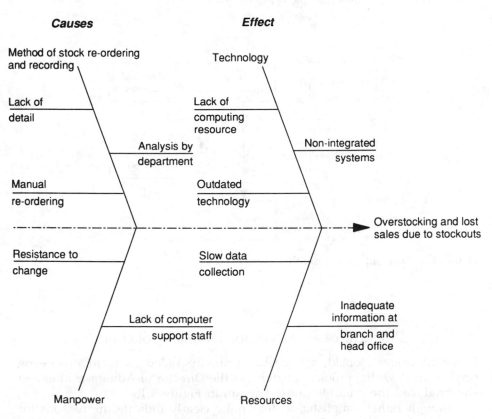

Figure 3.19 Fish-bone cause and effect diagram.

required features of the new system. It also proved a useful means of assisting in the communication of the impending change to the word processor operatives and acted as a focus for initial management/operative discussions.

Practical case: Texstyle World Ltd

The Terley, Texstyle World, stock problem was previously introduced and the associated systems map produced. The rationale behind the need for a review of the existing computerized system is neatly summed up by the cause and effect diagram which the problem owners produced. The diagram utilizes a fish-bone format and can be seen in Figure 3.19.

A MULTI-DISCIPLINARY APPROACH

Please note that diagramming alone, although offering significant assistance to management, is unlikely to meet all our analytical and research needs in the field of change management. Many other useful techniques will be mentioned in later chapters such as brainstorming, Delphi, focus groups, interviewing, financial analysis and project planning. The successful management of complex situations calls upon many disciplines and the application of a wide range of theories and techniques, so it truly requires a multi-disciplinary approach.

Part 2

The Intervention Strategy Model: for Systems Intervention

4
Intervention Strategies

THE SYSTEMS APPROACH

In change management, the systems approach is the term given to the analysis of change situations which are based on a systems view of the problem. The Intervention Strategy Model (ISM), which forms the basis of this chapter, is designed with the belief that messy change situations may be effectively managed through the application of systems thinking.

The application of the systems approach is not limited to the 'hard' end of the change spectrum. All management processes and structures may be described in systems terms. Therefore a systems analysis of the change situation, no matter how complex and people-oriented the transition may be, will provide meaningful results for the problem owner(s). It would be incorrect to suggest that the application of an intervention model such as ISM, to an extreme organizational change would produce in itself a detailed solution. It could, however, provide a framework for initial investigation, and/or a mechanism for more detailed analysis of specific change issues within the Organizational Development Model, which is the subject of Part 3.

Prior to considering the actual framework of an intervention model it is necessary to develop an understanding of systems-related terminology.

WHAT IS A SYSTEM?

From the perspective of managing change a system may be defined as being an organized assembly of components, which are related in such a way that the behaviour of any individual component will influence the overall status of the system. It is impossible to think of any physical mechanism or process which cannot be described in systems terms. Similarly most managerial processes and functions may also be described in a systematic manner. All systems, physical or 'soft', must have a predetermined objective which the interrelated components strive to achieve.

Given that a system must have an objective and that it is interrelated with other systems associated with its environment, then the accomplishment of the objective must be of interest to the other related systems. It is this shared interest that warrants the application of a systems approach. Any system which impinges on the activities of others must be investigated in the light of its associations. Changes in any given system will affect both its own internal workings and very possibly those of interrelated external systems. There is therefore a need to accurately define the system environment experiencing a change prior to the development of a transition path which

Table 4.1 Inter-related systems dependencies

Systems Level	Status	Objective
The car	System	To transport occupants and associated artefacts.
The driver	Sub-system	To manage and direct the system.
The engine	Sub-system	To provide the driving force.
The gear box	Sub-system	To engage the driving force.
The fuel pump	Component	To provide petrol to the combustion chamber.
The gear shift	Element	To provide link between the driver and the gear box.

will lead to an eventual solution. This requirement highlights the importance of the previous chapter which illustrated the use of diagramming techniques for the purpose of achieving systems definitions. Such techniques assist the problem owner in defining the nature and impact of systems-related changes from both a physical and organizational perspective.

The motor car, when considered in terms of its basic transportation role, provides a simple example of interrelated systems dependencies as Table 4.1 illustrates. The definition of the systems under study depends, to a great extent, on both the position of the reviewer in relation to the system and the purpose of the study. The driver is a sub-system of the car, as the review is taking place from a position which is concerned simply with the car as a means of transportation. However, a doctor assessing medical competence associated with driving, or a manager selecting a delivery driver, may consider the 'driver' to be a total system in its own right. The fuel pump may be regarded as a total system by a mechanic working on a problem within its many mechanisms. The car itself may be seen as a sub-system if one considers the household and its operations as the greater system. The term element is also introduced to describe the gear shift. An element is that part of a system or component which cannot or need not be broken down any further.

System objectives need not be singular, as they are in this example. The car's objective is to provide transport but this may be sub-divided and thus provide a greater insight into the system as a whole. It is important to consider not only the prime objective but also any associated sub-objectives as they may be of particular interest to both internal analysis of the system under study and any other related external systems. Let us again take the car as an example and consider a possible objectives tree as shown in Figure 4.1.

Transport may be the primary objective but economy and safety could be secondary aims, provided that the car still offers reasonable looks, adequate performance and offers personal esteem to the owner.

Objective trees, similar in construction to the one illustrated above, are produced in most systems investigations. It is seldom enough simply to

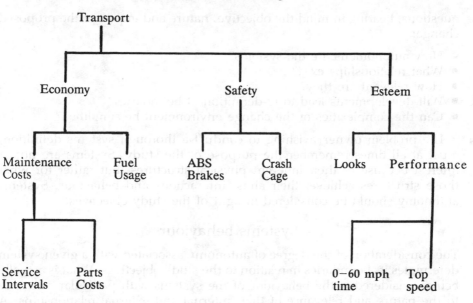

Figure 4.1 Car objectives tree.

consider the primary purpose of a system or the macro-objective of a proposed change. The various elements of the associated change environment may place greater emphasis on particular sub-objectives; to ignore this possibility could lead to a problem owner ill-defining the relationships within the affected environment.

SYSTEMS AUTONOMY AND BEHAVIOUR

Systems autonomy

The diagramming techniques previously introduced, along with the construction of objective trees, provide the problem owner with the ability to define the systems environment effectively, either prior to and/or during a change event. Care must be taken to define the scope of the change environment in an accurate manner. To accomplish this, consideration and effort must be devoted to determining the degree of systems autonomy existing within the change environment. Within any given environment its systems and their internal workings will have both collective and individual boundaries. The problem owner must ensure that these boundaries are set when defining the change in such a way as to exclude any non-essential relationships. A change environment consists of all systems both directly and indirectly affected; it also includes all associated sub-systems. It is part of the 'art' of systems diagramming, to set the boundaries at the appropriate level, so as to include all relevant factors, but exclude all irrelevancies.

It is therefore necessary for the systems investigator(s) to determine the degree to which the core system under investigation may be considered in isolation. Throughout an investigation we must constantly ask the following questions, bearing in mind the objective, nature and impact of the proposed change:

- How autonomous are the systems?
- What relationships exist?
- How relevant are they?
- Will developments lead to re-definition of boundaries?
- Can the complexities of the change environment be simplified?

The problem owner, wishing to conduct a thorough systems definition, must at all times remember the purpose of the study. Systems are not of interest because of their inherent physical structures, but rather for what those structures achieve, their aims, interactions and behaviour. Systems autonomy should be considered in light of the study objectives.

Systems behaviour

The consideration of the degree of autonomy associated with a given system determines its boundaries in relation to the study objectives. What is actually being considered is the behaviour of the systems with particular reference to the nature and relevance of their internal and external relationships. A study of systems behaviour requires that the following three process areas be reviewed:

(1) The physical processes constituting the operational system.
(2) The communications processes handling the transfer of 'information' within and between systems.
(3) The monitoring processes maintaining system stability.

By reviewing the process linkages one may begin to determine the degree of autonomy existing within the various constituent parts of the system. It is how the system behaves, in relation to both internal and external change stimuli, that the problem owner must consider. A systems investigation should commence with a detailed specification and analysis of the change environment. Having determined the general environment, the investigator then focuses on eliminating irrelevancies. This is achieved by considering the study objectives with reference to the behaviour and autonomy of the systems under review.

THE INTERVENTION STRATEGY

The previous chapters have examined both the nature of change and the means of coping with its inherent complexity. Now what is required is some means of handling, in a structured manner, the analysis and implementation of a change situation. An intervention strategy may be regarded as the procedural methodology for successfully intervening in the working processes of the original system, with the purpose of bringing about an effective change in that system. The ultimate result should be a stable new environment, which incorporates the desired changes.

The remainder of this chapter is dedicated to the introduction and examination of a practical systems intervention model which has been termed the Intervention Strategy Model (ISM). This is very much a hybrid model which is firmly based on the traditional investigative techniques associated with the schools of operational and systems management. Elements and underlying premises associated with Systems Intervention Strategy (SIS) developed by the Open Business School and the Total Project Management Model (TPMM), which is the subject of Chapter 6, a product of the University of Glasgow Business School (Paton and Southern, 1990), have been incorporated within the ISM. All three models have been extensively tried and tested on countless practising managers, and their associated organizations, while they studied for their MBA qualifications. ISM forms the basis of the Change Management course and TPMM features heavily in the Operations Management programme of the Glasgow MBA. In addition, both models have been employed on a number of successful consultancy projects. User feedback has at all times been positive and the models have found a place in the professional managers' book shelves and tool bags.

In Chapter 2, the basic investigative procedure associated with the operational and systems management school was introduced:

(1) Objective clarification,
(2) Data capture and performance indicators,
(3) Systems diagnostics,
(4) Systems analysis,
(5) Determination of solution options,
(6) Solution evaluation,
(7) Solution implementation,
(8) Appraisal and monitoring.

As we can see, the core of this procedure consists of three phases. The definition phase defines the objectives, the general problem environment and sets the investigative framework. This is followed by an evaluation or design phase, of which the first step is to determine the most appropriate analytical and/or research procedures to employ. Having made this selection the data collected in the definition phase are analysed to produce a range of potential solutions. These solutions are then subsequently evaluated against the performance criteria associated with the investigations' objectives and an optimal solution identified. The final phase is that of implementation during which the plan for introducing and monitoring the solution is devised.

Systems intervention models all share this basic three-phase approach. The actual terminology used to describe component parts of the model and the emphasis placed upon various elements within each phase may differ, but the underlying framework remains unchanged. However, the intervention strategies are much more than basic decision-making frameworks. They, for example, stress the importance of systems analysis, participative group work, iterative mechanisms, organizational issues and much more, as the following sections and the remainder of Part 2 will illustrate.

The ISM methodology emphasizes the linkages between phases two and three. In particular the need to consider implementation issues within the design and evaluation phase to ensure acceptance of the change at a later date is stressed. The user is also implored to ensure the incorporation of the 'softer' issues associated with the project and where appropriate employ organizational development practices. The word 'system' has been deliberately omitted from the title, as the model can be applied to both specific systems-related change and more general management problem-solving situations.

Change, no matter what its nature, be it technological, personal, organizational or operational, must at some point impinge upon a 'system'. A system's view of the process, operation, relationship and/or culture experiencing a transition phase is an essential feature of the ISM. However, the word 'system' often alienates those of a non-technical background. ISM does not require the user to be familiar with system analysis and design. The diagrams employed have been outlined in the previous chapter and cannot be considered overly technical or complex and their subsequent analysis need not be of a particularly quantitative nature.

By defining a change situation in systems terms, the problem owner may clearly define the nature of the change, those affected by the change, the boundary and scope of the change, the relationships affected by the change, etc. A systems-based intervention strategy is a powerful change management tool.

THE THREE PHASES OF INTERVENTION

Successful systems intervention, or problem formulation and solution, requires the management team, or the individual, to proceed through the three interdependent phases until the management objectives have been achieved. The three basic phases of ISM are highlighted in Figure 4.2.

Problem initialization may sound impressive and conjure up images of a complex management process but in reality its meaning is relatively simple, namely, that a need to investigate a change situation has been identified and that the process of managing the change is about to commence. A problem owner and possibly a supporting group will have been identified and charged with handling the transition from the old to the new. Chapter 2 stressed the importance of ensuring that the problem owner was committed to the task at hand and possessed or had access to the necessary managerial expertise and skill to manage the transition process effectively. For the purposes of this review of ISM the problem owner will be deemed to be the actual manager of the transition process. Those individuals, along with the problem owner, who eventually are identified as being part of the managing team will be termed the change agents. The nucleus of the management team will be formed during problem initialization. It may grow to reflect the environment affected by the change and the skills required to manage the problem.

The definition phase involves the in-depth specification and study of the change situation, both from an historical and futuristic viewpoint. The second phase generates and evaluates the potential solution options; the third phase, that of implementation, develops the action plans which should successfully introduce the outputs of the design phase. Due to the inherent dynamic nature of operational, organizational and business environments,

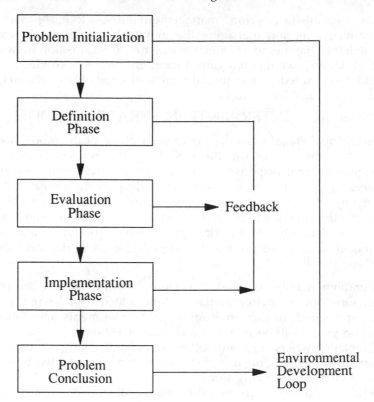

Figure 4.2 The basic phases of the Intervention Strategy Model.

it is essential that, during each of the phases, the systems affected are constantly monitored, both on an internal and external basis, to ensure the validity of associated assumptions, objectives, information and analysis. At any point, it may be necessary to iterate back to an earlier stage for the purpose of incorporating a new development, or factor, which may influence the outcome.

Iterations are an essential feature of an effective change or problem management strategy. For this reason, it is often advisable to conduct a 'quick and dirty' analysis of the change, prior to a more formal and detailed investigation. This should reduce the need for numerous time-consuming iterations once the 'intervention' has formally commenced.

Figure 4.2 shows an environmental development feedback loop, linking the final outcome, the 'new environment', with that of the 'initial situation'. The purpose of this loop is simply to illustrate that the change cycle is never complete. Dynamic environmental factors will, over a period of time, necessitate the need for additional change and so the process will once more commence. As operational, organizational and competitive environments continue to develop, management must adopt a proactive stance, thus anticipating and managing the inevitable change to their advantage. The ability to handle, in an effective manner, the transition between 'steady state' situations, within an organizational environment conducive to change, should be regarded as a potential source of competitive advantage.

THE INTERVENTION STRATEGY MODEL

The individual stages associated with each phase of the model are shown in Figure 4.3. The adoption of the model, by the problem owner and/or the management team responsible for the effective transition from the existing systems status to the desired situation, will provide a means of managing the change cycle in a structured, logical, interactive and visible manner. It facilitates the total planning and control of a systems-oriented change.

There are a number of important points which should be noted concerning the model as a whole prior to investigating each of the individual stages. They are as follows:

(1) Iterations may be required at any point, within or between phases, due to developing environmental factors. Once the desired position has been reached, further environmental developments may cause the transition process to be re-entered at some later date.
(2) Problem owners and any other associated change agents should be involved throughout. It is essential they are committed to the initiative as they are the driving force.
(3) There is a tendency to rush through the diagnostic phase, with problem owners basing assumptions on their own brand of 'common sense'. Time spent getting it right first time is seldom wasted. Specification and description are crucial to the problem owners' understanding of a change situation.
(4) It is always advisable to attempt to produce quantifiable performance indicators in Stage 3 as they will simplify the evaluation process in Stage 6.
(5) It is virtually impossible not to start thinking about options during the diagnostic phase, especially on a 'live' problem. There is no harm in this, but do not skip stages. Put the options aside until Stage 4.
(6) Having generated a host of options, some form of 'sensitive' screening must take place. Often one will find that certain options may be eliminated for implementation reasons, or because they are dependent upon uncontrollable factors. Such options should be removed prior to more formal evaluation. Occasionally some options may have been entertained simply for 'political' reasons. For example, during an option-generating session suggestions which are less than suitable may have to be tolerated to avoid alienation of the proposer, or because they come from key players who expect to be listened to and acknowledged. Such options may be edited out at this stage; they may be lost or forgotten for long enough to allow more plausible options to take hold.
(7) The options and solutions generated and evaluated within the second phase need not relate to individual and unrelated entities. It is often the

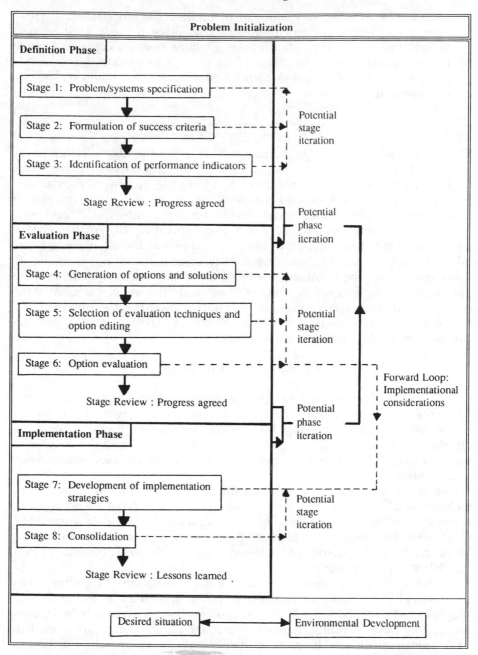

Figure 4.3 The Intervention Strategy Model.

case that chains of interrelated options and solutions have to be dealt with and care taken to ensure they are evaluated as a total entity.

(8) The distinction between phases two and three is rather cloudy. Phase two, concludes with the option evaluation. Implementation, phase three,

commences with the development of implementation strategies. However, for effective implementation to take place it must itself be considered during the evaluation phase. Options may on occasion have to be considered in the light of their ease of implementation. Users of ISM must be prepared to jump forward during the evaluation phase to consider implementation.

THE STAGES OF ISM

The key to successful change management is firstly the identification of the appropriate problem owners and secondly the selection of a management methodology to provide the means of handling the transition. Provision of adequate resources and support is also rather crucial. Assuming the players have been identified, they must decide on their subsequent course of action. ISM should be selected when the impending or existing change situation exhibits tendencies towards the hard end of the change spectrum, when in fact it can be clearly seen that systems, and not attitudes or relationships, are the dominant issues. It should be noted that the systems approach can on occasion be employed to tackle the initial stages of softer organizational problems. Long-term solutions would not be generated, but the problem owner would have 'kick-started' the change process and this can be useful when time is of the essence.

Phase one: definition

Stage 1: problem/system specification and description
Management must, through the problem owner(s) and with the assistance of interested parties, develop their understanding of the situation. The change, or problem, must be specified in systems terms and the complexity reduced so as to isolate and determine the systems interactions, relationships and cultures.

It is at this stage that one employs the previously outlined diagramming techniques as a means of assisting definition and analysis. Meetings and interviews will be conducted, experience sought and historical data examined, in an effort to construct an accurate picture of the present system and the likely impact of the changes to systems components and elements, of both the 'hard' and 'soft' variety.

As this is likely to represent the first formal notification of the change one must tread lightly; unfreeze the present system in such a way as to minimize the likelihood of resistance and non-co-operation. Mistakes here in communicating the impending change to interested parties will create immediate and future difficulties. The problem owner requires co-operation if the true nature and impact of the change is to be defined. In messy change situations, diagramming and defining the change must be seen as a group activity.

Stage 2: formulation of success criteria
The success criteria associated with a particular change situation may be defined in two ways. The first, and most common, involves the determination

of objectives and constraints. The second is merely a corruption of the first in that it generates options or paths which are tagged on to the original objective. For analytical and communicative purposes it is always best to produce objectives and constraints. They are simpler to understand and can be more readily associated with performance measures. Options are messy to deal with and have to be broken down at a later stage to determine specific measures of success.

An example of an option masquerading as an objective could be a phrase such as 'Improve productivity by reducing manning levels'. The objective has been followed by a solution or option. This tends to result in the problem owner(s) focusing in on this option without fully considering alternatives; a dangerous and unimaginative course of action.

Objectives may be derived from the rationale behind the change and constraints generally emerge from the resources which have been allocated to the task, or more accurately the lack of them. It would be fair to say that the normal constraints facing management in change situations are time and money. Constraints may also be traced to both the nature of the systems and the cultures affected.

Even when objectives and constraints appear to be clear and unambiguous the problem owner(s) must ensure that any less obvious sub-objectives, along with any associated constraints, have been identified. When one is faced with less obvious objectives and more dynamic constraints exhibiting characteristics tending towards the 'softer' end of the change spectrum, then the situation which is about to be encountered is liable to be rather complex and messy, and no doubt will call upon recourse to the organizational development practices.

It is always advisable to construct a prioritized objectives tree, with associated constraints incorporated. Figure 4.4 illustrates such a tree. It

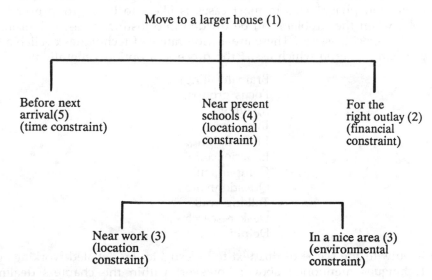

Figure 4.4 Prioritized objectives tree.

considers the objectives and their ranking which may be associated with the need to upgrade the size of the family home due to a pending 'population explosion'. Priorities (as are constraints) are shown in parentheses, with the number '1' indicating the greatest priority. Figure 4.4 is only a first draft, but it could quickly develop into a complex network of interrelated objectives.

This objective tree can, during the evaluation Stages 4, 5 and 6, be developed further to include the options for achieving the objectives. In turn the generated option paths can then form the basis of an implementation strategy.

Stage 3: identification of performance measures

Having decided what the objectives of the exercise are, it is necessary to formulate appropriate measures for each one. If this is not done at this point, then how can the problem owner evaluate the options generated subsequently?

It is always advisable to try and identify quantifiable measures, such as costs, savings, volume, labour and time. When this is not possible, then the measures should be graded in some way, e.g. seeding or ranking could be employed. Measures can be entered on the objectives tree, thus providing one descriptive representation of what is to be achieved and how its success will be measured. This provides an ideal focal point for the subsequent evaluation phase and also communicates in a logical fashion the aims of the change.

Phase two: evaluation

Stage 4: generation of options or solutions

As in the definition phase, the nature of the change dictated the scope of the investigation and the composition of the management team, so too in the evaluation phase. This in most cases is likely to be a group exercise. Possibly, when the problem can be divided into distinct areas, sub-groups may tackle specific issues. There are a wide range of techniques available to the problem owner(s) which assist the process of option generation:

> Brainstorming,
> Focus groups,
> Meetings,
> Interviews,
> Ideas writing,
> Experience,
> Comparison,
> Questionnaires,
> Talking wall,
> Desk research,
> Delphi.

It is outwith the scope of this text to investigate the detailed workings of the techniques mentioned above; however, within the chapters dealing with case studies the reader will see many of them being both referenced and demonstrated. By far the most popular techniques involve some form of 'brainstorming'. Meetings are held with appropriate groups in attendance, and a brainstorming session follows which generates a range of options. Another popular technique is 'comparison', by which we mean examining what is done elsewhere, learning from someone else's experience and mistakes.

It is most important not to take too blinkered a view of the change during the option-generating sessions. A variety of possibilities and opportunities should be considered. There is no need to worry about 100% relevance, as any sub-optimal options may be screened out in the subsequent evaluation during Stages 5 and 6.

Such sessions must be seen by the participating individuals and groups as being constructive and influential. They should not become cosmetic smoke-screens for the tabling of preconceived options. If this happens, those involved may withdraw support and take a more reactive stance. To this end sensitivity must be shown towards the promoter of even the most ridiculous options.

Some form of team building exercise is often required prior to commencing the option-generation stage when the group involved has limited knowledge of each other and the actual process. Such group sessions may be conducted by an external facilitator if the problem owner either wishes to remain impartial or lacks the required group management skills.

Stage 5: selection of appropriate evaluation techniques and option editing

The options and indeed potential solutions must now be considered in greater depth to establish their true viability. The problem owner(s) should, prior to formal analysis, eliminate all suggestions which are not considered worthy of further investigation. This should be done in a sensitive and non-alienating manner.

There are a number of techniques and processes available which will be of assistance in providing more detailed analytical information. The data gained from this stage will not only eliminate certain options, it will also form the basis of the final evaluation which follows. The following processes and techniques may be of assistance in editing the options. It is the responsibility of the problem owner and any associated management team to select the appropriate techniques. Once again a detailed analysis of them is outwith the scope of this text.

(1) Examination and manipulation of the systems diagrams.
(2) Physical or computer simulations.
(3) Investment analysis.
(4) Cost−benefit analysis.
(5) Network analysis.
(6) Cash flow analysis.
(7) Strategy analysis.
(8) Cultural analysis.
(9) Experimental techniques, etc.

This initial formal screening should eliminate sub-optimal options, as well as developing an understanding of the interrelationships and order of option paths and linkages. Remember that options need not be stand-alone activities, they may form paths, courses of activities which must be considered as a group. The analysis within this stage need not be quantitative. Subjective assessments of an option's suitability may be conducted when there are non-quantifiable performance indicators associated with particular objectives and constraints. Subjective assessments are best conducted in an open and participative manner, thus ensuring that accusations of bias and skulduggery are minimized.

Stage 6: option evaluation

This stage constitutes the final hurdle of the evaluation phase. It is essentially the final decision point, and its product will be the solution to the problem. Here, options are evaluated against the previously determined change objectives, in particular, the performance measures previously identified in Stage 3.

A tabular format may be used to conduct the evaluation. Objectives, along with their associated performance measures, are entered as a prioritized listing on the left. Individual options and/or option chains are entered along the top. Factual data and/or calculated weightings are entered in the appropriate box corresponding to the option's performance against a particular objective measure, such information being in the main a product of the analysis conducted in the previous editing phase.

The example shown, Table 4.2, illustrates the use of such a format for the selection of a new family car based on four objectives and a choice of four models. Objectives C and D can only be assessed against subjective values derived from data gleaned from the motoring press. A grading system would have to be employed. Given the indicated priority for each objective the selected option would be model B. Modifications to any of the variables can be easily introduced and the priority system altered to illustrate greater differentials. For example, let us assume that the driver, due to a recent addition to the family, increases the priority on safety to '1' and cost, objective A, to '2', while downgrading performance and esteem to a negative digit. The selection may then alter to option and model D.

This simple example illustrates the visual impact of the tabular presentation and indicates how it may be used as a focal point for discussion and the consideration of 'what if?' scenarios.

The process of option evaluation must be conducted with reference to subsequent implementation. A 'forward loop' is incorporated within the model to emphasize the importance of this factor. The problem owner must look forward to the implementation phase and build into the evaluation some consideration of the implementation difficulties associated with each option. This can be formally addressed by ensuring that implementation objectives are built into the original objectives tree, thus resulting in the production of at least subjective measures of success relating to implementation issues. The existence of such measures will ensure the consideration of implementation during the evaluation phase.

Table 4.2 Evaluation table

Objective/ measure	Priority	Options					Optimal
		Option A	Option B	Option C	Option D		
Cost £s (constraint: <£25,000)	3	10,000	22,000	15,000	12,500		A
Performance 0–60 mph ~ s ~ mph top speed	1	10 s 99 mph	8 s 130 mph	8 s 116 mph	12 s 109 mph		B
Safety	4	Low	High?	High	Med		C
Esteem	2	Low	High	Med	Med		B

Phase three: implementation

Stage 7: development of implementation strategies

By this stage in the change management process, or in any other form of problem analysis or systems investigation, the detailed foundations of a successful conclusion to the project have been laid. Objectives are clear and current, options selected and reviewed and the system well defined and understood. Now all that is left is to package the findings into a coherent whole and introduce the changes to the system.

It may sound simple, but never is. It is at the point of implementation that the full impact of the change will be recognized by all those likely to be affected. Only now will the problem owner discover the extent to which a shared perception was reached. In problems with truly 'hard' systems there will be no resistance, the physical change will go ahead, but as one gravitates toward the 'softer' end of the change continuum the risk of latent resistance is always a worrying factor.

The implementation strategy, to be successful, must be carefully planned. Tools are available to assist with the physical planning process, such as network analysis, bar and Gantt charts, etc., but they do not take into account the human dimension. Care must be taken to minimize the risk of adverse reactions and maximize the likelihood of co-operation.

There are essentially only three basic implementation strategies available and they are as follows:

(1) Pilot studies leading eventually to change,
(2) Parallel running,
(3) Big bang.

Pilot studies provide the greatest opportunity for subsequent review of the change. Assumptions and procedures can be tested, arguments developed and the likely future acceptance of the fully implemented change increased. But they also delay full implementation, and they allow those who may wish to resist the change to adopt delaying tactics. In addition, the environment does not stand still; delays to implementation may render the original solution sub-optimal and therefore necessitate a review of the whole process. Often the proposed changes will have a dramatic effect on not only those parts of the system directly affected but also on all associated systems. In such cases one may adopt a parallel-running implementation strategy. Slowly phase out the old system as the new becomes more reliable and understood. Big Bang implementation maximizes the speed of change but it can also generate the maximum resistance to the change, at least in the short term. Like most things in life, compromise generally provides the answer, and a blend of the three strategies is normally found.

Later chapters will deal with the development of implementation strategies in more depth, from both a systems and organizational development perspective. But for the present, remember that to gain a shared perception of a problem and commitment for its solution, it is essential to involve those affected by it in the decision-making process and to ensure that they have the knowledge, skills and tools to handle the change.

Stage 8: consolidation

Armed with an implementation strategy designed to maximize the probability of success and acceptance, the change is introduced, but we have not yet finished. Old systems and practices, just like old habits, die hard. It takes time for a new system or change to be fully accepted. Skilful communication, visual support from above and provision of adequate support to those affected, are required throughout this stage. Initial changes must be followed up, and both protection and enforcement of the new system will be required. It is up to the problem owners, the agents of the change, to nurture the growth of the new, while encouraging the peaceful demise of the old.

Change cannot be avoided, all systems must be constantly monitored in the light of developments in technology, materials, management practices and the business environment. Only through anticipation of change events can management address them in a proactive and opportunistic manner.

KEY SUCCESS FACTORS ASSOCIATED WITH ISM

ISM, in common with all other systems intervention strategies, can only be successfully employed when those handling the change recognize the importance of the factors and features outlined within this section. These points represent the essential components of effective systems intervention:

(1) The development of a comprehensive systems definition lays the foundation for an effective change management process. The importance of ensuring that the environmental impact of the change is fully defined and understood cannot be overstated. One would be well advised to follow the highway code prior to taking any action: 'Stop, look and listen — then act!'

(2) Those affected by the change, the 'users', should be involved and consulted as early as possible. They may be identified from the initial review of the systems environment.

(3) Change management is usually a multi-disciplinary process. The problem owner, or any other associated change agent(s), must seek assistance when they are faced with difficulties outwith their own realm of expertise.

(4) Internal, or external consultants may be required to provide objectivity, knowledge and skill. Not only do they provide expertise, they can also be used as the ideal 'scapegoats'. Consultants have been, and will continue to be, blamed for unpopular actions and for sub-optimal project solutions over which they had little control.

(5) Support from senior management is essential, it must be vocal, visual and provide authority and leadership. Change agents must be seen to have the full support of their superiors; they need either the informal or formal authority to act.

(6) Constructive critical comments must be listened to and incorporated where warranted, and logically argued against when damaging or inapplicable. Problem owners are cursed like all others with their own brand of common sense, and they must strive to be objective.

(7) Effective communication is essential.

(8) Effective teamwork and the facilitation of group activities are essential.

(9) Sensitivity must be used when dealing with affected parties as change is often a threatening experience. The chapters on organization development address the issues facing those affected by change, and propose a number of models and techniques which will assist the change agents in securing a safe passage for the change.

(10) Resistance to change is likely to be experienced, in at least one of its many forms, at some stage in the transaction process:

  (a) Physical damage/sabotage (e.g. latter-day Luddites).

  (b) Direct refusal to co-operate (e.g. industrial disputes).

  (c) Conflicting and negative arguments and schemes, proposed to both delay the project and create an atmosphere of misinformation.

  (d) Total agreement on the surface, but no real action (e.g. the back-stabbers).

  (e) Blocking moves (e.g. working parties, special committees, etc.).

  By following the maxim that prevention is always better than the cure the change agent should endeavour at all times to ensure:

  (i)   openness and understanding from the commencement of the transition.

  (ii) visible senior management support.

  (iii) participation and involvement throughout the transition process.

  (iv) education and development aimed at promoting greater understanding of the process and a shared perception of the rationale.

  (v)   the development of a proactive culture.

  (vi) provision of appropriate training prior to direct exposure to the changed environment.

(11) The necessary skills, knowledge and resources must be provided both to those who will manage the change process and to those who will be affected by the final outcome.

(12) Technological change, due to its dynamic impact on existing systems and also its threatening image, can create many challenges for the change agent. Being at the forefront of technology within any organization can be exceptionally lonely. The emphasis which must be placed on gaining the shared perception and co-operation at as early a stage as possible in the change process when dealing with such 'futuristic' developments cannot be overstated.

(13) By adopting a proactive stance to change, opportunities, rather than threats, may be seized. Again, the existing organizational culture will influence the perception of change situations. An enterprising and participative culture will tend to be more proactive.

(14) Change is a continuous process, systems must be monitored regularly to ensure their continued appropriateness to environmental factors. One's guard cannot be relaxed. To maintain a competitive position within the business environment, management must ensure the constant monitoring of systems with regard to developments in technology, the market-place, management practices, competitors' actions, etc.

THE 'QUICK AND DIRTY' ANALYSIS

The impression may have been given that the adoption of the ISM will force the change agents, the problem owners, into a protracted period of consultation, negotiation and deliberation. In many instances the nature of the change will be such that its magnitude will necessitate a lengthy and meticulous transition process if the desired outcome is to be effectively managed. In situations where either the nature of the change is such that its impact will be limited or the time scales involved dictate a speedy conclusion to the problem, or both, the application of ISM may be conducted in what may be termed a 'Quick and Dirty' manner, Q & D for short. A small group can drive themselves through the model and arrive at a solution which may not be the optimal one, but it will at least have addressed and incorporated the key factors associated with the change environment.

A Q & D analysis can also be a useful starting point for the change agents tackling a more complex problem. It will indicate key factors and potential barriers to change, it will highlight the principal players and give an indication of resource requirements. Such an analysis will at an early stage set the scene for things to come and provide the change agents with a valuable insight into the complexities of the transition process.

THE ITERATIVE NATURE OF THE MODEL

A principal aspect of the model is its iterative nature. Although the model has been described in a stage-by-stage sequential manner, one must not forget the feedback loops which have been incorporated into the design to facilitate the return to previously completed stages in the light of environmental changes. In addition, each phase is concluded with a review activity. The first two phases conclude with an agreement from those involved that the stage sequence is complete and that all agree with the decisions and conclusions reached. Ownership of the problem as it develops is thus maintained. The final phase concludes with a debrief activity. What were the management lessons associated with the transition process and how can things be improved the next time?

To date, this chapter has mainly highlighted the 'macro' aspects of the model's iterative nature, in particular the need to be aware of the continuous cycle of change which affects all systems and therefore must be monitored to ensure a proactive response when the time comes to act. But the need for what may be termed 'micro' iterations also exists. Such iterations take place during 'real time', while the transition process is actually occurring. The model design incorporates feedback loops between each of the stages so as to emphasize the importance to the user of constantly updating and monitoring the system environment.

Environmental shifts which affect the basic definition of the system(s) undergoing change must be incorporated into the first phase of the model, and their impact assessed. If the impact is such that the system definitions and relationships are altered then this must be appropriately incorporated in the subsequent stages of the model. Iterations may not all result in a complete reappraisal of the definition phase. The feedback may be from the implementation to the design phase; such would be the case if resource allocations altered prior to implementation and rendered a selected solution path redundant. The new situation would be incorporated into the option evaluation table and a previously sub-optimal option selected. Failure to find an alternative would result in a return to the first phase.

5

Practical Applications of the Intervention Strategy Model

INTRODUCTION

The previous chapter concentrated on the technicalities of the Intervention Strategy Model (ISM). Each phase and its associated stages were described in a sequential manner. The iterative nature of the model was highlighted, which facilitates the return to earlier stages in the light of changes in either the internal or external environments. Key points concerning the model's application were emphasized. The need to consider certain of the models and techniques associated with Part 3 of this text, namely organizational development and design, which deals with the 'softer' people issues, was raised. Effective implementation can only be accomplished when both participation and commitment have been sought and won.

This chapter aims to illustrate the detailed use of ISM by introducing a number of short case studies from a range of 'real life' practical applications. They will be presented in a sequential manner in accordance with the ISM's format.

THE DEFINITION PHASE

Stage 1: problem/systems specification and description

Chapter 3 dealt with systems diagramming and in general the definition and initial analysis of change situations. There is therefore little point in dwelling on this area of systems definition. Stage 1 should produce a clear and concise definition of the affected systems and their relationships. To illustrate this point let us briefly consider the systems change described below.

Case A: British Gas, Scotland

An example from the purchasing department of British Gas (Scotland) plc illustrates how a systems problem should be entered. A policy decision was made and justified at the corporate level of the company, to the effect that the stock holding of items termed 'one-time-buys' (otherwise denoted as OTBs) would commence and that the more frequently used OTBs would be held at two central locations. The aim of this exercise was to reduce the delivery time of such items and thus improve the quality of service to the end customer. Traditionally these were items ordered by purchasing clerks directly from suppliers as and when requested. The numbers involved and the frequency of orders did not, on a regional basis, justify internal stock holding.

The policy change, designed to improve delivery performance, would result in the bulk of the OTBs being held in a central warehouse facility with the regions ordering directly from this internally held stock. Delivery time, in the region of 15 days when ordering directly from the manufacturer, would be reduced dramatically.

The purchasing manager, in effect the problem owner, was directed to manage the change and had an imposed target date to work to. He quickly identified another two key change agents and brought them on to the team. Firstly, the spares buyer who had line responsibility for the clerks who dealt with OTBs, and secondly the purchasing department's own systems development officer. They then, as a group, set about defining the exact nature and impact of the change. The first steps they took on entering and defining the change were as follows:

(1) The ordering clerks were notified of the proposed change and the rationale behind it and the proposed change management process was explained.
(2) A flow chart was developed by the change agents, with the assistance of the clerks, which detailed the internal OTB ordering system (in effect a sub-system of the total ordering system) to assist in the understanding of the existing process.
(3) The change agents then constructed an activity sequence diagram to determine how the new system would impact on the old, thus determining the scope of the change.
(4) Next they produced a systems map detailing both internal and external systems associated with the OTB ordering process.
(5) A relationship map was then developed to aid their understanding of the nature of the linkages between the systems involved.
(6) An investigation then took place into the relative magnitude of the conflicting forces which existed, to determine their effect on the likelihood of success. Force field analysis was employed.

On completion of the sixth step the change agents had a clear picture of the systems involved, their relationships and status. By this point it was obvious to all concerned that they were faced with a reasonably 'hard' systems change, with minimal people issues, as the clerks' function would be retained and retraining was unlikely to be significant. This case, along with the diagrams mentioned above, will be dealt with in more depth in Chapter 10.

Stage 2/3: formulation of success criteria and identification of performance indicators

Having fully defined the change environment as far as is possible and necessary, the next stage may be entered. The example which follows, taken from ABC Ltd, details the objectives, constraints and measures developed to assist in solving a particularly 'hard' problem.

Case B: ABC Ltd

This case involved the possible automation of calibration and monitoring systems on an engine test rig. The problem was defined as being of a particularly 'hard' nature by the problem owner, namely the test controller, who cited the following reasons in support of an ISM-based solution:

(1) Time scales: as soon as possible to maintain competitive advantage over other test facilities.
(2) Clear objectives: the introduction of an automatic recording system to a test rig with the purpose of reducing costs and improving the quality of data.
(3) System boundary: clearly defined and limited to the test facility.
(4) Source: internally driven by the testing facility management.
(5) Control: essentially fully under the control of the testing facility management.
(6) Resources: limited financial budget.
(7) Motivation: a high degree of interest and commitment existed amongst staff.

The above review of the nature of the change facing the test controller deals with the issues raised by the TROPICS test introduced in Chapter 2, which is designed to highlight the key factors affecting the location of a change situation on the change spectrum:

> Time scales,
> Resources,
> Objectives,
> Perceptions,
> Interest,
> Control,
> Source.

All the above factors were considered, with the term motivation being employed loosely to cover the areas of perception and interest. Diagrams were produced which vindicated the initial assumption that this was indeed a 'hard' systems change. Subsequent production of the objectives and constraints listing, along with the associated performance measures, also indicated a straightforward systems change. The products of ISM Stages 2 and 3 are shown in Table 5.1.

It is at this point that ABC Ltd strayed from the ISM path. The diagrams produced were constructed by like-minded engineering managers who focused on the technical aspects of the system. They entered the formulation stage as one and did not think forward in sufficient detail to the implementation phase.

The millwrights, who were the shop-floor operatives most directly involved in the existing manual process, were not fully briefed nor adequately consulted during the planning process. The 'softer' issues were not identified in the definition phase as the emphasis had been on technical specifications and systems. The result was that the management of the project was impeded

Table 5.1 Objective and performance measures for ISM stages 2 and 3

Objective	Performance measure
a. Quality improvement	% of correct data
b. Test time reduction	Hours
c. Reduced calibration time	Hours
d. Removal of manual inputs	Hours
e. Reduced fuel useage	Gallons
f. A more reliable system	% down time

Constraint and performance indicator listing:
    Cost restraint (£), limited budget for hardware and software development
    Resistance of operatives and unions (recognized but not acted upon)

just as the implementation phase was being entered. The co-operation of the operatives and their union could not be relied upon. Insufficient attention had been paid to the operators' perception of a loss in status due to the automation of their task and the possible resulting redeployment of their resource.

The situation was resolved by an iteration back to the definition phase to incorporate the 'softer' elements of change into the overall systems definition. The implementation was put on ice until the education and involvement of the operatives had been effectively incorporated into the solution.

THE EVALUATION PHASE

Stage 4/5: the generation and editing of options and solutions

As we saw in the relevant section of Chapter 4 there are a host of techniques available to the problem owner to assist in both the generation of options and their subsequent reduction of numbers. The appraisal and subsequent selection of the evaluation techniques employed, their degree of sophistication and method of application, will depend almost wholly on the nature of the problem and the availability of resources.

The ABC Ltd example introduced in the previous section followed the ISM protocol as outlined below:

(1) Option generation. Due to the perceived need for haste, given the expressed desire to maintain their competitive edge, the generation of options was conducted via a single brainstorming session led by the test controller. Representatives of the following groups took part, their presence being justified by their key positions within the original systems definition:

> computer systems,
> instrument technicians,
> engine performance analysts,
> testers.

The above group produced the following list of options:

> hire or buy equipment;
> 'in-house' designed system;
> externally designed system;
> partial system – data collection only;
> complete system – no manual intervention;
> external equipment maintenance;
> 'in-house' equipment maintenance;
> tester-operated;
> tester-operated with instrument technician back-up;
> tester-operated with staff back-up.

The reader should note that the above list is not as extensive nor as detailed as that produced by the team during their option-generation session. The technical nature of many of the options and their explanation was such that their reproduction would simply lead to confusion.

(2) Option editing. Having generated the options the group then set about editing out those which were unsuitable or at least impracticable given the existing system environment:

Option	Rejection Criteria
Tester operated with staff back-up.	Shift working problems.
'In-house' systems design.	Insufficient expertise.
'In-house' equipment maintenance.	No facilities.

As we can see, there is no need to become involved in complicated procedures and protracted discussions. These options were eliminated without recourse to any form of financial analysis.

Stage 6: option evaluation

Following on from the editing stage, the group moved to the evaluation of the remaining options. The data required to formally evaluate the options were gathered and generated by the problem owner and the other change agents. Much of the information came from financial and operational analysis of existing in-house data and literature provided by equipment manufacturers. Various breakeven style analyses were conducted to establish both costings and performance profiles for all the options. The necessary information along with the objectives and options were collated and presented in a tabular format as shown in Table 5.2.

The agreed solution was as follows: 'The recording system should be externally designed and 'complete', allowing auto-calibration and recording of data to be directly transferred to the mainframe computer. The equipment should be hired and operated by the tester with support from the instrument technician.'

THE IMPLEMENTATION PHASE

The importance of this phase must not be underestimated. One of the most frequent faults associated with poor change management occurs in this

Table 5.2 Option evaluation (test rig)

	Options					
Objective	Buy	Rent	Data record only	Data record & transfer	Complete system	Tester & technician
Improve data quality	N/A	N/A	90%	95%	98%	98%
Reduce testing time	N/A	N/A	1 h	1 h	1 h	N/A
Reduce fuel consumption	N/A	N/A	150 gal	150 gal	150 gal	N/A
Reduce calibration time	N/A	N/A	0 h	0 h	8 h	N/A
System reliability	N/A	N/A	N/A	N/A	N/A	2%
Reduce costs	Buy	N/A	£50k	£75k	£100k	N/A
	Rent	N/A	*	*	*	
Reduce manual input	N/A	N/A	0 h	2 h	2 h	N/A

* Rental costs will be 30% less than the associated purchase cost.
N/A denotes not applicable.

phase. The problem owner, along with any other relevant change agents, having just completed a major project evaluation exercise, possibly very effectively, may rush into the implementation phase without fully preparing the way ahead. Implementation strategies are required which address issues such as timing of events, scheduling of activities, sourcing and delivery of resources and the development of the human resource support structures. Implementation issues need not be left until the final stages of ISM. They will naturally emerge during both the discussion and evaluation of options and solutions. Previous discussions regarding sound implementation strategy emphasized the need to build implementation issues and objectives into the actual evaluation process.

There is much more to developing an implementation strategy than engaging in network-based planning exercises and the construction of elaborate control charts and budgetary monitoring devices. No one would deny the value of such techniques nor the importance of seriously considering the harder issues. However, the vast majority of competent managers are capable of dealing with both the planning techniques and monitoring mechanisms, either directly or by seeking expert assistance when required. The technical aspects of project planning are not generally associated with project failure. It is the 'softer' people-based issues, which are often neglected and they therefore can have a tremendous detrimental impact on the successful implementation of a project.

The two cases chosen for this section have been selected not for their complexities of planning but rather for the emphasis they place on the management of people. A recent study, entitled the *Glasgow Management Development Initiative* (Brownlie et al., 1990), contacted many employers and their managers, through both focus groups and questionnaires, in an effort to establish the health or otherwise of management development. By far the most sought-after category of management development, expressed by both the employers and their managers, was people management. Managers themselves know that the key to success lies in their ability to effectively manage people in an enterprising manner towards the fulfilment of mutually agreeable objectives.

Stage 7/8: develop implementation strategies and consolidation

The first case, Froud Consine Limited (FCL), demonstrates the benefits of generating a shared perception of a problem and ensuring that the principal players are 'onside' prior to implementation. To make sense of the implementation phase, the case must be joined at the conclusion of the formulation phase.

Case C: Froud Consine Ltd (FCL)

FCL is a medium-sized engineering company involved in the design, manufacture and contracting of high-technology test equipment. The company was acquired by Babcock International (BI) in 1985. Prior to the BI take-over, FCL had experienced a succession of management teams endeavouring to improve the firm's performance, mainly through diversification of a technological and vertical nature. The company found itself providing a service as well as a product, but did not successfully restructure its manufacturing and management systems accordingly. FCL was a traditional engineering company, they had their own way of doing things and had managed to survive in their original base in Worcester for almost a century.

The problem owner, part of a four-man management team from BI, was faced with an organization set in its ways and fast developing a substantial inertia to change, of which it had seen quite enough over recent years. There were of course many issues which the BI team addressed, but for this example the emphasis will be placed on the objective of improving the commercial control of contracts in line with the increasingly important customer-servicing requirements.

As one might have expected from the project objective and the nature of the company, the change was not going to be one of simply updating a few physical management systems. There would be a number of complex organizational issues. This was recognized within the management of the change process and every effort was made during the early stages of the systems change to identify and involve the principal parties who would play a key role in securing the successful adoption of the change. Although the organizational issues were significant, the management team opted for a systems-based solution methodology. In the aftermath of a take-over and faced with tight schedules the aim was to secure immediate improvements with minimal opposition. The more protracted and open nature of organizational development solution methodologies were not considered to be positive factors in this particular change environment. This is not to say that BI did not wish to see organizational change, but at the time of the take-over this was seen as being a longer-term objective.

The option evaluation table, Table 5.3, produced by the problem owner along with the change agents, reflects the importance of organizational issues within this particular change environment.

The preferred option was the establishment of a dedicated contract management function. As Table 5.3 illustrates, all the generated options dealt with the organizational issues associated with the proposed change. ISM produced a solution to what at least was superficially a non-systems problem. It identified the optimal route forward and by ensuring, in the traditions of best practice, that the principal change agents were involved and committed from an early stage, it simplified the process of implementation. The new contract management function would later employ the systems approach to address more specific procedural changes, while the company and the new function went through a period of managerial development.

Implementation was dealt with as follows:

(1) Detailed planning to establish the new function. Conducted by the BI team and the proposed contract managers.
(2) Immediate transfer of staff from their existing functions (see point 3).

Table 5.3 Option evaluation (restructuring)

Objectives	Options		
Improvements in:	Dedicated contract management function	Improve administration effort and employ progress chasers	Place contract responsibility on functional department heads
Contract control	Responsibility defined: good chance of success	No single point of responsibility	Difficult to view the whole problem and act: poor chance of success
Cost control	Requires contract budget system	No budget responsibility	No overall contract cost control
Quality of customer contact	Single contact point	Multiple contact points	Multiple contact points
Team spirit	Facilitating role: independent of functions	No effect	No cross-functional benefit
Internal communications	All significant communication via contract manager	Possible improvement within functions only	Possible improvement at middle management level only

(3) The transferred staff, ten in total, acted as 'product champions'. These individuals had in the past, out of necessity, been acting as contract managers for large orders. As a result they were keen to promote the concept and generated a great deal of enthusiasm in others. In addition they possessed both a practical knowledge of the existing systems and understood the organizational issues.

(4) The contract managers, within their new department, developed the control systems.

(5) Resistance to the change was minimal as the new systems did not replace any existing control mechanisms. Remember that this function had not previously existed.

Over a period of time the contract management function established itself and in so doing produced a dramatic improvement in the handling of contracts. BI involvement continued until the change had been consolidated. They acted as an external driving force providing the change agents with authority and encouragement.

Case D: Caledonian Airmotive Ltd

The change situation which is about to be discussed was previously referred to when the case study from Caledonian Airmotive was used to demonstrate certain diagramming techniques in Chapter 3. As they also form the basis for one of the cases in Chapter 10, this review of their implementation strategy, concerning the development of an existing workshop area, will remain brief.

An autonomous accessory workshop is the desired outcome of the following implementation strategy:

(1) Parallel running of the proposed autonomous system along with the existing integrated set-up designed to minimize production disruptions.

(2) Building modifications to create purpose-built space for the new facility.

(3) Installation of an additional testing facility to ease capacity problems.

(4) Selection of additional supervisors for the new facility, with recruitment taking place from the existing systems personnel to minimize employee resistance.

(5) Erection of a new storage area to service the new facility.

(6) Selection and training of store personnel.

(7) Additional training of the mechanics about to enter the new autonomous working group.

(8) Final organizational change.

The sequential nature of the implementation strategy reflects the physical aspects of the change. Training and development, points 4, 6 and 7 above, are running alongside the physical construction activities. Discussions dealing with the finer detail of the organizational change are also scheduled to take account of the construction completion date. As would be expected, the greater emphasis on physical systems within the Airmotive case has produced a typical project planning solution of a sequential nature, but people issues have been identified and are receiving attention alongside the technical aspects of the change.

ITERATIONS

The example taken from the ABC testing facility illustrated a typical iteration. Too great an emphasis was placed on one aspect of the problem, in this case the technical features of the proposed system, which resulted in a key systems relationship, namely the role of the operatives within the new system, being overlooked until implementation loomed. In any project dealing with new and/or complex issues iterations are inevitable. The ISM methodology recognizes the need to formally introduce mechanisms which facilitate a number of feedback loops, and which may be utilized without casting aspersions on the abilities of the project management team.

6
Total Project Management

INTRODUCTION

Practising managers, especially those from an operational or systems back-ground, often express the view, when first faced with an intervention-strategy model, that they have no need for yet another investigative methodology based on the traditional phases of definition, design and implementation. They generally consider themselves to be proficient in the use of network and budgetary based planning and fully understand the decision-making process. However, with a little prompting they will very quickly admit that the problems they face when managing a complex project, a transition from one state to another, a change in effect, are often traceable to people-related management issues. When they are then forced to examine the planning and control tools they employ in project management, along with their decision-making methodologies, they realize that they do not incorporate the facilities necessary to integrate the organizational complexities with the physical planning mechanisms.

When exposed in a practical manner to the features of the intervention model described in Chapter 4 managers readily identify with the rationale behind its design. The emphasis placed on a systems review, which forces one to consider both the 'hard' and the 'soft' issues, to fully define the change environment and identify potential trouble spots well in advance of implementation, is often initially hailed as simple common sense. But do they follow this so-called common-sense approach? The answer is generally 'No' and that is why it must be emphasized within the model. Having agreed to the need for a thorough definition of the project environment it takes little effort to convince sceptics of the next step, namely, to fully specify both objectives and constraints, along with their associated perform-ance indicators, while always bearing in mind the forces and relationships identified during the definition phase. In addition, they warmly welcome the requirement to include in these early discussions potential change agents and other interested parties. However, they are not all enthusiastic about managing such an open and participative process, their enthusiasm seems to depend both on their discipline or function and the culture of their organization. Although a generalization, it would appear that managers from traditional engineering, manufacturing and construction industries tend to prefer to concentrate on the technical and scheduling aspects of a project or change. They recognize the benefits of a participative approach but do not feel their organizational culture, or their peer and subordinate colleagues, are ready for such a progressive step as talking about a problem.

The need to adapt the intervention strategy concept to reflect the processes and demands of project management was first identified, at least at the

Glasgow Business School, when staff detected an interesting development in the Operations Management course. A practical assignment designed to explore various facets of project management, within the course-participants' organization, began to be submitted in a format which reflected the content of a previously studied course. The Intervention Strategy Model, ISM, from the Change Management course was being employed to investigate and formulate responses to the project management assignment. The usage of ISM was such that the relevant staff members decided to investigate the rationale behind the shift towards this new approach to project management problems. Focus groups were organized. The participants expressed the view that existing network-based planning tools, computerized or not, did not fully address the 'softer' management problems, raised by projects which required organizational development issues to be tackled alongside the implementation of physical systems.

To assist the project manager in adopting an interventionist approach, in parallel with the more traditional planning and control techniques, members of staff at the University of Glasgow Business School commenced work on developing an integrated model, which was later to be called the Total Project Management Model, or TPMM for short. The basic aim of the model is to present to the project manager a package which integrates the intervention strategies associated with planning and managing change and the mechanistic planning tools associated with the scientific management approach. A model such as TPMM cannot teach a manager to manage in a more participative manner, which is the task of management development and training, but it can highlight the points within a typical project cycle when a more liberal and open management approach should be employed, or at least sought.

A project manager, as far as this text is concerned, is a term used to denote the individual charged with handling a specific project. They therefore in the course of normal events need not hold the title 'Project Manager' in a functional sense. They may or may not be skilled in the application of project planning techniques, but they will at least acknowledge their existence and seek out project team members skilled in their application. Such assumptions concerning the capabilities and knowledge bases of professional and appointed project managers are in this text's view valid, given the nature of its target audience, namely, potential or accomplished professional managers engaged in an advanced programme of managerial development.

This chapter will introduce the TPMM and develop its key features associated with both personal and organizational development in such a way as to lead into Part 3 of the text, which deals in more specific terms with organizational design and development.

TOTAL PROJECT MANAGEMENT

The introductory section of this chapter noted that project management has traditionally been treated as a systematic process with the emphasis firmly placed on the physical activities of the planning process, rather than on the actual practical non-technical managerial problems associated with the implementation of the plan. The planning process has been in the past and often continues to be, according to the feedback from Glasgow MBA students, solely conducted by those deemed to be directly responsible for the 'management' of the project. This project team will consist of planners and possibly technical experts with specific expertise associated with the project at hand. They will not experience the actual implementation of their plans from a managerial viewpoint. Many of the individuals and groups who will be both affected by and involved in the implementation of the planning outcomes are excluded. Yet surely it is this 'excluded' group who will ultimately determine the degree of success associated with the venture?

An example which rather dramatically illustrates this need for consultation involved the construction of an office block in the mid 1970s. The clients for whom the office block was to form a new headquarters, through their architects and consulting engineers, specified and subsequently had installed an air-conditioning system. Such systems were not common in Scotland at this time (although the year-round tropical climate does make them a necessity!) and people's knowledge of them was therefore limited. On occupying the premises the clients' staff, the ultimate users of the system, discovered that the windows did not open, and created such a fuss that at considerable expense to the client a large number of windows were removed and replaced with the standard opening variety. No one, from the clients to the contractors, had ever thought of asking the users what they desired in terms of work-place design. If they had, they may have discovered the need for some form of direct control over the working environment. The clients were never told that one of the advantages of air-conditioning, namely the automatically controlled working environment, negated the use of independently controlled window openings.

An investigation of the project environments along the lines advocated by ISM and TPMM would have indicated the need to consult the end users. This in itself would only have highlighted the potential conflict. By involving the users in the planning process and engaging in a programme of explanation as to why air-conditioning was required, and education of the benefits to the employees associated with its introduction, then the project managers may have reached some form of compromise prior to installation.

COMPLEX PROJECTS

At what point does a project cross the boundary from being one which can be adequately handled by considering only the physical planning activities into one which must be tackled, due to its complex nature, by considering physical and organizational issues in parallel? There is unfortunately no simple answer to this question. Chapters 2 and 3 dealt with the classification of the nature of change and the subsequent definition of a change environment. A project manager must employ the techniques and follow the procedural steps outlined in these chapters and then assess whether or not a particular project tends towards the 'hard' or 'soft' end of the change spectrum. The greater the tendency towards the 'softer' end of the spectrum then the greater the probability that the project falls into the complex category. In

Table 6.1 Comparison between mechanistic and complex projects

Complex projects	Mechanistic projects
Unclear objectives	Clear objectives
Large number of activities	Limited number of activities
Activity sequences and boundaries are unclear	Clear activity sequences and boundaries
Activities are not technically orientated or the technical aspects are not well known (e.g. new technology)	Activities are technically orientated and the technical aspects are well known and understood
Activities have indeterminate durations and resource requirements	Activities have a fairly determinate duration, and resource requirements are at least approximately known
Activity successes are largely dependent upon motivating people	Activity successes are linked to known technologies and systems, with limited human interfaces

such cases a purely 'hard' approach will not provide an optimal solution; that is not to say that the project will fail to be implemented, just that it will not arrive at its conclusion without creating a great deal of controversy and resistance. Any disruption to a project causes concern as delays generally mean that some form of financial penalty will be incurred.

One of the most important factors which differentiates a complex from a mechanistic physical project is the degree of dependency placed on the co-operation and acceptance of those directly affected by the outcomes of the planning process. The successful implementation of complex projects will ultimately depend on the effective management of organizational issues throughout the total planning process. Characteristics associated with complex and mechanistic projects are compared in Table 6.1.

The success of the project management process depends on the appropriate selection of a planning methodology. By fully defining the project in systems terms, the manager gains an insight into the complexities associated with the planning process. In situations where the project activities work towards the achievement of a specific and well-defined objective and the technologies, along with the environment, are equally well defined, then traditional planning tools should suffice. If any doubt exists as to the nature of the problems facing the project team and/or the environmental impact is difficult to define, then it is always safer to adopt an intervention-based strategy such as TPMM.

THE TOTAL PROJECT MANAGEMENT MODEL

The TPMM recognizes that a technically oriented approach to the management of complex projects must be augmented by the adoption of 'softer' people-centred planning mechanisms. As already stated, projects consist of both technological (or systems-based), and organizational (or people-based) elements. A systems-based planning technique is needed to handle technological or physical change; after all, it is in fact the systems which are being manipulated. However, adopting a purely systematic approach to the 'people' components of the project environment is likely to lead to subsequent difficulties during the implementation phase. TPMM addresses both 'hard' and 'soft' issues, by focusing on the technical and more physical aspects of a project from a systems point of view, and by adopting techniques associated with organization development (French & Bell, 1984) to address 'softer' aspects. Both areas are thus treated in an integrated manner, utilizing cross-functional teams, drawn from key areas of the project environment, who will bring to the problem a range of appropriate managerial skills and knowledge bases to effectively manage the 'total' project (McCalman, 1988).

The TPMM is an iterative and systems-based planning technique, which integrates 'softer' management philosophies and techniques into a traditional project management process. The model is outlined in Figure 6.1. Again the familiar three-phase format, similar to that adopted within ISM in Chapter 4, is employed, with terminology and activity modifications to reflect the specific emphasis on project management as opposed to the management of change.

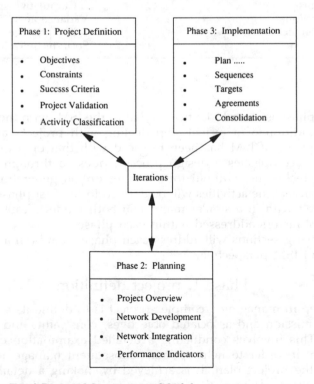

Figure 6.1 The Total Project Management Model.

Table 6.2 TPMM phase descriptions

Factors addressed	Techniques employed
Phase 1: Project definition	
Definition of the current position	Brainstorming techniques
Specification of environment	Team building
Evaluation of project	Systems diagramming
Definition of project owners	Factor ranking
Definition of preferred position	Decision trees
Project objectives	Investment appraisal
Resource constraint	
Resource requirements	
Success criteria	
Activity classification	
Phase 2: Planning	
Integrated project plan	Gantt charts
Performance indicators	Critical path methods
Potential iterations	Resource scheduling
	Investment appraisal
Phase 3: Implementation	
Presentation of plan	Charting methods ....
Application and monitoring of	Process charts
review systems	Cumulative spend charts
Potential iterations	Variance analysis ....
Autopsy of project	Exception reporting
	Socio-technical change models

The first phase is almost identical to that of the ISM, with the only change being the addition of a formal step dealing with project validation. The evaluation phase of ISM has been replaced with that of planning, which, although it accomplishes a design process, does so through a prescribed networking technique, without the need for option generation and evaluation. In a project the activities will be defined in the first phase. Implementation is dealt with in a similar manner in both models. Table 6.2 outlines the principal factors addressed within each phase.

The following sections will address each phase from both a project management and ISM perspective.

Phase 1: project definition

The first step in managing a complex project is to define its scope in terms of primary mission and associated objectives, constraints and performance measures. This involves conducting a detailed examination of the project environment in order to help optimize subsequent management decisions relating to the project plan. It is achieved by making a detailed, systems-oriented analysis of the project environment in association with any individuals or groups who have a vested interest. Within this analysis the activities and resources required to complete the project will be identified and detailed. In stressing the need for such an environmental analysis, TPMM is no different from ISM, and similar techniques would be employed in accomplishing the definition.

TPMM possibly emphasizes the need to indulge in team-building activities to a greater extent than ISM. This reflects the fact that project managers are often dealing with environments which change in terms of their composition from project to project. As TPMM suggests, the best way of ensuring that organizational issues are incorporated into the plan is to create and develop a cross-functional team representing key system areas and relationships from the project environment. As this team is likely to vary between projects, every effort must be made to ensure a team approach to the planning process is developed. To this end TPMM advocates the use of brainstorming techniques and planning sessions, within the definition phase, which emphasize a participative team involvement in specifying the project in terms of objectives, constraints, resources and environmental factors. Given the diverse nature of the project team, in terms of their hierarchical position, disciplines and roles, a non-threatening and open means of generating information for the definition phase is required (Paton, Southern and Houghton, 1989).

Project validation, involving investment appraisal techniques, within the first phase of analysis is not normally associated with ISM. It is employed to deal with a change which possibly, for many reasons, cannot be avoided. A project manager often finds it necessary to justify future actions by either proving the need to go ahead or validating someone else's initial proposals. TPMM also identifies the project activities and resources required within this first phase; these will be required to complete the network plans associated with Phase 2.

Phase 2: planning

Having fully specified the project environment in the initial diagnostic phase, the project team can now progress to a formulation phase, during which they will be confident of their system's assumptions, targets and resources. By evaluating the plans produced at this stage against the previously defined performance measures, the team will be able to evaluate planning alternatives effectively. In addition, since the total project environment has been considered, they should be aware and ready to deal with any obstructions which may delay implementation.

The planning process itself consists of four steps.

(1) Project overview: This is conducted by the project team and consists of the identification of major components, key events, component relationships, and human resource requirements (Boddy, 1987).
(2) Network development: This is conducted by a component team (i.e. a sub-group of the project team) identified during the previous step. This stage consists of task definition, resource requirement definition, and then network design (Lockyer, 1984).

(3) Integration of component networks: This is conducted by the total project team and consists of potential iterations back to component networks, formulation of the total project network, and referral back to objectives and measures identified in Phase 1.

(4) Performance indicators identification: This again is conducted by the total project team and consists of identification of specific performance indicators and iterations back to Phase 1 and Step 3 above. The indicators will be used for control and assessment purposes.

The planning phase of TPMM follows the traditional project planning route, utilizing networking techniques, to facilitate the actual physical planning of the project. The actions required to address the organizational issues identified within the definition phase, along with any others discovered during this phase, should be incorporated into the network planning process. These may include educational and training programmes and/or the limited involvement of additional key players in the actual planning process. In the similar ISM phase there is unlikely to be such a clear path to follow as one must first determine the potential solution paths and appropriate analysis techniques, prior to even considering sequencing solution options.

Phase 3: implementation

The final phase, that of implementation, consists primarily of the mechanisms to present the plan to relevant parties, and to put in place the necessary monitoring and correction systems. It is reached only after exhaustive examination of the environment has been completed, and the results are incorporated into the planning stage. As factors concerned with implementation are part of the planning process they will have already been considered earlier. Hence the presentation and monitoring mechanisms already developed to ensure successful implementation are integrated into the plan, and are more likely to be easily administered and understood.

Implementation involves the integration of the network analysis exercises of Phase 2, together with a thorough appraisal and action plan concerning any organizational issues, such as education, development and negotiation identified in earlier stages. Consolidation in the case of TPMM involves the project manager in monitoring the control mechanisms and taking corrective action as and when required. TPMM must deal with similar implementation issues as those addressed in ISM. All too often project planning teams reach the final hurdle of 'implementation', only to find that a lack of consideration in the earlier environmental definition has led them to neglect a key factor associated with successful implementation. By fully specifying the problem in systems terms and subsequently analysing the interactions to identify areas of interdependence and resistance, the project team will have the ability to forecast and deal with potential difficulties during Phases 1 and 2. The major difficulties associated with implementation will have then been removed.

If 'external' business and organizational developments alter the project environment between Phases 1 and 3, then the TPMM model, with its built-in iterations, can backtrack and incorporate the developments. Phase 3 ends with a post-mortem of the TPMM cycle, any lessons learned may be identified and incorporated into the project team's subsequent planning processes. The net result of the adoption of the TPMM philosophy will be effective project management allied to the development of an integrated design team. The use of socio-technical models to effect the final implementation is included to emphasize the point that TPMM, just as ISM, may require to employ, when dealing with a particularly messy change situation, techniques and process associated with organizational development and design.

ADMINISTRATIVE AND ORGANIZATIONAL POINTS

TPMM is a multi-disciplinary approach to the process of project planning. A cross-functional team brought together to manage the project, with each function bringing its own managerial skills and environmental knowledge, through the integrative nature of planning sessions and the facilitating skills of the project leader, will produce a project plan geared to the total solution of the problem or task at hand. This multi-disciplinary and cross-functional approach to project planning, along with the required estab-lishment of a team approach, often necessitates the need for extensive management development of the core project team. The provision of tech-nical planning skills is not enough, and managers must be made aware of, and provided with the skills to cope with, the 'softer', people-related issues, associated with effective project management (Boddy & Buchanan, 1986).

Project planning is conducted in a dynamic environment; the variability of both external and internal factors necessitates that the TPMM concept incorporates iterative feedback loops. Iterations, as mentioned previously, are particularly important during the implementation phase, but they may occur within and/or between any of the aforementioned phases. They may be seen as the reaction to the dynamic nature of associated variables. Iterations may be minimized through the development of a proactive stance by the project team. Changes in the environment associated with the project must be managed and incorporated within the developing plan (Wright and Rhodes, 1985).

Total project management, as in the case of the intervention strategies previously discussed, may be regarded as a hybrid planning tool. Its com-ponent parts are not revolutionary, it is the packaging of the systems and organizational disciplines into a cohesive whole which creates the positive results. Such a complete planning package, when effectively managed, cannot fail to increase the likelihood of successful project implementation. It also reflects the changing nature of today's management structures and strategies. Total quality programmes, customer awareness initiatives, just-in-time and the globalization of markets, must surely necessitate the development and implementation of innovative planning procedures which reflect manage-ment's overall strategy. Networking techniques, computerized or not, can no longer be seen as an independently sufficient means of achieving effective project planning.

ORGANIZATIONAL DEVELOPMENT AND DESIGN: ITS ROLE IN SYSTEMS INTERVENTIONS

In both the ISM and the TPMM much is made of the need to ensure participation and involvement, with the aim of achieving firstly a shared perception of the problem and secondly commitment to finding a solution. A systems-based solution methodology can not achieve this without redress to management techniques and processes associated with the field of organizational development and design. Unless the change or project is of a particularly 'hard' nature then the problem owners and project managers must endeavour to encourage those affected to accept the situation and thereafter assist in implementing a solution to the problem. Adoption of the 'softer' management approaches within a systems-based investigative framework should encourage the management team concerned to integrate more fully with those at the sharp end of the change.

Let us now consider five factors which help people accept change:

(1) Involvement:
   (a) Involve them by explaining the nature of the change and discussing its implications in an open and frank manner.
   (b) Gain participation by seeking out and fostering their ideas.

(2) Communication:
   Communicate, don't lecture, by means of:
   >Meetings and discussions,
   >Presentations,
   >Education and training.

(3) Perceptions:
   Consider people's worries. Think about:
   (a) Individuals' objections and how one could deal with their fears.
   (b) The benefits of the change and how they could be sold.

(4) Resource:
   Recruit and transfer in advance to allow assimilation of the new environment and facilitate training.

(5) Schedule:
   (a) Avoid scheduling the change and/or associated activities during work peaks.
   (b) Inconvenience can lead to resistance.

These people factors are dealt with in greater depth in Part 3 on organization development. They are also one of the major concerns in Case 5 in Chapter 11, in particular Figure 11.1 dealing with the management of change and people problems.

The above factors must be integrated with the 'harder', systems-based, approaches. In earlier chapters, organizational culture was noted as an important factor in promoting a climate of change, along with the need to formulate a proactive stance towards change and therefore encourage it to be viewed as an opportunity rather than a threat. Opportunistic and proactive actions are encouraged within cultures which exhibit enterprising features and open structures which foster challenging ideas. The creation of such cultures is far beyond the remit of systems-based intervention models. The power of the intervention model as a change management tool increases dramatically when it is employed in a progressive and co-operative environment. The organizational development chapters which follow in Part 3 of this text contain the means by which soft, people-based, change can be accomplished.

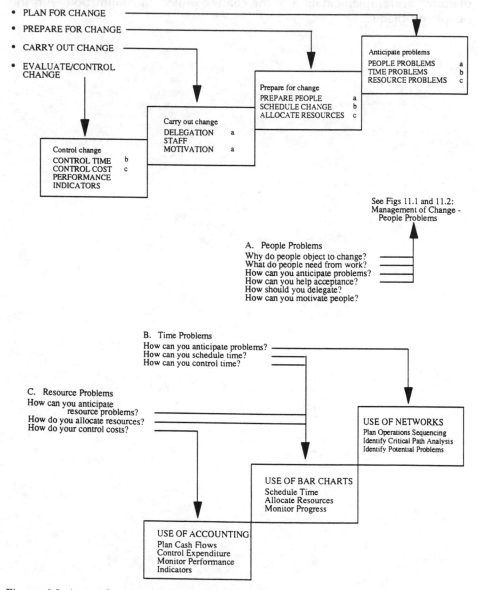

Figure 6.2 A step-by-step guide to managing change.

To provide a link between the systems intervention model and that of organization development, we recommend that the reader study Figure 6.2. This provides analysis of a step-by-step guide to managing change used by one of our case-study organizations, MTC Ltd. Figure 6.2 examines the people element of change as part of a total systems approach where the emphasis is on preparatory work for change. The harder issues addressed are grouped under resource and time problems. These groupings reflect the more technical features of the TPMM and are used to manage the control, planning and implementation of the change project in conjunction with the people problems.

Part 3

The Organization Development Model

7

People Management

The bulk of the scientific evidence suggests that the more the individual is enabled to exercise control over his task, and to relate his efforts to those of his fellows, the more likely he is to accept a positive commitment. This positive commitment shows in a number of ways, not the least of which is the release of that personal initiative and creativity which constitute the basis of a democratic climate.

(Einar Thorsurd, 1972)

You firmly believe that sound management means executives on one side and workers on the other, on one side men who think and on the other men who can only work. For you, management is the art of smoothly transferring the executives' ideas into the workers' hands.

(Konosuke Matsushita, 1988)

INTRODUCTION

An examination of any of the current, vogue examples of 'successful' companies reveals that two underlying themes are ever-present. Firstly, there is an emphasis on meeting customer satisfaction, to the highest standards. The quality criterion is what guarantees success in any business you care to mention. Secondly, the successful organization, no matter which country it comes from, how long it has been in existence, or what products or services it produces, takes care of its people. That is to say, success comes from customer satisfaction which is generated from motivated people. The ability of an organization to manufacture products or provide services, rests on its ability to gain commitment from the people within that organization. This seemingly simple process is complicated, however, by the approaches adopted by organizations, and by managers within those organizations in terms of their behaviour and attitudes towards the individual within the organization.

There is the potential for conflict in all organizations. In fact, conflict occurs on a daily basis. The argument with your secretary over a report that is needed for the board meeting, the screaming match between marketing and the factory floor, the formal warning given for consistent lateness, are all examples of conflict between individuals who theoretically share the same objectives. Buchanan and Huczynski (1985, p. 9) view this as an organizational dilemma: 'Many of the 'human' problems of organizations can be identified as conflicts between individual human needs, and the constraints imposed on individuals in the interests of the collective purpose of the organization.'

Similarly, March and Simon (1958, p. 26) note that, 'An organization is, after all, a collection of people and what the organization does is done by people. Therefore, ...propositions about organizations are statements about human behaviour.'

The simple logic in these statements is only lost on us when we begin to view organizations as something more than what they are. When the issues are confused by organization structure, management roles and the role of technology, we begin to lose sight of what the real basics are. If we build organizations for performance, then it is the people within such organizations that deliver the performance we require.

Part 3 of this book, and this chapter in particular, deals with three fundamental concepts:

(1) Organizations are about people.
(2) Management assumptions about people often lead to ineffective design of organizations and this hinders performance.
(3) People are the most important asset, and their commitment goes a long way in determining effective organizational design and development.

People in organizations can be provided with the opportunities for growth and development if the organization itself is designed to do so. It is the recognition of this which drives the basic principles of organization development. We introduce here the concept of design and development within the organization as it relates to people. The Organization Development Model (ODM) propounded in Chapter 8 is not new, nor is it radically different from the writings of many of the leading authors in the field. What it does is place design and development in the context of managing change. To do so requires that people, structures and systems change, and this creates the potential for conflict. Avoiding conflict is as much a state of mind as it is a manageable process. If the manager believes in employee involvement, the freedom to exercise control over tasks, then the design element should reflect this. The difficulty, as Konosuke Matsushita points out, at the beginning of this chapter, is that a lot of managers in organizations in the Western world believe in the division of labour − the separation of initiative from performance of the task, thinking from doing, manager from employee.

This raises a number of questions which the following three chapters will hope to address. For example, why does this type of thinking still occur in the 1990s, why is it so prevalent in Western economies, what are the consequences of adopting these approaches, and lastly, can we do anything about it? This chapter sets out to address these questions by looking at how and why the ODM is needed. We begin by looking at why some form of people management is necessary in all organizations. From there we go on to look at the concept of design in organizations and various ideas related to how to deal with organization design and development in the firm.

The latter part of this chapter begins to look at the weaknesses of Western management. In particular it addresses managers' perceptions as they relate to the desire for control in organizations, the way in which they perceive design as an analytical exercise, the lack of resolution to delegate responsibility, and the lack of philosophy and values about the organization. These are serious accusations that are laid at the door of managers in organizations in the Western world. However, there are two justifications for putting them so blatantly. First, it reflects a level of truth associated with them. Management in Western economies, to a large extent, still operates with traditional forms of work organization which are epitomized by the application of assembly style manufacture. This may be a gross generalization, and some of you may work in what can be termed enlightened companies. But many will not, and this is what we need to address. For example, why do companies in the Western world look to Japan and ponder how they do it? One answer is to look at how Japanese firms believe they do it. The quote from Konosuke Matsushita at the beginning of this chapter continues: 'We are beyond the Taylor model; business, we know, is so complex and difficult, the survival of firms so hazardous in an environment increasingly unpredictable, competitive and fraught with danger, that their continued existence depends on the day-to-day mobilization of every ounce of intelligence.'

There is a current management joke doing the rounds of conferences and presentations. It goes something like this. Three chief executives, one American, one Scottish and one Japanese, are taken hostage by Arab terrorists. On failure by their companies to pay ransom they are all sentenced to death. In time-honoured fashion their captors grant them a last wish. The Scottish manager chooses a bottle of whisky to drown his sorrows and remind him of the old country. The Japanese manager asks for a Sony Walkman to record for posterity how his company managed to become world leader in its field. The American manager asks to be immediately executed, 'So that I don't have to sit through another lecture on successful Japanese management practices!'

In a world that is highly competitive, firms in the United States, Britain and other European countries quite rightly look enviously east to Japan and repeat the question, 'How do they do it?' If the need for change in the organization design of Western firms was not so crucial this question would not be asked so often. Our first justification is based on the assumption that firms look for alternative models of design and behaviour where they perceive that a need exists. In the past, the need for change was not so prevalent — the old ways of manufacture brought profitable returns. This is no longer the case. The reasons why managers ask why the Japanese perform so much better than we do are based on the need to search for solutions that will ensure competitive survival in the market-place. Many firms operate traditionally because they know of no other way. This is the way that it has always been done, and it brought profitable return. However, when the market-place demands change, for example products geared to specific customer needs, traditional concepts such as the long production-run no longer become feasible, and change is therefore needed.

Second, we wish to see firms actively address these organizational and managerial issues in a positive sense by looking at alternatives; by using the Intervention Strategy and Organization Development Models to consider options; and by implementing changes which make for effective organizations. We all have a vested interest in the survival and growth of organizations in the UK. By overtly opening up the discussion in this way we hope to suggest (in Chapter 8) that there is a need to look at organization design and development and view it as being as important as product development. It is only in this way that managers begin to recognize its importance for effective performance.

WHY MANAGE PEOPLE?

Extremism is a popular concept in management. Both in the theoretical underpinnings and the everyday practice, analogies are used which portray the two extreme elements of management characterized by an either/or exchange deal: good and bad management practice, 'hard' and 'soft' management techniques, manufacturing versus sales and marketing trade-offs, technology or people. The reality is that continuum which Simon (1957) recognized as bounded rationality. That is, all managerial decisions are made by individual choice based on economic (business) and social (humanistic) concerns. One of the outcomes of these concomitants of economic and social rationality is that there is a dependence and independence among individuals in organizations.

McGregor (1960, p. 26) argued that the individual in American industry existed in a state of partial dependence, 'Authority, as a means of influence, is certainly not useless, but for many purposes it is less appropriate than persuasion or professional help. Exclusive reliance upon authority encourages countermeasures, minimal performance, even open rebellion.'

If this was true of the American organization of the 1960s, then it is also true of Western societies in the 1990s. The power of the individual has assumed greater prominence over the last decade, fuelled by the cult of entrepreneurialism, the alteration in demographic make-up of the working population, the increasing educational awareness of the workforce, and the erosion of the middle management layer in organizations. What we have in today's society is a workforce which matches ideally that propounded by the early organization design and development writers: 'Interdependence is a central characteristic of the modern, complex society. In every aspect of life we depend upon each other in achieving our goals...the desirable end of the growth process is an ability to strike a balance – to tolerate certain forms of dependence without being unduly frustrated' (McGregor, 1960, p. 27).

This is one of the major issues concerning the management of people today; how does the manager tread the fine line between complete dependence of the individual on the one hand, and complete independence on the other? This brings us back to extremism again. Down one path (dependence) leads the conceptualization of the individual as specialist in the organization process. This is the Tayloristic view of structure and design of the firm: everyone in their place. Down the other path, many would see the managers' worst nightmare, organizations without management. As was hinted at earlier, the reality is the middle ground, what McGregor and others would refer to as interdependence.

The need to manage people effectively is the desire to attain what is termed the 'helicopter' approach to management, that is being able to take the longer-term view without becoming involved in the day-to-day operational issues. These are workforce issues and are most comfortably dealt with at that level. A manager in one of our leading electronics companies explained how this process should work, and why it does not:

Let me give you an example of how you manage it. It's dead easy and the analogy is so straightforward that even some of our managers can understand it. You have an important meeting to get to in London on Monday afternoon and you discover that your car isn't working on Friday night. What do you do? Obviously, you contact the garage first thing Saturday morning, get them to come round, take it away and fix it for you. You also find out if they can get it back to you later that day or Monday morning. You then go ahead and make alternative plans for your meeting if necessary, plan what you are going to do at the meeting, and in reality enjoy the rest of the weekend. You know, enjoy the Chablis over a good meal on Saturday night, oversleep Sunday morning, spend the afternoon over *The Sunday Times*, watch *The Cosby Show*, etc., etc. What you don't do, and this is where you get the message home, is stand over the mechanic whilst he repairs your car, telling him what to do. He knows what to do for Christ's sake! If it's good enough as a personal example then it's good enough in a workplace scenario. The manager has to let go. He has to be able to let the people for whom he is responsible get on with their own jobs, secure in the knowledge that they have the competence, the capability and the commitment to deliver the goods on time. This leaves the manager free to do other things; planning is an example, dealing with customers and suppliers, both internal and external to the business. The difficulty we have is that so many of our managers find it painful letting go of the everyday reins of what they consider management. It's basic insecurity on their part, they have to be seen to be doing something, and overtly managing the work is the best showpiece they have. It's silly really.

One of the key elements of managing change in the 1990s will be to develop this 'hands-off management' approach. Peters (1987, p. 369) notes that, 'In this new role, the middle manager must become: (1) expediter/barrier-destroyer/facilitator, (2) on-call expert, and (3) diffuser of good news. In short, the middle manager must practise fast-paced 'horizontal management' not traditional, delaying, 'vertical management'.

Similarly, Kanter (1989) stresses the importance of change in organizations, away from formalized structures and rules towards greater personal commitment,

In the traditional bureaucratic corporation, roles were so circumscribed that most relationships tended to be rather formal and impersonal. Narrowly defined jobs constricted by rules and procedures also tended to stifle initiative and creativity, and the atmosphere was emotionally repressive. The post-entrepreneurial corporation, in contrast, with its stress on teamwork and co-operation...brings people closer together, making the personal dimension of relationships more important.

(Kanter, 1989, p. 280)

The difficulty with these visions of the future is that making the change is difficult and painful, and not too many managers truly believe that the changes are essential to business survival. Why is this the case? If there is any truth to what we are saying here then why do managers not want to make the necessary changes that ensure survival, growth, customer satisfaction, and success? The answers have a self-accusing, almost frightening tone to them.

THE ENEMY IS US

Most managers when they look at their employees see a need for control. Tom Peters summarizes this approach quite eloquently.

> You have to ask yourself what you see, what you really see, when you look into the eye of a front-line employee. Do you see a ne'er-do-well that needs that span of control of 1 to 10 prevalent in your organization, that'll rip you off if you turn your back for more than three or four nanoseconds? Or do you see a person that could literally fly to the moon without a face-mask if only you would just train the hell out them, get the hell out of their way, and give them something decent to do?
> (Quote from 'Tom Peters — Business Evangelist', *Business Matters*,
> BBC Television, 1989)

It is this concept which lies at the heart of the control versus commitment argument of management. From an organization-development perspective, organizations are about people, about their development, enhancing their performance and building the organization on that performance. The essence of rigid control is an onerous one in the development of the organization. It is obvious that every organization needs a set of rules and guidelines against which individual and group behaviour is judged. However, in most modern organizations, these tools and methods are traditional and no matter how well refined and expertly applied, they are insufficient mechanisms for the development of the organization towards higher standards of performance. Why? Let us look at a common and persistent example.

Task fragmentation is a popular system in firms (Buchanan and McCalman, 1989, p. 11). It can have a number of advantages for the organization that applies it. The individual employee does not need too much expensive, time-consuming training, those who leave are easily replaced because the job is simple to learn, employees can do their tasks at great speed, and less skill is required, hence lower-paid workers. For the manager it is also easier to control employees who undertake simple tasks. However, fragmentation also has a number of serious drawbacks. For one, the job is repetitive and boring. The employee working on a fragmented task has no idea what his or her contribution to the organization as a whole is. This boredom costs money — absenteeism, apathy, carelessness, even sabotage. The employee develops no skills which can lead to promotion, a greater degree of contribution, or higher standards of performance. But it is these facets which are exactly what we require from every employee to allow the firm to survive and grow in the global economy of the 1990s. And yet, the procedure for fragmenting manufacturing or service tasks is common and accepted in most of British industry today.

One therefore has to ask oneself why are these techniques and practices still applied so widely? Management models and theories have existed for most of this century. Many of them are widely known and practised. However, many are inappropriate models for today's organizations. Designed in the early part of this century, they work on assumptions that no longer exist. So in this sense we practise the wrong stuff, and many Western organizations stick by these theories as if they were written on tablets of stone. The idea of removing the need for time and motion analysis is as much an anathema as removing the organization and methods specialist in a large number of organizations. The same can be said for the way companies are structured and the bureaucratic forms, rules, procedures and role allocations that take place within them. How can a company like Compaq Computers come from nowhere to become a $3 billion multinational enterprise in the space of ten years with a fraction of the manpower that other electronics companies employ? The reason is they allow their people to make decisions. The company is founded on the belief that the people within it are what makes it successful.

There has been a growth in interest in the concepts of work organization and development through the latter part of the 1980s and early 1990s. The reasons for this are fairly straightforward. The circumstances that organizations face today are related to speed and flexibility of response to changing market situations. For example, five years ago the concept of doing business with companies in Poland and Czechoslovakia would have been inconceivable. Things change, and today Czech firms, such as the world's only manufacturer of Semtex explosives, are on the open market. Management concern is associated with being able to deal with changing markets, how to make best use of sophisticated levels of technology application, and how to meet the rising expectations of customers as they relate to quality, reliability and delivery. This means that issues related to the people element of firms become more important. As Kanter notes:

> You watch human resource policies move in British firms, from being a sort of backwater, 'they're the people who do the paperwork', to being a much more significant piece of strategic thinking for the firm because everybody is going to compete for people in the 1990s. In fact the quality of people is going to make a bigger difference than the quality of products or the quality of services.
>
> (Rosabeth Moss Kanter, from *Business Matters*, BBC Television, 1990)

Buchanan and McCalman (1989, p. 6) argue that these issues have meant that a movement has occurred in the management of people in organizations. This movement is one away from 'personnel administration' (the hiring and firing) to 'human resource management' (development of the individual in the organization). As problems have become more serious, what were traditionally accepted as the boundaries placed on work organization have been widened. One could argue that human resource management is no longer acceptable unless it is accompanied by organization strategy and improvement. The argument here is that traditional personnel departments need to become involved in people and organizational development at the same time, to assist the organization in dealing with more complex issues than were apparent in the 1960s and 1970s. The world is a different place in the 1990s and organizations have to behave accordingly. Nor is it the sole remit of personnel departments. Effective people management affects the overall operating profitability of the organization and must therefore involve management at all levels from the boardroom to the shopfloor.

There are important issues at stake here. In earlier chapters we have emphasized how systems intervention could help resolve what we classified as 'hard' issues – questions such as technology allocation, priorities, etc. In Part 3 we also want to place emphasis on the concept of what would be considered by many as 'soft' issues. The concern here is with people management as part of the 'big picture'. Here the concern is with getting the best level of performance from the human assets which the organization invests in. These are not incidental issues. Effective human resource management makes money, guarantees profitability and ensures effective performance. We may classify these as 'soft' issues by comparison to systems intervention strategy, but the returns on getting it right in terms of organizational development are equally as important as the issues dealt with in Part 2. The significant questions associated with people management are:

How do we manage people to best effect?

What systems do we put in place to ensure that this effective management of the human resource occurs?

To the extent that effective human resource management systems have been widely known since the 1930s and 1940s, there is a third, and ultimately damning question:

Why are these systems and styles not applied?

The answers have a familiar, self-analytical tone to them. We manage organizations according to our perceptions about the individual and about the organization. We do not apply models where we believe they are likely to upset the apple-cart. In other words, we have met the enemy – it is us. The answer to the question 'Why are these systems not applied?' is that there is a fundamental problem in the way managers think and then educate people in organizations. It may be rather a simplistic way of putting it, but it is managers that design and run organizations. If these organizations are unable to compete in the market-places of the 1990s, then the design is wrong and the blame ultimately rests with those responsible for that design. This is what Konosuke Matsushita was getting at in the quote at the beginning of this chapter. He describes his view of the victory of Japanese industry over that of the West as a victory associated with organization design, and with the management of people. In this sense the battleground is over the correct and appropriate division of labour. Laurence V. C. Megson, European Organization Consulting, Digital Equipment Corporation, argued in 1988 that:

Six major issues seem to be at the core of building organizations that perform exquisitely. These in my experience are the major educational hurdles we have to overcome if our quest for more effectiveness is to bear further fruit.

1. The way we think is THE root cause. We use analytical and mechanistic thinking inappropriately. With organizations we need to use systemic and synthetic thinking instead.
2. Our models of organizations are too limiting. Produced by analysis they run on analysis. Machines are their analogues.
3. We have no purpose. Preposterous? Organizations are inward looking and purpose can only be found beyond their boundaries. So if we don't look in the right place for purpose we will not have the right one, which is as bad, if not worse, than none at all.
4. We have no vision or sense of mission. Without this any organization cannot achieve really high performance.
5. We lack the resolution to delegate. We simply do not treat our subordinates as we expect our bosses to treat us — and if they feel 'less than', their contribution is 'less than' as well.
6. We have no values nor philosophy — about work and people that are explicit, shared and identify the part people play in the scheme of things.

As a result, there are a number of elements associated with the choices that are made in relation to people management in organizations today.

First, because the root cause is the way we think, we tend to use models for organization design which are too limiting for our needs. Managers use and concentrate on the machine theory of design, and place capital equipment above and before people in the design element. The machine system analyses the problem, produces the desired design and installs that design, in-company, by analysis. The difficulty here is that the reason for designing the organization in this way is to meet an internal purpose when purpose is to be found beyond the boundary of the firm. An example of this would be where managers design systems that are technologically driven but ignore human contributions and/or customer demands.

Second, very little time and attention is paid to the concept of design from an organizational perspective. The research and design of a product can take years from initial idea to final product delivery. Market research, advertising and placement of that product can command massive budgets in ensuring that everything is right when the product hits the market-place. The amount of time spent *designing a new organization system to cope with change* within a firm is minimal, if it takes place at all! It is more often than not done on the back of an envelope, with little consultation with those likely to be affected by the changes involved, and little consideration given to the likely outcomes of the change. The reasons for this are related to the way managers think about their organizations. Analytical and mechanistic thinking are encouraged (especially at business schools and on MBA programmes) when they are highly inappropriate. If an organization is an organic system, then systemic thinking is necessary.

Third, the behaviour of managers in organizations suggests that there is a distinct lack of resolution to delegate within organizations. This was referred to earlier on and the examples from Thorsurd and Matsushita explain the impact that this has. There is an unwillingness to treat subordinates in the same manner that managers expect to be treated by their own superiors. This has knock-on implications for motivation. Place yourself in the position of a front-line operator. Ask yourself the Megson question — 'If I am treated as "less than" by my immediate boss, then is it surprising that my response in terms of commitment is "less than"?' If the answer is no, which it should be, then managers have to ask themselves, 'What types of hell-holes have we as managers created?' (Tom Peters, *Business Matters*, 1989).

Fourth, managers lack any form of systematic thinking about core values and philosophy of the nature of work and people in work that are explicit, shared and identify the part that people in organizations play within the grand scheme of things. If you do not understand the 'big picture' yourself, how can you see how others fit into it?

It is these issues which need to be addressed in order to create a clearer understanding of what the big picture is, and how people fit into it. This leads us on to Chapter 8 which sketches out the Organization Development Model and how it can be used by organizations. The remainder of this chapter takes each of the comments associated with the main management issues outlined above by Megson (1988) and explains them in more detail. We look at why these issues occur, how they manifest themselves in organizations, and what is needed to change. The accounts given here are largely prescriptive in the sense that we specifically set out what is being done wrong, and what is needed to make it right. They are also set in fairly provocative and challenging terms — deliberately so. We want you to think about them, see if they are true, see if they apply to your organization, and then think what can be done to resolve them. However, we have also attempted to be descriptive and present particular events and circumstances that managers would be expected to come across during the course of their job in order to provide illustrations of what we mean. You should be able to sympathize and associate with these. You should also be able to recognize and begin to think about the changes that are needed. One important point needs to be emphasized here. Suspend your initial judgements and firm belief that, 'This wouldn't happen to me, so I can ignore it'.

THE MODELS WE USE ARE TOO LIMITING

The way managers think in the Western world is very much conditioned by their approach to the management profession. It is most readily summed up in that well-worn (and flawed sentiment) that 'It's management's right to manage'. The noun 'right' in this instance connotes a prerogative, authority or desire to control or dominate. The right is that of position power in many instances and is based on nothing more than title. This is reflected in the traditional Tayloristic model of organization popularized in the early twentieth century. This views people, especially those on the shopfloor, as machine parts, elements, factors of production, cogs in the larger machine. In this sense, individuals only need to know as much as is necessary to play their part in the process. It is the manager's role to organize, control and co-ordinate the bigger picture.

There are three reasons why models such as Taylorism retain their popularity (Buchanan and McCalman, 1989, pp. 12–13).

First, they are easy to apply. Taylorism, the division of labour, task specialization, etc., appears as a plausible and cheap set of techniques which appear to suit. The ideas are fairly straightforward by comparison to some of the models which are linked to organization development. Specialization for example, reduces the amount of work that progresses through the manufacturing system and consequently increases throughput. It also simplifies the production element: everyone has a place and everyone should be in that place: 'It is always easier to blame workers who have the wrong skills, wrong attitudes and wrong values, than to blame a systematically prepared job specification' (Buchanan and McCalman, 1989, p. 12).

Second, they perpetuate status. The status is that which Taylorism affords to managers. A greater degree of responsibility taken on by the workforce, who can control the performance of meaningful sections of an organization's operations, begins to threaten the legitimacy of management. It is easier (and more comforting to status) to have individual workers who have little or no identification with the whole organization and who have no idea how they fit into the bigger picture. Taylorism fragments tasks, hides contributions and maintains managerial status.

Third, managers are unaware of alternative forms of design and development for their organizations. This is not the managers' fault. The alternatives are couched in such obscure language (and journals) that their wider applicability is lost to the manager, and thus the credibility of such alternatives is eroded.

One of the difficulties with the old-fashioned view of management was that it failed to recognize the full potential of the individual in the organization. It is commonly accepted that for most organizations in the 1990s, survival and growth will stem from the full utilization of the intelligence, skills and commitment of the workforce, and from perceiving the labour element of production as an asset value instead of a factor cost.

It is not surprising that approaches to the concept of design are not new in organizations. The fact that industrial organizations have been in existence for 150 years or more would suggest that at some time during this period a body of public knowledge on how best to organize and design the firm would have built up. There are a number of approaches that can be considered. Many are couched in the language of the period in which they were developed, and many show signs of age as we approach a new century. However, there are schools of thought which try to integrate differing variables associated with design to effect more appropriate forms of business performance.

Four models are briefly outlined in this section. We freely admit to not doing them justice here, and the reader should seek these out for future reading (see Huczynski and Buchanan, 1991). The models have an historical, sequential development beginning with machine theory or scientific management (Taylorism), moving on to the human relations movement, the contingency theorists, and finally the organization development movement.

Scientific management (Taylorism)

One of the first models of organizational and management behaviour was that developed in the early part of this century by Frederick Winslow Taylor. The concepts of what is now widely referred to as 'Taylorism' lay in the division between manual and mental work in the organization. The basis of Taylor's theories was that work could be divided into sub-units or specializations which could be performed by individuals. Taylor started from the basic principle that work could be scientifically determined and that 'one best way' to perform a task could be found, made standard practice, and that the individual and organization could benefit. We do not have the time or space here to go into the details of the Taylorist model, but we mentioned earlier the reasons for the popularity of this. Organizations have also attempted to move on from Taylorism in the search for more appropriate models.

The human relations movement

The second school of thought related to organizational effectiveness and behaviour stemmed from the studies of Elton Mayo and Fritz Roethlisberger at Western Electric's Hawthorne plant near Chicago during the 1920s and 1930s (Roethlisberger and Dickson, 1939). Whereas the scientific management studies of Taylor focused attention on mechanistic, machine theories of organization, the Hawthorne studies drew attention to the humanistic approach and in particular to group behaviour and relations among group members and between group members and management. Effective performance was associated with understanding the linkages between the individual, his role among other members of the group at the workplace, and the degree of independence given to the group. In the human relations movement, increasing individual satisfaction within the group led to increased performance and greater organizational effectiveness. The human relations movement was also important in recognizing the importance of job design as a variable in organizational performance.

The contingency theorists

By the early 1960s, further research in the area of organizational behaviour suggested the development of a series of contingency theories based on an open-systems concept or view of the organization. These organizational theorists advocated no single form of organizational structure or style of management. Concepts such as structure and managerial style were dependent on the organization's business and its environment, or numerous other influencing variables. There were a number of contingency theorists, each with their own specific view of the influencing variables which determined the way an organization was designed. We shall look at two in particular – Burns and Stalker, and Lawrence and Lorsch.

In an examination of twenty British firms during the 1960s, Burns and Stalker identified two types of effective organization – mechanistic and organic. Both types were effective under different circumstances. The mechanistic firm prospered in stable markets whereas the organic firm succeeded in rapidly changing markets and technologies. The mechanistic organization has the following characteristics:

(1) Task differentiation and specialization;
(2) Hierarchy for co-ordination of tasks, control and communications;
(3) Control of incoming/outgoing communications from the top and tendency for information to be provided on a need-to-know basis;
(4) Interaction and emphasis placed on vertical reporting lines;
(5) Loyalty to the organization and its officers;
(6) Value placed on internal knowledge and experience, in contrast to more general knowledge.

(Burns and Stalker, 1961, p. 119)

By contrast, the organic organization was characterized by:

(1) Continuous assessment of task allocation through interaction to utilize knowledge which solves real problems;
(2) The use of expertise power relationships and commitment to total task. Sharing of responsibility;
(3) Open and widely used communication patterns which incorporate horizontal and diagonal as well as vertical channels;
(4) Commitment to task accomplishment, development and growth of the organization rather than loyalty to officials;
(5) Value placed on general skills which are relevant to the organization.

(Burns and Stalker, 1961, pp. 120−5)

Burns and Stalker's research work was important in the sense that their studies identified differentiation between types of organization, and the belief that the organization could change its design, structure and approach dependent on the situation in relation to its environment.

In a similar vein, the basis of the Lawrence and Lorsch analysis of organization (1967, 1969) was that structure and management depended on the environment the firm found itself in, and because of this, the more complex the environment, the more decentralized and flexible management needed to be. They suggested that successful organizations were structured according to the environment. Patterns emerged which suggested that the nature of *differentiation* occurring in the organization determined the degree of centralization/decentralization that took place. This differentiation within the organization could be measured by examination of the following characteristics:

(1) Formal structure (rules, regulations, procedures, etc.)
(2) Certainty of goals (are they clear and easily measured or uncertain?)
(3) The timing of feedback (are results seen in the short or long term?)
(4) Interpersonal interaction (level of interpersonal and intergroup communication and co-operation).

Let us look at this in practical terms by considering the example of the structure and management of firms in the hardware and software sectors of the electronics industry. Both the internal and external environment for software manufacturers is extremely complicated. Firms deal in the concept of, and trading of, pure knowledge — the expertise of their software writers. Policy is largely flexible, being a function of current demand in many instances. Instantaneous feedback and interpersonal communication are a way of life. Structure is largely informal (for example, relaxed dress codes, single status parking and restaurants). The environment changes rapidly and therefore the organization has to be able to monitor and react quickly to changes. This suggests a more relaxed, decentralized form of organization and management.

By comparison, in many of the hardware sectors of the electronics industry — defence and avionics, large mainframes, supercomputers, etc. — there is a more stable environment. Structures are more formalized, as are reporting and communication procedures. Although by comparison to other industries, change may be perceived as rapid, there is a tendency for more centralization, longer-term goals and results feedback, and precise policies and procedures that are adhered to.

Which of these types of design, structure and management are correct? The answer, according to Lawrence and Lorsch, is that they both are, because they both fit the organization's environment. One of the key elements to emerge from the work of Lawrence and Lorsch was that predictability of the task was a basic condition variable in the choice of organizational form. That meant that both internal and external criteria had to be taken into consideration.

The Organization Development Model

Chapter 8 deals specifically with the history, systems and application of organization development. However, it is important here to emphasize that it is a design model that has been developed extensively over the last twenty years by authors both here and in the United States. A wide body of literature exists on the subject of organizational development and design. It is important here to classify what we mean by organization development and the concerns it attempts to address. Warner Burke (1987) classifies organization development as 'a planned process of change in an organization's culture through the utilization of behavioural science technologies, research and theory'. The importance though is that,

> OD practitioners are concerned with change that will more fully integrate individual needs with organizational goals; change that will lead to greater organizational effectiveness through better utilization of resources, especially human resources; and change that will provide more involvement of organization members in the decisions that directly affect them and their working conditions.

> (Warner Burke, 1987, p. 11)

This is the model which we are looking for in terms of people management. However, we still have to take into account the limiting issues mentioned by Megson. Figure 7.1 is a schematic model for organization used at Digital Equipment Corporation. The first point to note is that it is a bounded

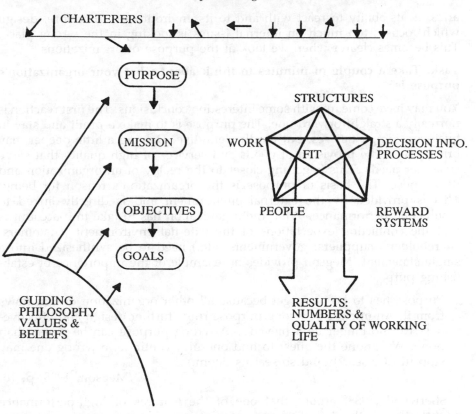

Figure 7.1 The organization development model at Digital (Megson, 1988, *Building Organizations for Performance*, Digital Equipment Corporation, unpublished).

model. It places the organization within an environment (this pays heed to the work of Lawrence and Lorsch) represented by 'charterers'. The word charterer is used to convey importance to those outside the organization, those that give the organization its reason for being. Mechanistic models of organizations ignore them or assume that their needs, having previously been established, do not need to be reviewed. However, for survival, organizations need to identify expectations of charterers, and synthesize these into a statement of purpose.

OUR ORGANIZATIONS HAVE NO PURPOSE

If the accepted design norm is that most organizations are/were designed using the process of analytical thinking, breaking the job down into constituent parts for task specialization, then this machine analogy finds its purpose by reference to an internal focus. However, as many organization theorists point out, the purpose of an organization is found outwith its own boundaries, in its ability to react with and to its environment. Therefore, design which focuses too much on internal issues is looking in the wrong place. This becomes clearer when we look at the purpose of organizations.

Task: Take a couple of minutes to think about what your organization's purpose is.

You may have come up with some interesting conclusions. The first reaction is normally a straightforward one. The purpose is to make a profit and stay in business. Simplistic, yes, but hardly definitive. Delving a little deeper may bring you to the provision of goods and services of high quality that serve customer needs. This is getting closer to the reality of an organization and its purpose. The basis of purpose is the organization's reason for being. This is provided by the external environment and is directly linked to results and performance. What the organization has to take into account is that the conflicting expectations of the external environment (customers, shareholders, suppliers, governments, etc.) need to be synthesized into a single statement. Megson provides an example of the importance of establishing purpose:

> Purpose has to be on target because all other organization design flows from it. An unclear or wrong purpose ruins further design and effectiveness can no longer be achieved...A wrong purpose can be worse than none. With none the quest to find one may continue, a wrong one may stop further search and so seal its doom.
>
> (Megson, 1988, p. 10)

Sherwood (1988) argues that one of the features of high-performance organizations is the definition and organization-wide awareness of purpose:

> A shared sense of purpose entails sharing a vision that is based on a clearly stated set of values describing both the organization's mission (purpose) and the methods for realizing it. An organization's vision provides energy and direction...It empowers individual employees and forms the basis of a planned culture.
>
> (Sherwood, 1988, p. 9)

Organizations have to be able to define their purpose in clear, unambiguous terms which enable them to create a precise design to fit the purpose. The most effective means of doing so is to look to the external environment to find the purpose of the organization (provision of product on time, negotiation of supply contracts that benefit both sides, etc.). This provides the work that an organization needs to accomplish, and then the organization executes the work. The other variables in the diagram operate to assist in the accomplishment of purpose. Define the purpose, do the work, achieve the result and effective performance is gained. This appears too easy. The reality is that design is complicated because of what we have argued earlier. We are not geared towards thinking in these terms. They are seen as 'woolly' and too far removed from reality and the everyday pressures of work. We would argue that this is because many organizations lack the vision or sense of mission to think in these terms.

OUR ORGANIZATIONS LACK VISION OR SENSE OF MISSION

The mission statement in organizations is a popular tool for clarifying operational strategy. A sense of mission, in an organizational sense, is for the people working in that organization to develop. The level at which mission is defined determines the level of awareness and commitment to it. The most popular form of mission definition is that provided by the boss. It is quick but shuts out the rest of the organization. Mission defined by a senior management team takes longer but the pay-off is more powerful. Mission determined by the whole organization is rare, takes an enormous amount of time, and may prove impossible to develop. Whoever sets it, mission is about aspiration values within the organization. By not sharing these aspirations, the opportunity to build an effective organization team is lost. In developing vision and mission, the organization also has to look at the needs and wants of the individual. People do not get energized unless they see their own needs and wants in parallel with those of the organization. If purpose tells the organization what it needs to do, then mission gives the organization what it wants to do as well. There are opportunities to structure work that has to be done to fit the purpose in ways that meet individual needs and wants. However, these needs are often ignored. Organizations require to develop their mission, to tap into the talents and energies of the people within it.

MANAGERS LACK THE RESOLUTION TO DELEGATE

Many managers do not treat their subordinates as they expect to be treated by their bosses. As a manager, your expectation is that your immediate superior will give you space. You can manage yourself — true? However, managers expect obedience from those who work for them. Managers see themselves as committed to the organization and to its purpose as well as their own. Yet managers expect loyalty from subordinates without considering their needs and wants. The manager expects to use his or her own talents to the full, yet they tell people what to do. As a manager you see yourself as open, candid and courageous, yet you see subordinates as less-than with all that this implies for shutting off candour and making argument feel like a test of courage or a career decision. Managers often treat employees as less-than in terms of their own initiative to contribute, and it is hardly surprising therefore, that their response is less-than. There is a need to empower subordinates to see themselves as equals.

In Chapter 8 we will look at some of the practical applications of organization development. One of these is the use of autonomous or semi-autonomous workgroups where employees are empowered to take responsibility for their own actions in a workplace setting. However, this is difficult for the manager to deal with because it involves a 'hands-off' management approach. The structure of these workgroups sets up the requirement for employees to be treated as equals. Managers have trouble with this because most of them do not really believe that they are or can be equal. Because of this managers do not have the necessary values which are consistent with the concept of delegated responsibility. Without this delegated responsibility there is never full commitment, and hence the potential of employees remains underutilized.

ORGANIZATIONS OFTEN HAVE NO VALUES

This is a mistake. Everyone has their own values and philosophy which guide them through life. However, in an organizational setting what is lacking is a shared set of values and philosophy. Philosophy and values relate to how organizations deal with their beliefs about people and work. Deal and Kennedy note that,

> In our work and study, we have found that successful companies place a great deal of emphasis on values. In general, these companies shared three characteristics.
> They stand for something − that is, they have a clear and explicit philosophy about how they aim to conduct their business.
> Management pays a great deal of attention to shaping and fine-tuning these values to conform to the economic and business environment of the company and to communicating them to the organization.
> These values are known and shared by all the people who work for the company − from the lowliest production worker right through to the ranks of senior management.
>
> (Deal and Kennedy, 1982, p. 22)

These fundamental beliefs and philosophy guide the design of organizational life. They need to be defined and shared with organizational members in order that people understand and make sense of their working life, how and where they fit into the big picture. Megson, in describing the guiding values and beliefs at Digital comments that,

> They are based on a Philosophy that I describe as follows:
>   People are the most important asset we have.
>   They want and need to grow.
>   Without growth interest wanes and talents waste away.
>   With growth interest flourishes and talents develop.
>   People really do care. They do exquisite work − if it is designed to
>   enable them to grow.
> In other words, personal growth is the engine that drives organization performance.
>
> (Megson, 1988, p. 16)

It is the ability to put these guiding values and beliefs into practice which is at the heart of the Organization Development Model which we deal with in the next chapter. The key is to design work that fits people and not the other way round. If we accept that effective performance comes from people being energized towards their needs and wants as well as those of the organization, then the design has to take account of this.

THE CONCEPT OF DESIGN IN ORGANIZATIONS

All firms have to consider the element of design. To the extent that every firm exists, it has a design associated with it. The small business operating out of a garage and employing ten people has a structure and is designed according to the owner's wishes. The corporate multinational operating across five continents and employing 400,000 people also has to consider design. The commonalty is associated with the attainment of standards of performance and the need to deal with complexities of size and division of labour (Galbraith, 1977). The organization has to conceive an approach to satisfy the attainment of a number of factors. There are three factors, *the goals and purposes for which the organization exists, the patterns of labour division and co-ordination of different units within the organization, and the people who will do the work* (Galbraith, 1977, p. 5). The concept of design in organizations is associated with establishing a fit between these three areas of choice. The essence of design is the assessment of fit between the three areas, the examination of alternatives where the fit does not operate effectively, and the implementation of those alternatives in the form of a new design.

An example of how this concept operates in reality is provided by the case of Virgin plc.

Virgin plc: going public and learning to regret it

In 1986, the Virgin records, retailing and leisure group became a public company. Richard Branson, founder and bastion of the 'go for it' approach to business in Britain in the 1980s floated off his empire on the public stock exchange and 55,000 small investors rushed to participate in the 140p per share offer.

The reasons for the decision to go public were fourfold. First, there was the belief that going public would increase the profile of the Virgin group and so enhance its business prospects. Second, the public flotation would provide the wherewithal to make acquisitions. Third, it increased the group's borrowing capability for expansion. Fourth, it provided incentives to staff who could own shares in Virgin plc, as well as involving the public in the company.

By comparing Virgin's decision to go public with the basis for organization design we can see that the criteria of goals and purposes of the organization and the people who will do the work were considered as the basis for the decision. In terms of goals and purposes, the desire to go public served several needs. The private Virgin felt stifled by its overdraft facilities for the size of the concern and by its inability to expand as quickly as it would like. It also had an awareness that its image with the outside world did not fit that which it desired. Similarly, in terms of the people who do the work, there was a desire to instigate a new form of reward system by giving people the opportunity to acquire shares in the new group, thus providing incentive.

In 1988, Virgin plc went private. The reasons behind this return were both financial and organizational. In terms of the organizational issues, the question of co-ordination was one of the key lessons learned that drove Branson towards returning the firm to private ownership. As he commented,

> Being public is incredibly time-consuming. You have board meetings for non-executive directors; you have 'board meetings' the day before real board meetings; and every single thing has to be vetted by lawyers. You are tied up in tape...making sure everything was done by the book — and worrying about the next quarter's results, rather than planning for the long term. And so we thought, *'Let's try to get out of this'*.
>
> (Eglin, 1990−1, p. 24)

The desire to design the Virgin organization for the third time in two years was the wish to get back to co-ordinating activities which fitted its goals and purposes. Again Branson commented,

> If the people who run the company feel free, they can make the rest of the people who work for the company enjoy it, and you can have a happy company. If the people at the top feel that their hands are tied and they can't make the kinds of decisions they feel are right for the company — and not just right for the shareholders and the city — then the company starts stifling.
>
> (Eglin, 1990−1, p. 26)

In this sense, the two Branson moves, the private to public to private again, can be seen as an approach to design which started out by an assessment of the degree of fit between goals and purposes, co-ordination of activities and the people element. This led them to the conclusion that there was a need to generate more capital than could be acquired privately and that there was a need to address image and reward issues. Secondly, Virgin considered alternative approaches to meet the needs of the business (in the first case going public, in the second returning to private hands). Finally, Virgin implemented changes according to the new design which were considered appropriate.

Virgin plc is also an example of an organization in which change occurs all the time, in which design elements are considered crucial to the well-being of the firm, and where the guiding values and beliefs specify that people are considered important enough to admit when mistakes are made.

The concept of design in organizations has to be congruent with people. Work needs to be designed in a manner in which people are engaged in meaningful tasks. The organization must fit work to people, not the other way around. Anything less is sub-optimal, and does not guarantee high performance. When designing the organization, we must consider how the work of the individual employee adds to the purpose of the enterprise. Work has to contain within it elements that achieve business purpose and can be measured. For example, in manufacturing, the mechanistically deter-mined fragmentation of tasks means that the individual employee knows his or her own job very well, but not the whole. This means that people miss the impact that the interactions of the parts have on their surroundings. The traditional mechanism for responding to this lack of interaction is supervision. The supervisor provides the overview and direction to the task players. Today, the pace of change is such that this level of supervision is questionable. It is an inadequate use of employee capabilities and is over-manning gone mad. Work that is designed to allow the employee to build product, test it and ship it provides contribution and meaning. People understand where they fit into the system, and performance is easy to assess in terms of results that are important — quality, cost, time to customer, etc. It provides the employee with work that demands commitment.

This is largely where we came in. Management in organizations today is largely people management. If people are the important asset of the 1990s, their effective management is related to how managers perceive the individual in the organization, how people relate to one another in an organizational setting, how we get the maximum contribution from the individual in the organization, and how we go about changing from a situation which is seen to be ineffective to one which ensures higher standards of performance. In Chapter 8 we set out the Organization Development Model as an approach to managing change. It is one which lays emphasis very much on people issues. In this chapter we have tried to lay the groundwork in a challenging manner. We doubt whether organizations are as black as we have painted them in terms of purpose, mission, delegation, etc. But when dealing with the people element of managing change it is important to continually question why we are doing things. It is how we perceive people that matters. It is how we perceive the organization that matters. It is how we perceive the manager's role that matters. We are fortunate to live in an era of rapid change. It gives us the *raison d'être* to ask questions, try new concepts, question things, and most importantly be aware of the pervasive nature of change. The goals associated with the 'soft' issues — organization develop-ment — are related to communication within the organization, to decision-making styles and systems, and to problem-solving. The values are human-istic and are aimed at developing maximum potential for the individual, the group and the organization as a whole. The requirement is for the encourage-ment of open relationships in the organization. Understanding the import-ance of people is the first step.

8
Organizations Can Develop

In the last few years, more and more organization leaders have realized that it is not enough to carry out piecemeal efforts to patch up an organization problem here, fix a procedure there, or change a job description. Today there is a need for longer-range, co-ordinated strategy to develop organization climates, ways of work, relationships, communications systems, and information systems that will be congruent with the predictable and unpredictable requirements of the years ahead.

(Richard Beckhard, 1969)

Let us make no mistake: the cultures of consent are not easy to run, or to work in. Authority in these organizations does not come automatically with the title; it has to be earned...based...on your ability to help others do better, by developing their skills, by liaising with the rest of the organization, by organizing their work more efficiently, by helping them to make the most of their resources, by continual encouragement and example.

(Charles Handy, 1989)

INTRODUCTION

There is a twenty year gap between Beckhard (1969) and Handy (1989) yet the issues being addressed have not really changed all that much. Beckhard, writing in 1969, identified that the business environment of the time had to deal with quite a few changes. These included internationalization of markets, shorter product life, the increased significance of marketing, relationships of line and staff management, new organization forms, and the changing nature of work (1969, pp. 5–6). Issues don't really change over time, only the degree of importance. How many of the changes identified by Beckhard are crucial today? We would argue that they all are.

Task: Inappropriate analysis of change...

Comparisons of American, British and other European companies by Ashridge Management Research Group found that British companies were likely to respond to change only as a result of major economic downturn or similar disaster (Wille, 1989). American and European companies were more likely to initiate change in their organizations to take advantage of opportunities or to avoid potential problems.

In 1990, the UK population totalled 57.3 million with 19% aged under fifteen years old. People in the 45–60 age group made up 16% of the population, while the old, those over seventy-five, made up only 6.9%. By the end of the 1990s, this age distribution will have changed markedly with the youngest age group making up 20% of the population, the middle-aged 18.5% and the over seventy-five, 7.4%.

The structure and size of the population has a major influence on the economic well-being of a country. Population demographics have a serious bearing on the profitability of certain industrial and service sectors.

What are the major implications of these changes for your organization in the 1990s?

In Chapter 7 we seemed to indicate that there was a great deal to be done in the area of organizational development in Western firms, especially in the United Kingdom. Our argument was that because of the nature of managerial behaviour, the full level of effective performance of an organization was hampered. The major element of this behaviour was reflected in approaches to the management of change. More often than not these are non-participatory, lack clear goals and objectives, and are undertaken in a piecemeal fashion. Our suggestion in this chapter is that the element of people management via organization development programmes is not given the same level of importance or thought as that attached to product development or market research development.

. . . leads to ineffective responses to opportunities

Most organizations in Britain during the 1990s are likely to be affected by changing demographic patterns to a greater or lesser degree. Two examples serve to show the crucial nature of being aware of the need for proactive change within organizations.

Two of the major beneficiaries of an ageing population are likely to be pharmaceutical giants and healthcare companies, such as AMI. An ageing population spends more per capita on healthcare than any other section of the population. Organizations such as BUPA may face a drain on their resources as an ever-ageing population begins to take advantage of the healthcare schemes that individuals have contributed to over the years. However, a generally healthier, more health-conscious population will not be such a drain on firms in the healthcare sector.

Secondly, in retailing, an increase in the middle-aged sector of the population may hold benefits for companies which specifically target this range of the population. Marks and Spencer will not go to the wall in the next decade because its traditional customer base is in the thirty-plus age group. However, the 'hot' retailers of the 1980s, companies such as NEXT and The Body Shop, may face mixed fortunes. The ecological and environmental concerns of a more aware population will ensure the survival of companies such as The Body Shop which operate sound environment policies, whereas NEXT is already trying to reposition its product range to take account of changes in markets, population and consumer tastes.

The importance of change management is not the extent to which these demographics are accurate, nor is it in whether the trends indicated actually come to fruition. The importance, in terms of change management, lies in thinking about the implications of issues, such as demographics, on company performance ten years down the road. How many of you, when thinking about demographics, thought about the impact on recruitment within your own organization?

In dealing with the often 'messy' problem of people management, many settle for the easy route of ignoring the problems and hoping that performance will be somehow maintained. What we argue in this chapter is that, given the current economic climate in the 1990s, organizations in the West can no longer afford to ignore the human element as part of the change process. All change in organizations is about people. Technological change includes a people element. Product design or improvement is likely to affect those who have to manufacture those products. Changes to services provided or markets served will have an influence on members of the organization. In this sense then, the people side of change cannot be ignored. Nor should it. We firmly advocate in this chapter that firms begin to use more refined mechanisms for instigating change that consider, include, seek out and involve those likely to be affected – the organization's members. What we recommend here is the use of an Organization Development Model (ODM). However, in doing so, we are not attempting to break new ground. The techniques that we describe and explain here are neither unique nor innovative. These techniques have been well known for at least twenty years, but not well practised by organizations in the United Kingdom to any great extent. The techniques of the ODM, however, will require a change of emphasis in management thought in a large number of cases. First and foremost, they require recognition that change implementation involves people and that gaining the involvement and active participation of the individual within the organization will assist the likelihood of success.

There are three areas with which we will concern ourselves. First, we look at where organization development stemmed from. To do so, involves an analysis of the work of a number of writers in the fields of behavioural and social science, what they suggest and how this impacts the individual, management and organization as a whole. Second, we detail what we mean by the ODM and how it can help organizations to manage change more effectively. Third, we comment on guiding values and beliefs which assist the movement towards effective performance.

SORRY, THERE ARE NO ROUTE MAPS

Martin and Nicholls (1987) describe three influencing factors which offer challenges for British managers. These challenges are well known and establish a certain number of needs related to how managers react and behave in organizations during the 1990s. Managers will need to learn to:

(1) manage people whose output is difficult to monitor directly – information workers;
(2) manage increasing technological complexity;
(3) manage to achieve a higher level of performance, given increased international competition.

To be able to meet these challenges, managers need to create (or more realistically recognize the existence of, and channel) commitment from the workforce towards new working relationships and more effective perform-ance. Martin and Nicholls (like so many others, including ourselves) recognize the problem, and offer potential solutions. As far as they are concerned, effective performance comes from having a committed workforce. This is accomplished by allowing people to have a sense of belonging to the organization, a sense of excitement in the job, and by confidence in manage-ment leadership (1987, p. 15). By using examples from British organizations such as Jaguar Cars, British Steel and Burtons, they proceed to show what can be done. However, and this is the nub of the matter, they cannot and do not attempt to tell other organizations how to go about it themselves. The difficulty with excellence programmes, as authors such as Peters and Waterman (1982) have found out to their cost, is that although many man-agement writers are aware of where organizations should be heading in the future, there are no route maps. We can describe the processes by which change should take place and the issues that need to be considered by management and workforce alike, but you cannot buy a stencilled guide to change management for your own organization − it doesn't exist.

Many managers, while accepting the overall argument about the need for change in organizations during the 1990s and the development of new organization structures and management styles, would like to see some beef. It is a common belief that there is a lack of adequate guidance on how to transform an organization and its employees, at all levels, in this direction. We will try to address this directly in Part 4 of this book when we look at practical cases of change management. What we will stress is that change is not effortless. However, when one pays attention to the experience of change as it is lived, then a more comprehensive perspective of organization change emerges (Buchanan and McCalman, 1989, pp. 50−7). One of the best ways of doing so is to look at examples of change management situations in some detail, analyse how and why they took place, and learn how to apply the benefits that accrued elsewhere.

What we attempt to address in this chapter is the process of organizational development from a people point of view. In the sense that we put forward a model here − the Organizational Development Model − it is not a panacea. It is the description of an approach, a school of thought on change, that has developed largely since the 1960s. This chapter sets out to describe the history of organization development; how organizations can use the ODM effectively for change; and what requirements firms need to have to operate effectively. In this sense, we offer a set of descriptive commentaries. However, we justify this by arguing that in this area of change, there is much commonality. The approaches adopted here are not crucially different from the work of other authors. The reasons for this are that organization development uses techniques from the behavioural and social sciences which are well known, have been around for a long time, and have been proven to be effective. What we have done is to place them within a context of change, to relate them to organizations based in Britain, and offer some checklists that the manager can use in his own organization to test the organization development water, so to speak.

Exercise: the manager, the organization, and design issues

Before we go any further we would like you to undertake a short, relatively painless exercise to try and gauge your own assumptions about your organization and the people who work in it. Below are ten sets of paired statements. We would like you to allocate TEN points per paired statements. For example, if you agree more with the first statement then allocate more points to that one than the second, etc., etc.

Points

1

There are very few people in my organization who come up with good ideas.   a . . . . . .

Given the chance most people in my organization will come up with good ideas.   b . . . . . .

2

The majority of people in my organization can and do exercise self-control and self-direction.   c . . . . . .

The majority of people in my organization prefer to be given direction.   d . . . . . .

3

People in my organization do not have enough experience to offer practical ideas.   e . . . . . .

Getting people to contribute ideas leads to the development of useful suggestions.   f . . . . . .

4

For the manager to admit that an employee is right and he or she is wrong weakens his or her status among other employees.   g . . . . . .

The manager's respect and reputation are enhanced by admitting to his or her mistakes.   h . . . . . .

5

A job that is interesting and challenging can go a long way towards eradicating complaints about pay and benefits.   j . . . . . .

Paying people enough for the job means that they are less bothered with responsibility and recognition.   k . . . . . .

6

If employees are allowed to set their own objectives and standards of performance, they tend to set them higher than their manager would.   l . . . . . .

If employees set their own standards, they tend to be lower than those set by the manager.   m . . . . . .

7

The more people know about their job and are free to make decisions about it, the more you have to keep an eye on them to keep them in line.   n . . . . . .

Knowledge of the job and freedom to make decisions means
fewer controls are needed to ensure competent performance.   p ......

8
The restrictions imposed by the job limit the ability of
people to show imagination and creativity.   q ......
In the workplace, people do not use imagination and inven-
tiveness because they do not have much of either.   r ......

9
When responsible for their own quality, people tend to raise
their standards.   t ......
Quality tends to fall off when it is not supervised and
imposed on people.   v ......

10
Truth is better than fiction and most people prefer the full
story no matter whether bad or good.   x ......
When there is bad news about the organization employees
prefer not to know.   z ......

Scoring

Add up the total points scored for each of the letters in the column below:

a   ....
d   ....
e   ....
g   ....
k   ....
m   ....
n   ....
q   ....
v   ....
z   ....
_____

_____ = Your X score

100 − X score = Your Y score

Score analysis

This simple exercise tells you something about the type of manager that you
are. It is based on McGregor's Theory X/Theory Y classifications. If you
have a high X score then the assumptions that you make about people and
the design of work in organizations operate around a certain set of values.
The framework you use is one that views the individual in the organization
as someone who needs to be directed, avoids responsibility, must be controlled and coerced into effort, and has an inherent dislike of work. If you
have a high Y score then your assumptions are that individual and organizational goals can be integrated and that the individual is a person that
strives for better performance, has commitment to the organization for
whom he or she works, and can contribute more than is currently being
asked of them.

We would certainly hope that your Y score is higher than your X score as it will assist in your willingness to use some of the ideas and concepts within the ODM. Either way, you should reflect on the scoring you have just achieved. That score is based on the assumptions *you* make about individuals in your organization, and hence influences how *you* go about managing change in organizations.

We now move on to examine organization development, where it came from, what it entails, how it can be used, and who is likely to be involved in an organization development change process.

WHERE DOES ORGANIZATION DEVELOPMENT COME FROM?

There are a number of broad definitions of the term organization development. However, there is a body of opinion from authors such as Beckhard, Bennis, Blake and Mouton, Lawrence and Lorsch, Schein, Walton, Warner Burke, and Lawler who regard organizational development as a process by which the members of an organization can influence change and help the organization to state and achieve its goals better. The ultimate aim here is achieving greater organizational effectiveness. The way this is accomplished is by a process of facilitation. This sets out to unblock issues which are currently hampering performance in the organization. The process of facilitation involves a change agent who helps members of the organization move forward towards an agreed set of goals and objectives which can then be implemented. This occurs at three levels within the organization and reflects both the organization and the people that make it up.

The first level is that of the individual and what motivates individuals to higher standards of performance. This emphasizes two areas of thought: need theory and expectancy theory. Need theory concentrates analysis on issues associated with how jobs are designed for best effect, career development, and human relations training. Expectancy theory concerns itself with needs and rewards systems. The second level is that of the group and inter-group perspective. This emphasizes the importance of group behaviour, group belonging and its effect on the motivation of the individual, and the use of the group as the major leverage point for change. The third level is organizational. Emphasis is placed on management style and approach, organization structure, and the organization in its environment.

The history of organization development

To get a better understanding of organization development it is useful to understand its historical progression. Rather than chart the history of the subject from time immemorial, we shall examine the progress of organization development in a number of subject areas and include a number of authors in these areas. We divide these into two phases. The first phase concerns the work of Douglas McGregor leading to Theory X and Y, and the work of Eric Trist and Ken Bamforth at the Tavistock Institute which led to the development of socio-technical systems design. The second phase looks at the growth of subject-specific work related to organization development techniques at individual, group and organizational levels, from the 1960s onwards.

McGregor and the human side of enterprise

One of the many starting points for organization development comes from the work of Douglas McGregor, author of *The Human Side of Enterprise* (1960) which set the tone for management thought during the 1960s. McGregor worked at the Sloan School of Management at Massachusetts Institute of Technology (MIT) and developed organization development programmes for many organizations including Union Carbide and Esso. These training programmes usually took the form of team-building events. McGregor, along with Beckhard, also worked on changing organization structures to enhance teamwork and increase decision making at the shopfloor level. They termed this work organization development. The publication of *The Human Side of Enterprise* clarified the role of management and created the concept of Theory X and Y. In this, McGregor classified managers' attitudes and perceptions about the worker and the design of organizations as falling into two categories.

Theory X assumptions

(1) The average human being has an inherent dislike of work and will avoid it if he can.
(2) Because of this human characteristic of dislike of work, most people must be coerced, controlled, directed, and threatened with punishment to get them to put forth adequate effort toward the achievement of organizational objectives.
(3) The average human being prefers to be directed, wishes to avoid responsibility, has relatively little ambition, and wants security above all.

Theory Y assumptions

(1) The expenditure of physical and mental effort in work is as natural as play or rest.
(2) External control and the threat of punishment are not the only means for bringing about effort toward organizational objectives. People will exercise self-direction and self-control in the service of objectives to which they are committed.
(3) Commitment to objectives is a function of the rewards associated with their achievement.
(4) The average human being learns, under proper conditions, not only to accept but to seek responsibility.
(5) The capacity to exercise a relatively high degree of imagination, ingenuity and creativity in the solution of organizational problems is widely, not narrowly, distributed in the population.
(6) Under the conditions of modern industrial life, the intellectual potentialities of the average human being are only partially utilized.

(McGregor, *The Human Side of Enterprise*, 1960)

The last exercise you completed placed you in one of the two camps. By creating a form of extremism in terms of management perceptions of the workforce and the design of organizations, McGregor intentionally set out to accomplish a particular objective:

It is not important that management accept the assumptions of Theory Y...It *is* important that management abandon limiting assumptions like those of Theory X, so that future inventions with respect to the human side of enterprise will be more than minor changes in already obsolescent conceptions of organized human effort.

(McGregor, 1960, p. 245)

At this point it may be useful to refer back to the exercise you completed a few pages back and reflect again on which side of the fence you came down on. We would suggest that if you came down heavily on the side of Theory X then the use of organization development techniques and the ODM will be difficult for you given its emphasis on participatory management techniques.

The Tavistock Institute and socio-technical systems

Not all theories and practices relevant to the ODM emanated from the United States. At around the same time that McGregor and others were undertaking research analysis in large American organizations on issues such as sensitivity training, a second influential body of research work was being undertaken at the Tavistock Institute of Human Relations in London. At the Tavistock, researchers such as Eric Trist, Ken Bamforth and A. K. Rice were developing the model of socio-technical systems design from their research work with Durham coalminers and textile workers at Ahmedabad, India.

The concept of socio-technical systems which resulted has had a great deal of influence in the field of organization development as it relates to elements such as work design and autonomous/semi-autonomous workgroups. The argument they put forward was that any organization exists both as a social and a technical sub-system and that both these sub-systems need to be taken into consideration when organizations contemplate change. It is a powerful technique in terms of work design but lacks popularity. One of the reasons for this is that the approach itself directly challenges the status and responsibilities of managers at supervisory levels whose duties can be taken on by self-managing groups. However, the concept has received a new lease of life during the 1980s and 1990s as problems within organizations have grown in significance. Radical solutions which call for a redefinition of the management function as well as reorganization of work become more acceptable and gain management credence under these circumstances. However, applications of this particular type of work design model have largely been the prerogative of large, multinational organizations (Buchanan and McCalman, 1989, pp. 209–12). The Tavistock model is outlined in Figure 8.1.

In analysing the effectiveness of socio-technical systems and especially the concept of autonomous or semi-autonomous work groups in organiz-

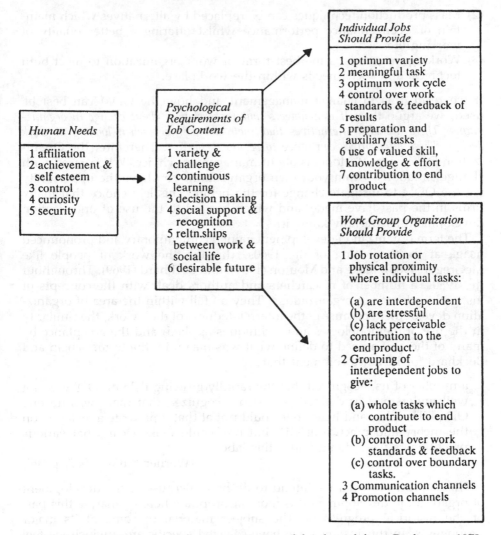

Figure 8.1 The Tavistock work organization model (adapted from Buchanan, 1979. *The Development of Job Design Theories*, Saxon House, Aldershot, p. 112).

ations, Hunt (1979, p. 259) comments that, 'Probably more than any other method, this approach recognizes the common sense of individuals who for decades have been treated as morons by managers of large organizations'.

Three important issues for organization development emerge from the Tavistock studies. We have not done the studies justice here and would suggest that the reader delves deeper into them. However, the important issues which emerge are:

(1) It is managers that make decisions about work organization, job allocations, the formation of groups, and the amount of discretion allowed to workers.

(2) Mass production techniques can be replaced by alternatives which maintain or even enhance performance whilst offering a better quality of working life.
(3) Working in groups is the best form of work organization to meet both technical and social needs within the workplace.

If we relate this to change management and how the ODM can best be used, we argue that: *It is managers that make choices about change in organizations. There are also alternatives that they can consider when looking at work design. These alternatives can prove to be more effective.* Therefore, the Organization Development Model is about management choice. When faced with change situations within your own organization, you have the opportunity via the ODM to instigate change for the better. This is a choice that many firms in the past have made, and which has led to the use of organization development as we now know it.

The term organization development gained contemporary and pronounced usage at the beginning of the 1960s, through the work of people like McGregor (1960), Blake and Mouton (1964), and Beckhard (1969). Throughout the 1960s, a number of researchers and authors dealt with the concepts of instigating change in organizations. They all fall within the area of organization development because of the interrelatedness of their work, the similarity in the use of methodologies and techniques applied, and the acceptance by many of them of a need to define what was meant by the term. Schein and Beckhard for instance comment that

> a number of us recognized that the rapidly growing field of 'OD' was not well understood or defined. We also recognized that there was no one OD philosophy, and hence one could not at that time write a textbook on the theory and practice of OD, but one could make clear what various practitioners were doing under this label.
>
> (Warner Burke, 1987, p. vii)

This is precisely what we intend to do here. Because of the development of organization development it is more appropriate here to analyse this part of the historical progress via the subject material of some of its major proponents. In this instance, we have selected specific areas which we feel best represent what is meant by the ODM that we shall propose later on in this chapter. These areas are: individual motivation at work, job and work design, interpersonal skills in groups, and participative management.

Motivation of the individual

One of the key areas of organization development is understanding human behaviour in organizations. The work of writers such as Vroom (1969) and Lawler (1969) is concerned with what motivates individuals to perform within their organization. Their research work led to the conclusion that motivation was dependent on situational and personality variables. In relation to this, Vroom (1969, p. 200) comments that 'The situational variables correspond to the amounts of different kinds of outcomes (e.g. pay, influence, variety) provided by the work roles, and the personality variables correspond to individual differences in the strength of their desire or aversion for these outcomes'.

Motivation was linked to three factors or assumptions concerning individual behaviour. The first pertained to what the individual saw as the expected outcome of their behaviour. For example, if an individual believes that the accomplishment of a certain task will lead to rewards then they will undertake that behaviour in the expectation that reward will be forthcoming. This belief is classified as performance-outcome expectancy. The second assumption was that the rewards associated with behaviour have a different value (valence) for different individuals. In this sense, what motivates some individuals may not motivate others to the same degree. For example, one individual may place a greater emphasis on monetary gain than another would. Third, individuals had to have a certain degree of belief that their behaviour would have a reasonable chance of success. For example, a manager may believe that he can finish a company report within ten days but his expectation that he can finish it within seven days is very low, no matter how hard he works on it.

Research work on motivation led to the conclusion that individuals would be personally motivated when they perceived that rewards would accrue, where they valued those rewards, and where they believed they could perform at a level where attainment of the rewards was feasible. Vroom also included a fourth variable related to past performance. That is the amount of reward that the individual expected to receive or had received in the past would also influence their behaviour within the organization (1969, pp. 200–8).

Lawler's work also extended into analysis of job design and the importance of issues such as meaningful contribution and feedback in stimulating motivation in the individual. In relation to this, Lawler comments that,

> it has been argued that when jobs are structured in a way that makes intrinsic rewards appear to result from good performance then the jobs themselves can be very effective motivators. In addition, the point was made that if job content is to be a source of motivation, the job must allow for meaningful feedback, test the individual's valued abilities and allow a great amount of self-control by the job holder.
>
> (Lawler, 1969, pp. 425–35).

The work of writers such as Lawler and Vroom is important in an organization development sense because of its emphasis on motivating the individual towards higher standards of performance. Their work is also crucial because its focus of attention is on job design and structure as well as the provision of feedback as mechanisms for enhancing organizational performance. Similarly, their work suggests that reward systems are an important variable in effective organization development change processes. These are issues we will look at in greater depth later in this chapter.

Job and work design

Work design is an important part of organization development models. The research work in this area, especially that of writers such as Hackman and

Oldham (1975), looks at work design from a position of need and expectancy theory. The focus of attention, in this instance, is how work design leads to greater worker satisfaction. The variables associated with greater worker satisfaction are: (1) meaningfulness of the work, (2) responsibility for the work and its outcomes, (3) performance feedback.

Hackman and Oldham (1975) attempted to separate the main features of work (core job dimensions) from critical psychological states (employee experience) to establish a causal link between job implementing concepts, such as natural work units and feedback channels; core job dimensions, such as task identity and autonomy; psychological states, such as responsibility for the work and knowledge of the results; and personal and work outcomes resulting in high internal work motivation, high quality work performance, etc. Figure 8.2 details the worker motivation, job satisfaction criteria associated with organization development.

Interpersonal relations

The work of writers such as Chris Argyris is important to organization development because of the emphasis placed on issues related to developing the individual within the organization. Argyris's work falls into two main streams as far as organization development is concerned: individual development towards maturity at work and interpersonal relations within the group at work. Argyris argues that what prevents maturity in individuals in the workplace is the approach of management and the lack of interpersonal competence. Developing on from the work of McGregor, he argued that certain behavioural patterns of management emerge in organizations. A manager may espouse Theory Y values but his pattern of behaviour (which Argyris referred to as pattern A) associates his managerial competence with that of Theory X (Argyris, 1970). In this sense, management self-perpetuates its own need for control:

> The increased use of management controls deprives employees of any opportunity of participating in the important decisions which affect their working life, leading to feelings of psychological failure. It is not they themselves but the control systems (such as work study and cost accounting) which define, inspect and evaluate the quality and quantity of their performance.
>
> (Pugh and Hickson, 1989, pp. 168–9)

In terms of change management, managers adopt a certain model of behaviour. Argyris and Schon (1978) argue that managers seek solutions in the form of a model of behaviour where they: (1) Take action based on valid information which has been freely and openly obtained; (2) Take action after consultation with those competent and relevant to that action based on their informed and free choice; (3) Sustain commitment to the choice made and monitor the preparedness of the organization for change and implementation of change itself.

The appropriateness of this approach for the model of organization development we are proposing is clear. The solutions proposed by Argyris and

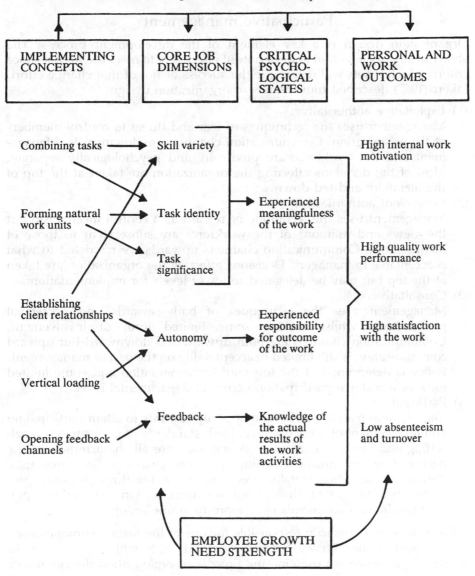

| IMPLEMENTING CONCEPTS | CORE JOB DIMENSIONS | CRITICAL PSYCHO- LOGICAL STATES | PERSONAL AND WORK OUTCOMES |

Combining tasks ──────→ Skill variety

Forming natural work units ──────→ Task identity

Task significance

Establishing client relationships

Autonomy

Vertical loading

Feedback

Opening feedback channels

Experienced meaningfulness of the work

Experienced responsibility for outcome of the work

Knowledge of the actual results of the work activities

High internal work motivation

High quality work performance

High satisfaction with the work

Low absenteeism and turnover

EMPLOYEE GROWTH NEED STRENGTH

Figure 8.2 The Hackman and Oldham job characteristics model (adapted from).

Schon assume that the manager in this instance adopts and displays an open and participatory approach to the process of change in organizations. There is a need here to remove the defensiveness associated with control orientation in order to obtain contribution from others likely to be affected by change. To do so, Argyris and Schon argue that the organization needs to be able to call on the assistance of outside agents, another characteristic of organization development.

Participative management

Organization design is a key element of the development process. The ability of any organization to design itself effectively to meet the performance criteria which it sets will determine the success or not of that change effort. Likert (1967) described four models of organization design:

(1) Exploitative authoritative:
  Management uses the techniques of fear and threat to control members of the organization. Communication channels are downwards. Management and the workforce are physically and psychologically separate. Most of the decisions affecting the organization are taken at the top of the hierarchy and fed down.
(2) Benevolent authoritative:
  Management uses the technique of reward as a control mechanism but the views and opinions of the workforce are subservient to those of management. Communication channels upwards are restricted to what is acceptable to managers. Decisions affecting the organization are taken at the top but may be delegated to lower levels for implementation.
(3) Consultative:
  Management uses the techniques of both rewards and occasional punishments whilst seeking some limited form of involvement. Communication channels are both upward and downward but upward communication is still limited to acceptability on the part of management. Policy is determined at the top with implementation and some limited form of workforce participation occurs at departmental level.
(4) Participative:
  Management uses the technique of group rewards to attain participation and involvement of the workforce. High standards of performance, goal-setting and improvement of work methods are all characteristic of the participative organization. Communication channels flow upwards, downwards and horizontally. Decisions are made through group processes and integrated throughout the organization via 'linking pin' individuals who are members of more than one group.

Likert was also primarily responsible for one of the main techniques used in OD models, the survey feedback method. This will be looked at in greater depth when we examine the process of organization development.

THE ORGANIZATION DEVELOPMENT MODEL: HOW DO ORGANIZATIONS DEVELOP EFFECTIVELY?

We now wish to look at some effective mechanisms and techniques for using organization development. What we are interested in is the concept of organization development, what it can do, what rules or issues bound it, and what specifics it can deal with. Here we begin to get into the technicalities or meat of the ODM. For example, in terms of what organization development expects to address, French (1969) identified seven objectives behind the use of organization development programmes. These objectives, it was argued, reflect problems which are very common in organizations;

1. To increase the level of trust and support among organizational members.
2. To increase the incidence of confrontation of organizational problems, both within groups and among groups, in contrast to 'sweeping problems under the rug'.
3. To create an environment in which authority of assigned role is augmented by authority based on knowledge and skill.
4. To increase openness of communications laterally, vertically, and diagonally.
5. To increase the level of personal enthusiasm and satisfaction in the organization.
6. To find synergistic solutions to problems with greater frequency.
7. To increase the level of self and group responsibility in planning and implementation.

(French, 1969, pp. 23−34)

Organizational development is about changing the organization from one situation, which is regarded as unsatisfactory, to another by means of social science techniques for change. In terms of organizational change, it is important to remember the concept of anticipation. The manager has to be always thinking ahead. The case study on change at Digital Equipment Corporation in Chapter 11 classically illustrates the need to think proactively instead of reactively. In a similar vein, Pugh (1978) argues that the effective manager anticipates change, diagnoses the nature of the change, and then manages the change process. In this, and the next chapter, we argue that the manager is often too near to the problem to be able to anticipate, diagnose, and manage the change themself. What is needed is the assistance of an outside agent, either internal to the organization, or brought in specifically for that task.

We will recommend that, in terms of managing change, the organization has to follow a five-step process of planned change which moves it through specific phases:

(1) *Recognition* by senior management that there is a need for change in the organization,
(2) *Establishment* of a change relationship,
(3) *Movement* towards the desired change by the organization and its members,
(4) *Stabilizing* the changes within the organization,
(5) *Allowing* the change agent to move on.

(Lippit, Watson and Westley, 1958)

When we look at change in organizations it is important to be able to understand why it is taking place. Pugh (1978) argues that there are four principal issues associated with the use of organization development and that to understand the basis of organization development, one has to place it within the context of the organization itself.

Pugh's four principles for understanding organizational change

(1) Organizations as organisms:
the organization is not a machine and change must be approached carefully and rationally. Do not make changes too frequently because they become dysfunctional or cosmetic.

(2) Organizations are occupational and political systems:
the reaction to change relates to what is best for the firm, how it affects individuals and groups, and how it affects the power, prestige and status of individuals and groups.

(3) Members of an organization operate in occupational, political and rational systems at the same time:
arguments for and against change will be presented using rational argument as well as occupational and political considerations.

(4) Change occurs most effectively where success and tension combine:
two factors are important here; confidence and motivation to change. Successful individuals or groups will have the confidence to change aspects of their work which are creating problems. Unsuccessful members of the organization are difficult to change because to protect themselves they will use their rigidity.

(Pugh, 1978)

Having established some basic principles related to the organization and how its members will react to, anticipate and deal with change as part of the organization, it is now useful to look at what attributes the model of organization development has which make it so attractive. Margulies and Raia identify thirteen characteristics common to organization development:

(1) It is a total organizational system approach.
(2) It adopts a systems approach to the organization.
(3) It is positively supported by top management.
(4) It uses third party change agents to develop the change process.
(5) It involves a planned change effort.
(6) It uses behavioural science knowledge to instigate change.
(7) It sets out to increase organizational competence.
(8) It is a long-term change process.
(9) It is an ongoing process.
(10) It relies on experiential learning techniques.
(11) It uses action-research as an intervention model.
(12) It emphasizes goal setting and action planning.
(13) It focuses on changing attitudes, behaviours and performance of groups or teams in the organization rather than individuals.

(Margulies and Raia, 1978)

Combining these characteristics with those mentioned by Lippit *et al.* (1958), French (1969), and Pugh (1978), we can put forward the following definition of organization development.

Definition

Organization development is an ongoing process of change aimed at resolving issues within an organization through the effective diagnosis and management of the organization's culture. This development process uses behavioural and social science techniques and methodologies through a consultant facilitator and employs action-research as one of the main mechanisms for instigating change in organizational groups.

This means that we are dealing with a philosophy of managing change which involves a number of skills and practices. This section does not intentionally set out to cover the entire field of organizational development and is seen more as an introductory phase. It is hoped that you will be stimulated to enhance your knowledge of the subject area further. We will cover the major aspects of organization development that we have used in our definitions such as the 'techniques and methodologies and action-research' as well as enhancing areas of particular interest. The philosophy of organization development is one of long-term change. The emphasis is on people issues to a large extent in an attempt to create greater interpersonal effectiveness within organizations. However, there are times when people in organizations cannot see the wood for the trees. The use of external consultants or facilitators is specifically warranted on such occasions to stimulate the change process. These can come from other parts of the organization or from outside. The long-term goal is to aid members of the organization in interpersonal problem resolution. The role of the change agent or consultant is dealt with at length in Chapter 9.

When considering using organization development as a means of managing change in the organization you need to be aware of its characteristics:

(1) Focus is on interdependencies and not on the individual. Therefore, team work is encouraged.
(2) A climate for change is sought rather than superimposed unilaterally.
(3) Interpersonal relationships are built upon using behavioural science techniques (role playing, problem-solving exercises).
(4) Goals relate to communication, decision making and problem-solving.
(5) The value system is humanistic aimed at maximizing development and encouraging open relationships in the organization.

The organizational development process is a tricky one to get hold of. It means sometimes having to re-evaluate how you manage people to get the best from them. It means looking at change with an open mind and adopting the attitude that you are prepared to lay down preconceptions about organizing for change where people are concerned.

Previous chapters have been concerned largely with the technical aspects of managing the change process. All that is about to change. What we are dealing with in relation to organization development is largely related to human resources in the organization and the ability of social science to assist in the management of change. One thing is crucial to the successful management of change – people matter.

Exercise

The following exercise is adapted from Huse (1975). Rule number one is to be honest with yourself. Do not try to second-guess the answers from what you *think* is wanted. Read carefully through the statements below and consider what your views on these are. As you read through each statement, you should allocate a mark to the statement depending on whether you agree with it or not. Mark your view in the column to the right using the following five-point scale:

5 Strongly agree,
4 Agree,
3 Neutral,
2 Disagree,
1 Strongly disagree.

Assumptions underlying OD activities.   Points

(1) Personal growth is the engine that drives organization
    performance. This is best provided for within an open
    and challenging environment.   . . . .

(2) The individual does not work in a vacuum and prefers
    to work within and is influenced by groups at the
    workplace.   . . . .

(3) The way organizations go about design leads to clashes
    of personality that are not of the individual's own
    making.   . . . .

(4) Work groups increase effectiveness by attaining
    individual needs and organizational requirements.
    Leadership in this instance is of a participatory nature.   . . . .

(5) Not considering people's feelings is likely to hinder
    leadership, communications and organizational
    effectiveness.   . . . .

(6) The formal organization forces people to conform. This
    prevents individual growth, innovation and wastes
    talent.   . . . .

(7) People are the most important asset an organization has,
    yet they are demotivated in formal organizations and do
    not take on more responsibility.   . . . .

(8) When problems arise in the organization, the ability to
    be open and honest in discussion helps both the
    individual concerned and the organization as a whole.   . . . .

(9) To be effective, organizations have to enhance the level
    of interpersonal trust and co-operation among
    individuals at all levels.   . . . .

(10) The way we structure and design the organization can
     reflect the needs of the individual, the group, and the
     organization as a whole.   . . . .

Scoring

Your rating of the items will give you an indication of your willingness to consider using organization development (OD) techniques to manage change. First calculate your total score on the 10 items in the table. The range of total scores goes from 10 to 50; the higher the score, the more you are in agreement with OD values.

The following scoring ratings indicate where you, as a manager, lie in terms of willingness to use OD as a model for change:

Score	Rating
40–50	You are largely in agreement with the principles and practices associated with OD. The way you feel about managing the organization, the people within the organization and the concept of attaining effective change is in line with basic organization development principles. You may pass GO and collect £200.
25–39	You agree with most of the OD principles and are quite willing to experiment with the concept for overall development of your organization. You have some doubts as to the efficacy of some of the ideas, but a willingness to experiment. Pass GO and collect your £200 next time round.
10–25	You have serious doubts about the basic concepts of organization development. You are willing to give some attention to the concepts but basically you want to see some evidence before being fully convinced. Do not pass GO. Do not collect £200.
<10	Go straight to JAIL, do not pass GO, do not even think of collecting £200! You probably know all the answers to Trivial Pursuit.

Most of us do not take the extreme views. The neutral point is 25, so that scores in the high twenties and the thirties would mean that on the whole you did agree with the OD approach, whereas scores in the teens would mean that you did not. If you have a more positive view, then the following will be useful in indicating the practical ways in which change can be accomplished without last-ditch resistance and loss of morale. This is because you accept that people at all levels in the organization have contributions to make which can be built on.

Organizations which use the OD process can be seen as falling into two straightforward 'black and white' categories. The 'white' category relates to the organization which has a well-defined OD strategy. This is tied into its overall business strategy and is used continuously as a mechanism of stimulating change at all levels. As with many innovative management practices, OD has been used more often in the United States, and by larger corporations facing constant change. The 'black' category is the organization that has got itself into such an internal mess through change that it needs to call on OD to help resolve large degrees of resistance to change within the organization. Resistance to change reflects bad management of the process of change. Where it does occur, however, there are a number of factors which may help recover what is seen as a lost position. The reality for most organizations falls within the shades of grey we mentioned in an earlier chapter where organizations use the OD process to solve particular issues of concern.

THE ORGANIZATION DEVELOPMENT PROCESS

Organization development, as it suggests, is about trying to progress change through more than one element within the firm. It is viewed very much as a long term, strategic mechanism for initiating change which places emphasis on the *process* of attaining change.

The purpose of training people in organization development techniques within organizations is to help increase the effectiveness of the organization by providing expertise and skilled resources to help manage the changes which take place. The amount of change that is undertaken is reflective of the environment of the firm. The type of work, the type and mix of skills, structures and systems, response times, performance measurement of operating units and people, and the way in which different parts of the organization are designed and operate are all factors which will have a bearing on organizational effectiveness. The main essence of organization development is trying to maintain control over an organization which is in a constant state of flux.

Why organization development is so important

(1) The volume of change in many organizations is massive.
(2) The economic scene places demands on managers while they are reluctant to change from tried and tested methods.
(3) The role of management is changing and new models are needed.
(4) Change management takes time.
(5) Some changes challenge basic assumptions − for example, the role of supervisory staff.
(6) The need for control remains − the skill is remaining in control when so much change is going on.
(7) More comprehensive strategic pictures are needed which integrate different changes in the organization and alleviate confusion.
(8) Organization design and re-design are *as important and necessary* as product, process or system design and are the responsibility of management and people in organizations, not just specialists.

By this point you will have reached the stage where you understand that change in the organization requires both planning and management. It does not occur on an *ad hoc* basis. There is a role for the social sciences in instigating change in organizations, and organizational development is one of the key methods of instigating and attaining successful change. There are four situations where organization development is needed:

(1) The current nature of the organization is leading to a failure to achieve objectives.
(2) Change is required to react faster to external alterations.
(3) Where the introduction of factors such as new technology requires change in the organization itself.
(4) Where the introduction of change allows a new approach to be adopted.

It was suggested at the outset that you test your own values and assumptions concerning organizational development. Similarly, the importance of factors such as group work have been expressed as important elements of organization development. As has been mentioned before, the process by which change is managed is a crucial aspect of instigating successful change. This pin-points the stages by which organization development instigates change. The important point to note here is that change is a continuous process of confrontation, identification, evaluation and action. The key is what is referred to in organization development as an action-research model. French (1969) argued that this model involved collaboration between the consultant (who could be an internal or external change agent, as we shall see in Chapter 9) and the client group towards data gathering, data discussion, action planning and action. Figure 8.3 details French's action-research model for organization development.

In terms of the process of organization development, there are a number of phases that an organization will go through. Lewin (1958) describes these as unfreezing, changing, and refreezing the organization into its new state. Warner Burke (1987) identifies seven phases which the organization experiences during a typical organization development change process. These are described below with appropriate examples, from our own experience.

Phase 1: entry

At this point an initial contact is made between the organization and the consultant to begin the entry phase. There may be many reasons for this initial contact, but largely this will be based on the organization's initiative as it has perceived a need for organization development. Both the organization and the consultant will explore the issues and establish a rapport or capability for working on the organization development intervention. From the organization's perspective it has to be sure that it has the right person for the job and that the consultant will be able to work with the organization. The consultant also has a number of criteria that have to be satisfied. These relate to factors such as whether he or she can work with the organization, whether or not there is a readiness for change, the motivation and values of the individual(s) within the organization calling on the consultant, their position within the organization as a leverage point for instigating change, and the amount of resources at hand for change (Warner Burke, 1987, p. 70).

It is also useful at this point for both the consultant and the organization to check that there is a clear understanding of the roles to be adopted by each prior to the establishment of the contract stage. In our experience, it is useful to leave the first meeting and provide the client with a copy of what we understood to be the salient points of the meeting and how both consultant and organization should proceed. This should be done as soon as possible after the first contact to maintain the flow and to check for any possible misinterpretations on the part of either party.

Phase 2: formalizing the contact

The second phase is the drafting of a contract which explains and clarifies what will be done. This is a two-way process in which the consultant lays

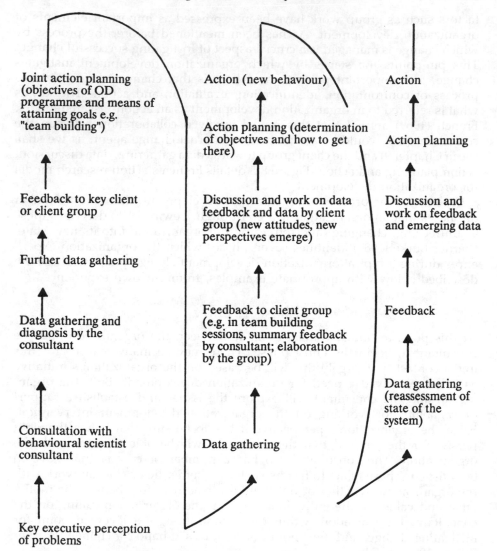

Joint action planning
(objectives of OD
programme and means of
attaining goals e.g.
"team building")

Action (new behaviour)

Action

Action planning (determination
of objectives and how to get
there)

Action planning

Feedback to key client
or client group

Discussion and work on data
feedback and data by client
group (new attitudes, new
perspectives emerge)

Discussion and
work on feedback
and emerging data

Further data gathering

Data gathering and
diagnosis by the
consultant

Feedback to client group
(e.g. in team building
sessions, summary feedback
by consultant; elaboration
by the group)

Feedback

Consultation with
behavioural scientist
consultant

Data gathering

Data gathering
(reassessment of
state of the
system)

Key executive perception
of problems

Figure 8.3 The action-research model for organization development (adapted from French, 1969, Organization development: objectives, assumptions and strategies, *California Management Review*, Vol. 12, no. 2, pp. 23–34).

out what he or she intends to do but also explains what the organization is contracting to do. At this point, the client organization will internally discuss the consultant's proposal with its key people and may propose amendments before agreeing to the terms. We would encourage organizations to view this phase as similar to any other negotiations which take place with any other type of supplier. Unless the consultant has a clear specification of what the client desires in terms of an organization development intervention, then he or she is unsure of issues such as what each expects of the other, how much time will be involved, the associated costs and the ground rules which will operate. Most organizations treat the organization development intervention by an external consultant in this way, even to the point of issuing a purchase order.

Phase 3: information gathering and analysis

Having successfully negotiated a contract, it is then up to the consultant in conjunction with the client organization to begin the diagnosis phase. There are two important elements here – getting the information required and being able to make sense of it. However, the two do not necessarily follow on from one another. The consultant will have begun the diagnosis from the initial entry point based on the information gathered, observations, gut feelings about the state of play in the organization, and in many cases from previous experience with similar issues.

French and Bell (1990, p. 63) comment that, 'organization development is at heart an action program based on valid information about the status quo, current problems and opportunities, and effects of actions as they relate to goal achievement. An OD program thus starts with diagnosis and continuously employs data collecting and data analyzing throughout.' Formal information gathering is therefore necessary and this usually comes in the form of interviews, staff surveys and organization records associated with the issue being analysed. Margerison (1988, p. 64) argues that this is a crucial stage in terms of what could be considered the diplomacy and partiality displayed on the part of the consultant towards whomever he or she gathers information from: 'A former colleague once gave me a phrase which has stuck with me as an important principle in all my work. "Selection implies rejection" he said. This is absolutely right. Make sure you don't offend people by ignoring their opinion.'

We would recommend that when gathering data, the consultant, whether internal or external, gleans information from all those likely to be affected by the organization development change programme, from a political and/or content perspective.

Phase 4: feedback

Having gathered the data, it is then up to the consultant to analyse it, summarize the information, and organize it into a format that can be readily understood by the organization's members to enable action to take place based on that information. This is the point where the organization development consultant will use his or her previous experience to draw conclusions from what they have observed, and to feed back data in a form, which is both understandable and acceptable to the organization, and which gets the necessary messages across. We would recommend two mechanisms for accomplishing these tasks. First, the preparation of a report of the work carried out and the consultant's conclusions from this, issues for the future, and proposals for change. This is distributed to all who took part in the data-gathering stage for their information and commentary and acts as a further source of information or feedback. Second, a presentation to the management body initiating the organization development change pro-gramme. This is likely to include those who will be affected by any change proposals and the consultant needs to be prepared to enter into what one might consider a 'lion's den' on many occasions. The important point here is to facilitate discussion of the data being presented.

The feedback session must contain three basic elements – summary of the data gathered and the consultant's initial analysis, a general discussion which clarifies points of confusion that may have arisen on the organization's side, and interpretation of what has taken place and how this will be carried forward. The consultant must also be flexible during this process as changes to his or her analysis and interpretation will often be generated in the feedback session.

Phase 5: planning the change process

This phase is a second stage in the change programme and sets out the action phase of the organization development intervention. The basis of all organization development programmes is to improve the organization's processes from what they are now, to what they will be in the future – the unfreezing, change, re-freezing process. There are two possibilities here. First, the planning for change stage may take place towards the end of the feedback session as the consultant and organization get a clearer picture of the steps that are likely to be needed. However, for more complex, larger organization development issues the planning process may be lengthened in time and include those likely to be involved in the process itself. The whole point of the planning for change phase is to look at what alternative actions are open to the organization in terms of response to the feedback given by the consultant, and to consider the best way forward or plan of action to take.

We would recommend that the consultant moves through this phase in collaboration with the organization in order to gain commitment both to the plan for change and its implementation. The consultant should act both as an idea generator, putting forward alternatives and getting the organization to consider the consequences of each proposal, and as a sounding board for the organization's proposals for the way forward, using his or her experiences of similar attempts at change. This is a crucial phase, but it is the organization, above all, that has to live with the consequences of decisions made during this phase. They should necessarily agree with proposals for the way forward.

Phase 6: implementing the changes

Once the organization has decided what action it will take in terms of an organization development intervention then the implementing of changes can take place. The consultant may or may not be involved at this stage depending on the actions to be taken, the degree of experience required within the organization to take these actions, and the consultant's own assessment of his or her role at this stage. Examples of organization develop-ment are given in the next section which looks at organization development strategies and develops an intervention matrix. We would suggest here that the consultant, even if not actively involved in the intervention phase, keeps an eye on the development of this phase. It is difficult to force an organization to change; those most likely to be negatively impacted by change will resist the strongest. As Warner Burke noted, 'the OD practitioner continues to work with the client system to help make the intervention successful' (1987, pp. 74–5). This is most effectively done with the consultant still involved as most failures at the implementation stage result from unanticipated consequences of the change process and it is here that the consultant may be able to help anticipate likely outcomes.

Phase 7: assessment

The final phase of the organization development process of change is to evaluate the results of what has taken place. Margerison (1988) argues that this should take the form of a review stage and that the principle of establishing a review stage assists in preventing all the previous work going astray. The process of assessment also assists the change effort by focusing attention on what has taken place. In our introduction to this book we referred to the layers of transition management. The final layer was associated with maintenance and renewal. The assessment phase is useful here in looking at what has gone before, what the current state of play is, and what action steps need to be taken to move the organization forward.

These then are the phases of an organization development intervention process for change. They are descriptive in terms of what happens, and the mechanisms by which an organization development intervention works out in reality. However, by necessity we have been lacking in describing what types of organization development change take place. This is because the organization development process can occur at many levels – individual, group or organizational. What is needed, therefore, is some form of development strategy outlining the types of organization development interventions that can take place at each of these levels. In the next section we outline development strategies for each of these levels in the form of an organization development matrix. This matrix is driven by the need for change in the organization, what level this takes place at, and what the nature of change is likely to be.

DEVELOPMENT STRATEGIES: AN ORGANIZATION DEVELOPMENT MATRIX

One of the important aspects of change is developing an appropriate strategy. This involves creating a matrix of change diagnosis and initiation associated with behaviour, structure and context at four levels; the organization as a whole, inter-group, group, and individual levels. The importance of this matrix concerns the two main factors that have to be identified in the organizational development process. These are:

> At what level do we focus our analysis?
> How much change has to take place?

Figure 8.4 details an organization development matrix conceptualized and developed by Derek Pugh of the Open University Business School (1986). The matrix is one of the keys for organizations in developing their organization development strategy. As such it needs to be understood in its two parts — the level of analysis required and the degree of intervention — as well as understanding where you start from in your analysis. To achieve this level of understanding means assessing the matrix. Go over the matrix

Diagnosis and methods of initiation of change

	Behaviour (What is happening now?)	Structure (What is the required system?)	Context (What is the setting?)
Organisational level	General climate of poor morale, pressure, anxiety, suspicion, lack of awareness of, or response to, environmental changes. *survey feedback, organisational mirroring*	Systems goals — poorly defined or inappropriate; strategy inappropriate and misunderstood; organisation structure inappropriate; centralisation, divisionalisation, standardisation: inadequacy of environmental monitoring mechanisms. *change the structure*	Geographical setting, market pressures, labour market, physical conditions, basic technology. *change strategy, location, physical set-up; culture (by saturation OD)*
Inter-group level	Lack of effective co-operation between sub-units, conflict, excessive competition, limited war, failure to confront differences in priorities, unresolved feelings. *inter-group confrontation (with third party as consultant), role negotiation*	Lack of integrated task perspective; sub-unit optimisation, required interaction difficult to achieve. *redefine responsibilities, change reporting relationships, improve co-ordination and liaison mechanisms*	Different sub-unit values, life style, physical distance. *reduce psychological and physical distance; exchange roles, attachments, cross-functional social overlay*
Group level	Inappropriate working relationships, atmosphere, participation, poor understanding and acceptance of goals, avoidance, inappropriate leadership style, leader not trusted, respected; leader in conflict with peers and superiors. *process consultation, team building*	Task requirements poorly defined; role relationships unclear or inappropriate; leader's role overloaded, inappropriate reporting procedures. *redesign work relationships (socio-technical systems), autonomous working groups*	Insufficient resources, poor group composition for cohesion, inadequate physical set-up, personality clashes. *change technology, layout, group composition*
Individual level	Failure to fulfil individual's needs; frustration responses; unwillingness to consider change, little chance for learning and development. *counselling, role analysis, career planning*	Poor job definition, task too easy or too difficult. *job restructuring/modification, redesign, enrichment, MbO*	Poor match of individual with job, poor selection or promotion, inadequate preparation and training, recognition and remuneration at variance with objectives. *personnel changes, improved selection and promotion procedures, improved training and education, bring recognition and remuneration in line with objectives.*

There are two dimensions to the matrix which represent the two main factors that have to be identified during the diagnosis stage of the OD process: level of analytical focus and degree of required intervention.

Figure 8.4 The organization development matrix (Pugh, 1986, *Planning and Managing Change, Block 4: Organizational Development*, Open University Business School, Milton Keynes).

slowly at first and be prepared to break the matrix into its constituent parts. It will be useful to do so by writing it out several times in individual areas. For example, take a specific case from your own organization (you will probably be able to cite an example at the individual level fairly easily) and work through the matrix.

If we were to identify any one part as being crucial to your understanding of organization development – this is it! Pugh's analysis of the most common strategies used in organization development provides an excellent example of diagnosing and initiating change. These are strategies that apply to organization development which depend on the level within the organization at which change is contemplated, and the approaches taken which correspond to these levels. Action at the organizational level is likely to be different from that at the individual level, although there are areas where overlap exists.

There are a number of aspects of the matrix which you may be unfamiliar with. For example, some of the methods of initiating change that are mentioned need explaining. Table 8.1 lists some of these methods of initiating change and provides some details of what is involved.

Table 8.1 Methods of initiating change in organizations

Method	Level	Explanation
Survey feedback	Group	Organization-wide review of attitudes and morale which is then used as basis for discussion of change
Inter-group confrontation (3rd party present)	Inter-group	Bringing together groups in presence of an external consultant to discuss and attain change
Role negotiation	Inter-group	Review process on the appropriate areas of concern for individuals and groups and levels of interaction between groups
Cross-functional social overlay	Inter-group	Attaining movement between groups which enhances cohesion through continuous interaction
Process consultation	Group	Review of work patterns and relationships for effective organization
Redesign work relationships (socio-technical systems)	Group	Effective co-ordination of people and technology in organization for a 'best fit' solution
Autonomous work groups	Group	Self-managing team approach to job design

If there is one underlying theme of organization development, then it is related to the need to be able to manage change. Taking care of the process by which an organization moves from an unsatisfactory state of affairs, through the recognition of this, identification of alternatives, communicating these and receiving feedback, educating the changes required, reviewing development in the light of experience, and progressing the change process forward is both a lengthy and messy process. Therefore, there is a need to manage this positively.

Organizations go through what can best be described as interlocking layers of perpetual change management which reflect aspects such as the trigger layer where opportunity or threat triggers response for change in the organization. This can sometimes create a vision of where the organization might be able to go. This visionary state then has to be communicated to individuals and groups and their commitment gained. Having gone through this process of change, what can best be described as a maintenance and renewal layer closes up the loop. Revision of what the organization sets out to do, and whether this is appropriate at this point in time, leads to a further process of change analysis.

This is related to the basic rules for managing a change process:

Rule 1   Establish that there is a need.
Rule 2   Think it through thoroughly.
Rule 3   Discuss it informally with those likely to be affected.
Rule 4   Encourage the expression of all objections.
Rule 5   Make sure you are willing to undertake change yourself.
Rule 6   Monitor the changes and reinforce them at all points.

(Adapted from Pugh, 1978)

GUIDING VALUES AND PHILOSOPHY

Before moving on to an analysis of the role of the consultant in the organization development change process, it is worthwhile considering what we have looked at over the last two chapters. The sceptical reader may not even have reached this point, but it is crucial here to summarize why we place such emphasis on people management and the organization development process of change. Basically, people matter. This is a guiding value and belief that organizations should have as the corner-stone of their operating philosophy – all successful organizations do.

Margulies and Raia wrote that the values of a fully functioning organization could be stated as:

(1) Providing opportunities for people to function as human beings rather than resources in the productive process.
(2) Providing opportunities for each organizational member, as well as the organization itself, to develop to full potential.
(3) Seeking to increase the effectiveness of the organization in terms of all its goals.
(4) Attempting to create an environment in which it is possible to find exciting and challenging work.

(5) Providing opportunities for people in organizations to influence the way in which they relate to work, the organization, and the environment.

(6) Treating each human being as a person with a complex set of needs, all of which are important in work and in life.

Individually, we each have our own sets of values or personal philosophy for life. The development of a *shared* set of values and philosophy about the organization is what is required. The organization needs a philosophy, a description of basic principles guiding its behaviour. The values are the beliefs which flow from these basic principles. All organizations have their own philosophy and values about human behaviour but seldom are these charted and used as a guide to organization design and development, as a guide to managerial and people policies, or as a checklist for daily practice.

We make no apologies for repeating what Megson in 1988 described as examples of the beliefs inherent in two of Digital Equipment Corporation's plants (one in the USA, the other in Scotland).

They are based on a philosophy that I describe as follows: People are the most important asset we have. They want and need to grow – without growth interest wanes and talents waste away, with growth interest flourishes and talents develop. People really do care, they do exquisite work if it is designed to enable them to grow. *In other words, personal growth is the engine that drives organization performance.*

Through the process of organization development it is possible to put expressions of values and philosophy such as these into practice at individual, group and organizational levels – to let the engine itself develop enough momentum to drive effective performance. Margulies and Raia (1988, p. 9) sum this up as, 'the usefulness and effectiveness of OD is dependent upon the degree to which organizational values become consistent with the core values of organizational development'.

In the next chapter we describe the role of the consultant in the ODM. The consultant can either be internal or external to the organization depending on the level of experience the organization has with organization development techniques, the strategy being adopted, and the level of change. What the consultant is, however, is the driver – the change agent. It is he or she who drives the change process, and as such occupies a linchpin role.

9

The Objective Outsider

INTRODUCTION

The use of organization development in stimulating and implementing change rests very much on the way in which it is handled. The successful use of the Organization Development Model (ODM) is influenced by a number of factors, not least of which are the purpose and process of change itself. One of the key underpinnings of this process is the role of the consultant acting as a facilitator of change. More often than not, an outsider is needed to move that part of the organization contemplating change to its new position. However, this outsider may well come from another part of the organization and thus actually be an internal figure. To this end, we prefer the term 'change agent'. Whether internal or external, the change agent facilitates change in the particular area in which it is needed.

Why is an outsider needed? What does facilitation mean? Why bother when the manager of the department in question knows what he or she wants, and knows how to get there? Good questions! But again the underlying assumption is that of predestination – the manager, in his or her infinite wisdom, knows best. Schein (1988) argues that managers in organizations need assistance in managing the process of change in order that they learn how to do it more effectively the next time round.

Seven reasons for using a change agent

(1) Clients/managers often do not know what is wrong and need special help in diagnosing what their problems actually are.
(2) Clients/managers often do not know what kinds of help consultants can give to them; they need to be helped to know what kind of help to seek.
(3) Most clients/managers have a constructive intent to improve things, but they need help in identifying what to improve, and how to improve it.
(4) Most organizations could be more effective than they are if they learn to diagnose and manage their own strengths and weaknesses.
(5) A consultant probably cannot, without exhaustive and time-consuming study or actual participation in the client organization, learn enough about the culture of the organization to suggest reliable new courses of action. Therefore, unless remedies are worked out jointly with members of the organization who do know what will and will not work in their culture, such remedies are likely either to be wrong or be resisted because they come from an outsider.
(6) Unless the client/manager learns to see the problem for himself and thinks through the remedy, he will not be able to implement the solution and, more importantly, will not learn to fix such problems should they recur.

(7) The essential function of process consultation is to pass on the skills of how to diagnose and fix organizational problems so that the client is more able to continue on his own to improve the organization.

(Schein, 1978)

When we look at who should be a change agent, we are concerned with the personality and style of the individual. Margulies and Raia (1972) note that there are three attributes that the individual needs to enable them to take on a consulting role in organization development.

The first is that of personality. As a result of the need to establish, maintain and work on relationships with people within the organization, the change agent needs to show an awareness and sensitivity to social issues. This means more than it actually says. The change agent has to feel comfortable with people, that is, have an ability to get on well with them, and be able to understand and recognize their worries and fears as well as their hopes and aspirations. In particular, he or she must not pay scant or transient attention to fears and aspirations as part of the process of accomplishing the change task. To do so, the change agent has to have an ability to listen to others and show empathy. This means that the change agent has to have numerous people-oriented skills. In essence, this is a flair or a natural empathy. The Theory X manager, described in Chapter 8, has few of these skills.

Second, to be able to enact the change process, the change agent requires both analytical and diagnostic skills, in combination. This enables him or her to identify and solve problems by using techniques which are available to facilitate the change process. However, the change agent has to be conscious that he or she is using these skills as part of the change process and not as an exploitive mechanism, as a means of 'going through the motions'.

Finally, the change agent needs to have client-related experience. We would quite rightly accept the definition of this as being what David A. Buchanan of Loughborough University describes as the 'been there, done that' school of experience related to expertise.

There is a degree of both expertise and facilitation associated with the change agent. The change agent has to come from outside the social system in which change is being contemplated. The reasons for this are fairly straightforward. It allows the change agent an unbiased viewpoint of the need for change, and also allows him or her to take a non-controversial line in considering actions for change. In addition, this is a mechanism which allows for all views within the change setting to be taken into consideration. To do so, the change agent has to be able to accomplish the following:

(1) Demonstrate a level of expertise which is linked to establishing credibility with those being affected by change;
(2) Demonstrate skill in the methods used to instigate and manage change;
(3) Possess personality characteristics which reflect certain social skills (the ability to listen to others, identify interpersonal conflicts and help resolve these, and to articulate differing viewpoints in an attempt to reach consensus).

To be able to place oneself in this position, the potential change agent has to be able to recognize and reconcile what type of person they intend being. The change agent, like most managers, is a person occupying a role for a particular period of time. To do so, they have to be able to determine what that role entails.

WHAT TYPE OF CHANGE AGENT IS REQUIRED?

The first issue that needs to be clarified when looking at the role played by the change agent in the change process is how that role is defined and implemented. The type of role adopted has a significant bearing on the results that one can expect to achieve using the ODM. The model most widely used by organization development practitioners is that of a collaborative approach which helps the client organization define, understand and act on process events which occur within their own environment (Schein, 1988). There are a number of characteristics associated with this model which follow on from Schein's assessment of the need for a joint change agent/client relationship. Margulies and Raia (1978) argue that these are,

...based upon the following assumptions and beliefs:

(1) Managers often do not know what is wrong and need special help in diagnosing what their problems actually are.
(2) They do not know what kinds of help to seek. Consequently, they need help in this regard.
(3) Organizations can be more effective if they learn how to diagnose their own strengths and weaknesses.
(4) The consultant cannot hope to learn all he or she needs to know about the culture of an organization to suggest reliable solutions. Therefore, it is necessary to work jointly with organization members who *do* know.
(5) Since the decision is the client's, it is important that the client learn to see the problem clearly, to share in the diagnosis, and to be actually involved in generating solutions.
(6) The consultant is an expert on how to diagnose processes and how to establish effective helping relationships with clients. Effective process consultation involves passing on *both* of these skills to the client system.

(Margulies and Raia, 1978, p. 111)

Based on these assumptions, what one might traditionally view as the role of the consultant, or in our terminology the change agent, becomes ineffective. The popular view of the consultant is that associated with the doctor—patient model of consultation. In this model, the organization brings in a consultant to find out what is wrong with it and the consultant then recommends change. This type of expert—client relationship has a number of problems when applied in an organization development setting. For one, it may hamper an individual's willingness to open up to the doctor. The patient is not totally involved in the diagnostic process and therefore feels left out of the solution. Similarly, the patient may be unable to understand the proposed solution or the mechanisms of achieving it.

Lippit and Lippit (1975) argue that the behaviour of the change agent runs along a continuum of eight different roles depending on whether the change agent is being directive or non-directive. These roles are not mutually exclusive and may vary according to the stage the change project has reached. They range from advocate, technical specialist, trainer or educator on the directive side, to collaborator in problem-solving, alternative identifier, fact finder, process specialist and reflector on the non-directive side. What Lippit and Lippit emphasize is the multiple role nature of the change agent, the situational focus which determines these roles, and the need to work in close conjunction with the client organization no matter what role is being used.

The collaborative nature of the process model of organization development defines the role to be adopted by the change agent. When taking up this role the change agent needs to be fully aware of a number of key criteria. First, in defining the problem the change agent works with the client organization to verify what the problem is. Second, the relationship between change agent and client is crucial to developing the change process and needs to be nurtured and developed. Third, the change agent's focus of attention is in helping the client organization itself discover and implement solutions to the problem. Fourth, the change agent's expertise is in diagnosing and facilitating the process of change — steering the organization through. Fifth, the change agent helps the organization improve its own diagnostic and problem-solving skills. Finally, the change agent assists the organization to a position where it can manage change itself (Margulies and Raia, 1978, p. 113).

The effective change agent takes on a number of roles:

(1) To help the organization define the problem by asking for a definition of what it is.
(2) To help the organization examine what causes the problem and diagnose how this can be overcome.
(3) To assist in getting the organization to offer alternative solutions.
(4) To provide direction in the implementation of alternative solutions.
(5) To transmit the learning process that allows the client to deal with change on an ongoing basis by itself in the future.

The type of change agent you are is dependent on the change situation with which you are faced. Broadly speaking, the change agent will tread a line between expert and process facilitator depending on his or her individual approach to the process, the skills and competencies which he or she possesses, the values and assumptions he or she makes about change in the organization, and his or her own personal characteristics. However, the change process will also be influenced by the experience of the organization in terms of its past dealings with change agents, their willingness to change, and the size and complexity of the problem. Similarly, the change situation itself will have a bearing on the role you adopt. Early on in the change process the role of the change agent is that of information-seeker. As the process develops and solutions emerge, the role of the change agent becomes more directive in terms of moving the organization through learning to the accomplishment of new procedures that solve the particular problem. In general, the change agent should try to take a position within the change process that serves to assist the organization in every way possible. This involves assessment of problems, attempts at resolution and implementation issues.

The role that the change agent adopts lays heavy emphasis on the process of facilitation to help expedite the organization from a position where there is a problem hindering effective performance to the resolution of that problem. This is done by taking on a role which combines, at various stages, gathering information, helping diagnose problems, assisting in planning change, providing a different perspective, integrating different viewpoints, providing continuity during the change process, and helping the organization learn how it has changed itself. The emphasis here is on the skills associated with helping others solve their own problems. If the change agent in an organization development setting can be said to have expertise, it is in facilitating this process. This is dependent on the way in which the organization and the change agent move towards change.

MOVING TOWARDS CHANGE

In Chapter 8 we noted that there were four situations where organization development is needed:

(1) The current nature of the organization is leading to failure to meet objectives;
(2) Change is required to react faster to external alterations;
(3) Where the introduction of one form of change (for example, new technology) requires change in other parts of the organization (work organization, reward systems, etc.);
(4) Where the introduction of change acts as the trigger for consideration of other new approaches.

We would like to give you the opportunity here to look at a situation where a change process has to be managed, and ask you to work your way through it, in terms of how you, as a potential change agent, would approach this situation. This is to be treated as a non-threatening, simulated example. There is not a right answer to it, but there are a number of different approaches, each with its own consequences. Read through the case described below, and write down how *you* would tackle this situation.

Case: Making friends at Quiltco

Bob Smeaton, the Managing Director of Quiltco, a West Midlands textile manufacturer, was quite pleased with himself. It was Friday afternoon and his flight from Tokyo was just about to land at Heathrow. In conjunction with his Sales Director, Peter Wilson, he had just returned from Japan where he had managed to successfully complete negotiations on a £2.5 million order from the Japanese golfing equipment manufacturer, Kokuna. The order was for the manufacture of a new range of golf sweaters and accessories and was the biggest single order that the company had dealt with in their five-year history. They had come up against stiff competition from other sportswear manufacturers in the United Kingdom and Japan.

To secure the order, Quiltco had to promise delivery of the first batch of newly designed golf wear within six weeks and bulk order shipments of 10,000 pullovers every two months. This created a problem. At capacity production, Quiltco could only manufacture and meet these order requirements by dropping 80 per cent of its ongoing business. It meant that three new computer-controlled manufacturing machines and a new computer-aided design system would be put to work to come up with the new styles and design and to manufacture the sweaters. These had been a heavy investment which the company had just made and therefore did not create any difficulties. The problem was who would operate the machinery and design systems in order to meet the order requirements, and what to do with Quiltco's current workload. Still, it had been a good trip and Bob had the weekend to plan the future development of the company.

Patricia Kennedy, Production Director at Quiltco, was called into the board meeting on the Monday morning. 'It's like this, Pat,' said Bob Smeaton, 'We need the new designs in a matter of weeks and they have to be computer-generated to fit straight into our new machinery. Our people haven't been trained on them yet so we'll have to subcontract this to some freelance designers who specialize in this field. They'll do the designs for us and we should be able to meet the six week deadline with some ease.'

Patricia paused, 'So who is going to actually make all these lovely new golf sweaters then, and who will tell Parks and Dencing that we can't provide them with any knitwear for the next nine months? You just can't tell the design shop that they are surplus to requirements for the next couple of weeks, and then tell P&D that we're sorry but they'll just have to wait. That's not how we do business, is it?'

Bob's reply was succinct and to the point, 'Pat, this is the 1990s. If this company is going to survive, it has to become an international concern. Sure, P&D's a big contract for us but we'll deal with that problem when it arises. As for the designers, I'm going to have a meeting with all operating staff this afternoon and let them have the good news.'

Work stopped at Quiltco at 4.30 p.m. that day. Bob Smeaton accompanied by Peter Wilson and Patricia Kennedy addressed the staff in the company cafeteria. Bob started off, in ebullient mood, 'Well, the situation facing us is one which I'm sure other companies would like to be in. I am sure you are aware by now that we have managed to win the biggest order in this company's short history, with the Japanese golfing company, Kokuna. This assures our future and means that jobs are secure. However, it does put us all under a bit of pressure. To this end I have made arrangements for an outside design and production team to join us temporarily to design and manufacture the Kokuna sweaters on our new equipment. This should allow the rest of you to carry on your normal duties whilst allowing us to meet the tight deadlines Kokuna have set. The outside team will be independent from the outset but will gradually bring in our own staff on design and production matters when they feel that the time to pass on the contract is right. To me, it's the best of both worlds and with a little bit of a squeeze we can do both the Kokuna work and satisfy the needs of our other customers like P&D. There are some good times ahead, lots of hard work, but I'm sure you'll agree with me that it'll be worth the struggle in the end.'

Smeaton's comments were met initially with stunned silence. However, it did not take long for murmurings to begin. The first came from one of the designers, 'Are you saying that we aren't good enough to do the design for the new sweaters?' 'Yeah, and we can't handle the new machinery so we'll buy in some smart alecs from outside, is that it?' The meeting soon deteriorated into a slanging match from the floor with comments such as, 'We're only good for the simple stuff', 'Who are these outsiders anyway?', and 'Don't you trust us to be able to deliver this for you?'

As the meeting finally began to get out of hand, Bob Smeaton turned to the assembled group and said, 'Who do you people think you are? We bring in the biggest order we've ever had and all you can think about is yourselves. Obviously we'll have to get this situation resolved before we go anywhere.' At that, he closed the meeting. However, on his way out of the cafeteria he turned to Patricia Kennedy, 'This bolshie lot need a good sorting out. Come and see me tomorrow morning, first thing, and we'll get to the bottom of this.'

Questions

Was Bob Smeaton wrong? How should he have approached the situation? What advice would you give Patricia before the Tuesday morning meeting? How should Quiltco try and recover the situation?

Case analysis

Quiltco is a good example of managing the process of change and also dealing with the potential for resistance to change. The manner in which change is brought about is an important determinant of the level of success associated with it. Huse (1975) argues that there are eight factors associated with reducing the level of resistance to change. One of the more important factors is that associated with allowing those likely to be affected by change a participatory role. So when considering the Quiltco case above, or any change process, three options are available.

Option one is likely to be the most unsuccessful. This is where change is introduced in a top-down manner with no consultation with those about to be affected. In this sense, the effect of change is likely to be more negative in its orientation. It is logical that those about to be affected, for example, by the introduction of new technology, should have their views and feelings taken into consideration prior to the change process taking place. Resistance to change is not resistance to the change itself, it is a reaction to the way in which change is introduced, and the levels of consultation and information provided related to that change.

Option two is likely to create the greatest chance of success, but is also likely to be time-consuming. This involves full participation by all likely to be affected by the forthcoming change. As Huse (1975) points out,

> The amount of opposition to change is reduced when those people who are to be changed and those who are to exert influence for a change have a strong sense of belonging to the same group. Change which comes from within is much less threatening and creates less opposition than change which is proposed from the outside. There are varying degrees of participation in this context.

The argument that Huse makes is relevant to the use of organization development as a model for instigating change in organizations because of its participatory nature, and the use of the change agent, especially one from within the organization. Full participation allows all to become involved and even enthused by change. However, it is a slow and time-consuming process and may not be appropriate where the need for change has been left too late, as in the Quiltco example.

Where change has to occur rapidly, for example to ensure company survival or growth, then option three, limited participation, is a more effective strategy. This is accomplished by targeting, selecting, and involving key members likely to be affected by change, and using them as a short-term project group to assess and implement the change process. This allows participation to occur as well as keeping to specific deadlines when these are crucial. The most obvious route (but not the only one) is to involve departmental managers, trade union representatives and a number of key staff.

The learning element for the change agent in terms of moving the organization, with which he or she is dealing with, towards change is that of allowing and taking advantage of participation. The individual problem will determine whether options two or three are pursued. However, in an OD setting, option one is anathema to successful change interventions. As Warner Burke (1987, p. 145) notes, 'Thus the primary though not exclusive function of OD consultants is to help clients learn how to help themselves more effectively. Although consultants occasionally provide expert information and may sometimes prescribe a remedy, their more typical mode of operating is facilitation'.

Dealing with change is one of the most crucial factors that a manager will have to experience within an organization. More often than not, it is resistance to change as a result of insufficient attention being paid to the process of change that causes problems.

Eight ways to reduce resistance to change

(1) Any change process needs to take into account the needs, attitudes, and beliefs of the individual(s) involved as well as the forces of the organization. The individual must see some personal benefit to be gained from the change before he or she will be willing to participate in the change process.

(2) The greater the prestige of the supervisor, the greater the influence he can exert for change. However, the official leader of a group and the actual (although informal) leader need not be the same individual. Frequently, an unofficial leader with high prestige and influence within the work group can be highly influential in the change process.

(3) Strong pressure for change in behaviour can be established by providing specific information desired by the group about itself and its behaviour. The more central, relevant and meaningful the information, the greater the possibility for change. For example, if properly used, data obtained through a survey questionnaire may be much more meaningful to a particular work group than data about attitudes in general.

(4) Strong pressures for change can be established by creating shared perceptions by the group members of the needs for change, thus making the pressure come from within the unit. In particular, the participation in analysis and interpretation helps to reduce or bypass resistance which comes from proceeding either too rapidly or too slowly.

(5) The amount of opposition to change is reduced when those people who are to be changed and those who are to exert influence for a change have a strong sense of belonging to the same group. Change which comes from within is much less threatening and creates less opposition than change which is proposed from the outside.

(6) In the matter of change, group cohesiveness or 'togetherness', may operate either to increase or reduce resistance to change, depending on the matter in which the group sees the change as being valuable or harmful.

(7) A group that has a continuing psychological meaning to an individual has more influence than does a group with only temporary membership. Therefore, a change process which involves bringing individuals together, off the job, in temporary groups, has less force for lasting change than those change processes which involve the individual in the immediate job situation.

(8) Information relating to the need for change, plans for change, and consequences of change must be shared by all relevant people in the group. A change process ordinarily requires the specific and deliberate opening of communication channels. Blocking these channels usually leads to distrust and hostility. Change processes which provide specific knowledge on the progress to date and specify the criteria against which improvement is to be measured are more successful in establishing and maintaining change than are change procedures which do not provide such specific knowledge and feedback.

(Adapted from Huse, 1975)

Huse's factors lay the framework for why organizational development is so important. At this point it is important to be able to relate the concepts of what is involved in the change process to your own organization, as well as highlighting that change is messy, affects many, requires systematic diagnosis and needs an effective strategy. Before moving on to examine the rules and procedures to be adopted by the change agent during the lifetime of a change project, it is worthwhile considering the implications of selecting a change agent from within the organization.

THE INTERNAL CHANGE AGENT: PROS AND CONS?

Many organizations today have invested resources to establish their own internal organization development consultants as a means of instigating change. In 1988, staff at Digital Equipment Corporation, Europe, prepared an organizational development training proposal. The purpose of this document was to secure internal company funding for the establishment of a training programme for internal OD consultants. Part of the introduction is quoted below. Why would an organization wish to become so heavily resourced in the area of organization development? One reason is that it is an investment in getting ahead and being able to manage change. The number of external OD consultants that can act as change agents for an organization in the UK is a severe limitation. Similarly, the costs involved in external change agents getting up to speed with the culture and values of an organization is expensive in time and money. There are several organizations willing to invest heavily in this field as a means of foregoing external costs via change consultants.

Organization development training at Digital

Purpose of training

The purpose of the Organization Development training is to help increase the effectiveness of manufacturing by providing expertise and skilled resources to help manage the massive changes now taking place in Digital's manufacturing operations in Europe.

The amount of change going on in manufacturing – the type of work, the type and mix of skills, structures and systems, response times, performance measurement of operating units and people, and in the way the manufacturing operations are designed and operate – is already high and is increasing. Manufacturing must change the way it operates in order to correspond with changes going on in customers, vendors, marketing and sales, and engineering. Products and processes are changing rapidly. Manufacturing also needs to influence the operations and style of these other organizations.

Training internal consultants drawn from existing, experienced Digital employees is preferred. This has the great advantage of providing resources who know how DEC works and who can actively re-design and make changes in the organization rather than just consult. The learning and the experience becomes embedded in the organization.

(From: Organization Development Training: Proposal for skills council funding (Digital Equipment Corporation, Europe, 1988). An in-house proposal for training managers in OD techniques and capabilities.)

The benefits of using an internal change agent are linked directly to two key issues – cost factors and access to information. By comparison, the costs associated with training an employee in the techniques and practices of organization development are minimal when the alternative is the use of an outside consultancy firm over a lengthy period of time. External consultants charge by the day and, more often than not, the cost of one change project can run into tens of thousands of pounds. The external consultancy firm has to build in overhead costs which runs up the bill.

On the other hand, the internal change agent may also have the benefit of having access to information that the external agent cannot hope to get to, no matter how long the project runs. However, as Margulies and Raia (1978) point out, to be effective the internal consultant is required to maintain a marginal status between being internal and being objective. The value of the internal change agent rests with being inside the organization and able to have information at hand whilst remaining objective towards the problem and the client organization. This is a particularly difficult situation for an employee of an organization to be in.

Factors hindering the internal change agent's objectivity are:

(1) Being too close to see what the problem is.
(2) Being part of the problem.
(3) Being unwilling to confront issues when promotion and pay issues are forthcoming.
(4) Being part of the power system being examined.
(5) Being aware of the needs and demands of superiors.

The use of internal change agents, who have been effectively trained in the techniques of managing change, will obviously benefit the organization. However, there are a number of issues that the change agent should be aware of that may inhibit their ability to influence change within the organization. Two of these relate to the method of entry into change projects and the nature of the voluntary relationship.

In terms of entry into a change management contract as facilitator, the internal change agent has to convince management and employees within a particular part of the organization of his or her expertise in this area. There is also a need to display the willingness to help. These issues are no different from those experienced by the external change agent and confidence and trust will come from successful change management projects within the organization. However, the internal change agent needs to use these successful change interventions as an open education process for the organization far more than the external ever has to.

The voluntary nature of the change project is one of the golden rules of change management outlined below. The internal change agent may not be given the opportunity to pick and choose clients from within the organization. Nor can they always expect to be free in their choice of the manner and mode of facilitation employed. The internal change agent is constrained by his or her involvement and participation in the organization and by their specified role which others may seek to exploit to their advantage.

The internal change agent must not and cannot become involved in change within his or her own area. Because most internal change agents are recruited from personnel, this often rules out change in this area, but leaves them free to deal with issues related to sales and marketing, manu-facturing, etc. Ideally, any organization training internal change agents would select a number of them from different departments to be able to deal with this difficulty.

In assessing the need for internal and external change agents, Margulies and Raia argue that,

> Organizations must learn to use external and internal consultants in more effective ways. Perhaps the best approach consists in the use of both. External consultants can bring objectivity, expertise and fresh approaches to organization problem solving. Internal consultants provide knowledge and understanding of organizational processes, information about cur-rent issues, and continuity of effort...a collaborative relationship pro-vides an opportunity to transfer the external consultant's skills to the client system...since the capacity for organization development must ultimately emerge from the organization itself.
>
> (Margulies and Raia, 1972, p. 477)

THE GOLDEN RULES OF THE CHANGE AGENT

The issues related to participation become apparent when we look in closer detail at the role and positioning of the change agent in the process of change itself. In essence, there are four 'golden' rules (Lippit, 1959) for the outside change agent that have to be observed.

Rule number one: The nature of the relationship

The relationship has to be seen as a voluntary one between the professional helper (the change agent) and the help-needing system. The most clear-cut example is that of a consultant from one of the large consultancy organizations who is brought in to assist the process of change in an organization.

In our work with organizations we make a point of stressing at the start of the process that it is a voluntary link between two parties which can be severed, at any time, by either party. We make the point of continually reiterating this at stages in the relationship, and to all concerned in the change process. The reasons for this are that it allows those who feel uncomfortable with the relationship to express their discomfort openly, allows both parties to begin to address this, if possible, and maintains an open and honest atmosphere. It also has the benefit of allowing the change agent to withdraw if he or she feels that the assistance being provided is not what is needed, or wanted.

Rule number two: To action an organization development process within any organization the change agent has to help solve a current or potential problem

The obvious is important. There are two issues here. First, the organization itself must recognize that a problem exists. This should come from senior management as the instigation of change stands a greater chance of success with top management support. Recognition of a need for change can take several forms. For example, an increase in employee absence figures should be recognized as an issue for concern that needs to be addressed. Absenteeism over a period of time costs money. Similarly, major changes in organization structure, the introduction of new technology being one example, are also situations where problems may occur and some form of organization development analysis may be required. The second issue relates to the help the change agent can provide. To help solve a problem, the change agent has to be able to offer some form of expertise. Traditionally, this is based on knowledge of the subject area. However, for the organization development agent, the knowledge, more often than not, is in dealing with people and helping the organization find its own solutions to structuring, absenteeism, etc. This is a skill that few have, and fewer still use effectively.

Rule number three: The relationship is a temporary one and the change agent and organization must accept the temporary nature of the assistance being provided

In effect, this means recognition of withdrawal from the system as a fact of life. One of the main criticisms of consultants is that they get others to solve their own problems, and charge them for the privilege, leaving the organization to manage the mess. Any change agent worth his or her salt cannot expect to stay in business long using this approach. The old adage that, 'If you ask a consultant the time, he'll ask if he can borrow your watch', may have a grain of truth to it, and can be applied in this context to the change agent. The important point is that the change agent has to be temporary but needs to see the project through to satisfactory completion. He or she is not employed, full-time, by the organization and, in the case of internal change agents, may have a day job in his or her own department! Both parties must recognize the need to sever the relationship at some point. This does not prevent the change agent from returning periodically to see how the organization is coping with the changes introduced, and some form of neutral or objective audit of change helps the process. However, this should occur after the initial change process has been completed and the change agent has withdrawn to allow the organization to manage its own affairs.

Rule number four: The change agent must be an outsider who is not part of the hierarchical power system in which the client organization is located

Why? Three main reasons immediately spring to mind. The first concerns the nature of being an objective outsider. Again, the obvious choice here is an external change agent. There is no particular axe to grind and therefore the nature of the assistance provided is that of being truly impartial. Change agents from within the confines of the organization, but from another department, may also be able to remain impartial, although the obstacles are greater. Second, as the change agent is from outside the immediate hierarchy, he or she is less likely to be influenced by the machinations of power, and therefore more likely to remain fair-minded. Third, to be truly effective in helping the client organization, the change agent has to be *seen* to be non-partisan by those within the client system who are likely to take part and be affected by the change and the process through which it occurs.

In our dealings with client organizations we make a point of stressing to all we come into contact with that we will remain objective, open-minded, and above all, free from influence. This is a difficult situation to maintain balance from. At the end of the day, the change process often involves payment to the change agent, and there is an argument that one has to be aware of whom one is working for. This would also be true for the internal change agent in terms of the intrinsic or extrinsic rewards associated with a successful change project.

These then are the rules which the change agent must accept as guiding the change process. Remember that it is a voluntary relationship in which you, as the change agent, are attempting to solve a current or potential problem on a temporary contract with the client organization.

THE CHANGE AGENT'S APPROACH TO CHANGE

In Chapter 8, we set out the process the change agent has to go through from the beginning to the end of a project in terms of negotiating access, undertaking the intervention, etc. In this section we outline, in more detail, the issues that the change agent will have to deal with in terms of each stage of the process. Where possible, we have tried to use examples from our own experience to highlight some of the issues that one can expect to encounter. We have also tried to relate these to some of the difficulties that an internal change agent can expect to meet under similar circumstances.

The first problem facing the change agent is one of definition. He or she has to ask: What is causing the problem?

This should be in terms of trying to define: What is it that is going wrong? What/who is causing the problem? Why does it continue to be a problem?

At this point, it is essential to be able to describe to oneself what the current situation is, why it exists, what is going on, etc. The ability to be able to apply a descriptive-analytical capability combines with the skill of diagnosis to enable the change agent to focus on the symptoms of the problem before drawing attention to the causes.

In our experience, this is where the change agent can make his or her first and perhaps fatal mistake. Under the doctor−patient scheme of system intervention, you tell me the symptoms and I prescribe the remedy. However, diagnosis via expertise may not be the most appropriate form of action in an organization development sense. This is related to why and how the change agent becomes involved in the process of change. At this point the change agent should ask the question: Why do I want to enter into this relationship?

If the answer is, to provide the solution via analysis, diagnosis and application of a cure by a fairly standard and mechanized means, then the damage inflicted may be greater than that which the actual problem warrants. The change agent has to be clear about his or her own goals and the reasons for motivating and influencing others. This is related to who sets the goals for the change process. These should be defined by the client organization and the change agent together. In an organization development mode, it has to be both, because of the nature of what is being changed. More often than not, this is people within a particular setting within the organization, and the change agent has to assist in helping people change themselves. Therefore, a description of what the problem is, what is causing it, and how it can be remedied has to come from both parties to the process working together. The doctor—patient relationship denies this mutual exchange as a two-way process.

In one of our first projects as external change agents, one of us was set the task of determining ways of making a customer sales department 'work smarter'. The definition of the problem was set by the client organization as a simple one of finding out how the people resources of that department could be better utilized. In the naivety of youth, the description of the problem and its analysis were accepted as straightforward. To diagnose the answer simply meant talking to the department's main internal customers to find out what better service they could provide. This ignored the fact that the customer services department could find its own way of 'working smarter', and that these ideas could and should be taken into consideration. The fundamental flaw was the process by which diagnosis was sought. This was externally driven and discounted the importance of getting those within the department involved in defining the problem and looking for solutions to it.

Having begun the process of defining what the problem is, in alliance with the client organization, the change agent should also look at what potential there is for change. The change agent needs to be sure that there is, within the organization, a motivation towards change. Otherwise, all attempts at instigating change with the client system may be hampered. The motivation can come from two main sources — ambition or dissatisfaction. Lippit (1959, p. 8) noted that in terms of the motivation for change among individuals, 'pain and dissatisfaction with the present situation are most frequently the dominating driving forces for change, but with groups very often one of the most important motivations is a desire to improve group efficiency...even though there may be no critical problems in the present situation'. Often the motivation for change by one part of the client system may be hampered by other parts of the organization. The change agent has to be aware of the potential for resistance from other areas, has to be aware that he or she may be viewed as 'on the side' of the immediate client organization, and has to be aware of the impact that both factors may have on the change process. The change agent should at the outset ask him- or herself:

Who is likely to be affected by change in this client system, and how are they likely to react?

Answers to these questions may go a long way in determining how successful change is likely to be, who is likely to be impacted by it, and how motivated the organization, as a whole, is to change.

Another important issue that the change agent needs to look at, and be honest about, is his or her own capabilities to manage the change process. In this sense, the change agent needs to ask the question:

What is it I can bring that can help this organization change?

This brings us back to the temporary nature of the change process and the full role of the change agent. The change agent in his or her role of facilitator is more often than not seen as being an individual who diagnoses problems and offers recommendations for improvement. However, the role is a temporary one and the change agent must also be seen to offer continuity in interpreting the consequences for change made in his or her recommendations. The logic behind this is fairly straightforward. Having assisted the organization to define its current problem, and helped it consider alternative solutions, the change agent should also assist in the process of working out the meaning of change for the organization in terms of practices, procedures and resultant design.

Change can create a level of disruption which, if not handled adequately, can lead to demoralization within the organization. Having gone through the diagnostic process and outlined the changes needed, the organization may also feel that it has insufficient capabilities to cope with the implications for change without the assistance of the change agent. It is therefore necessary, as a change agent, to be able to offer both diagnostic and application skills. Lippit (1959, p. 9) recommends that a consultative team is best placed to offer such solutions. Either way, walking away from the change process half-way through, would appear to be an inadequate means of dealing with change.

In our dealings with organizations we have often called on the resources of our own outside observer for a neutral standpoint. In this sense, what we get is the viewpoint from someone who has not been closely involved with the organization and may be able to look at the implications of change from a fresher viewpoint. More often than not, this confirms our diagnosis and assessment of the implications of change, but it would assist the change agent greatly, especially if he or she is an internal change agent, to have a 'sounding board' to bounce ideas off. What we recommend here is that organizations invest their resources in more than one individual as change agent, to provide the security and efficiency associated with a team.

There are two other important issues that the change agent needs to take into careful consideration during the course of managing a change project within an organization. The first relates to his or her role during the different phases of the project. The second is linked to establishing change as the norm within organizations.

In terms of the changing role of the change agent, the important question for the change agent here is:

Who should I be at certain points in time?

In essence this involves movement from information-gatherer towards a more active training role. Lippit *et al.* (1958) identified seven phases of change within what they term the consultant–client relationship:

(1) Development of the need for change.
(2) Establishment of the consultancy relationship.
(3) Clarification of the client problem.
(4) Examination of alternative solutions.

(5) Transformation of intentions to actual change.
(6) Generalization and stabilization of a new level of functioning or group structure.
(7) Achieving a terminal relationship with the consultant and the continuity of changeability.

The first crucial area is the move from change agent as information- and opinion-seeker towards that of facilitator and adviser/trainer. This occurs between stages 4 and 5 and involves taking on a more directive role with the client organization. This prevents the organization regressing backwards by allowing individuals to focus on the applications of the alternatives they helped develop. In this scenario, the change agent takes on more of a driving role for change. In this way the client organization will see what happens during the change process and will be able to learn from it and, hopefully, apply the techniques the next time.

In our experience, it is better for the change agent to deliberately separate the information gathering from the diagnosis and recommendations for change stages. In our dealings with organizations we make a point of using the summary session at the end of the information-gathering stages 1 through 4 to get a commitment that we can move forward in a different mode. This involves a form of contract renewal where we seek permission to either lead the transformation of intentions into actual change, or offer to act as observers of how the organization is managing this stage itself. The latter is preferable in terms of gaining the commitment from those being affected by change. It also assists in the termination of the relationship for the organization to be seen to be taking a greater participatory role. However, the change agent still has a role in terms of helping the organization learn new procedures and skills associated with the alternative solutions they have helped to establish. Our recommendation here is to be acutely aware of the change in role, not to hide behind the information-seeker phase, and to prepare to move on to the training and guidance role with the ultimate aim of removing the need for the change agent.

The second issue directly concerns the question of learning in the organization. The change agent should, during the change process, ask the question:

How do I get constant change in this organization?

The process of working through definition of the problem and possible solutions helps the organization learn to cope with the problems which initiated the need for change. It now knows what the causes were and is hopefully in a position to remedy them on its own should they occur again. However, if the change process has been successful, the organization will also have learned how to go about defining problems and clarifying them as they emerge. In this sense, they are learning directly from the change agent about the mechanisms he or she used to clarify problems as they emerged – the types of questions asked, the way in which meetings were run, the way the change agent communicated and got the involvement of all concerned. The organization learns when it has reached its own limits in dealing with problems, and hopefully learns about making decisions on when it needs to seek outside help.

One method that ensures that change becomes the norm is the fact that the organization calls in the change agent in the first place. This action means that the organization learns about new types of procedures for dealing with problems it may not have been fully aware of, and which it can now use itself to maintain the process when circumstances change themselves. One obvious example of this is information gathering.

We were asked by the VLSI (integrated circuit manufacture) business of Digital Equipment in Ayr, Scotland, to undertake a short review of the development of semi-autonomous work teams during 1989. This was a fairly straightforward process which involved the design of an opinion survey questionnaire, the running of a number of workshops on issues of concerns and critical success factors with operating staff, and conversations with managers within the business. We worked through the process of information gathering and analysis and provided feedback on how the teams were operating, what were the critical success factors, and a number of issues that gave cause for concern. However, one of the unexpected success criteria from our perspective was that having used the teams to help design and run the questionnaire and the workshops, the organization decided that this method of data collection and analysis could be successfully adopted inside the business and used as a mechanism for assessing where they were, what changes were likely to affect them, and what issues staff felt were likely to be problematic. The change agents, ourselves, had left the relationship, but the mechanisms for making change ongoing remained and had been built into the business. Digital's VLSI integrated circuit business is dealt with in greater depth in Chapter 11 when we examine organization development cases.

CONCLUSION: ORGANIZATION DEVELOPMENT AND THE EFFECTIVE CHANGE AGENT

We pointed out earlier on, that experience suggests that creating a sense of involvement with those likely to be affected by change encourages their commitment to change, and higher levels or standards of performance result. The mechanisms used during the process of change by the change agent, to ensure participation and involvement in the changes being contemplated, can increase the likelihood of a successful intervention.

The issues of involving people through consultation, participation and communication are all regarded as 'soft' criteria which everyone does. However, these issues still create a degree of controversy related to their timing, effectiveness and applicability, and they still generate debate and disagreement within organizations. However, there is a sincere logic behind the change agent adopting such an approach. Schein comments that,

> As long as organizations are networks of people engaged in achieving some common goals, there will be various kinds of processes occurring between them. Therefore, the more we understand about how to diagnose and improve such processes, the greater will be our chances of finding solutions to the more technical problems and of ensuring that such solutions will be accepted and used by members of the organization.
>
> (Schein, 1988, p. 12)

The effective change agent has to be able to manage the bridge between the manager's desire to solve the problem immediately and the time it takes the organization to solve its own problems via the change agent and his or her facilitation process. The effective change agent also has to remain on an unstable borderline, or what Margulies and Raia (1978) classify as 'marginality', between being in the organization and remaining aloof. Similarly, the change agent has to strike a balance between being the 'technical' expert – the person assumed to have the answers, and the process facilitator – the person with the techniques to allow the organization to find its own answers. Most effective change agents need to find a balance. This lies between what they know is the correct solution, having done it before and thus knowing what types of answers and solutions are likely to emerge, and the processes by which they get the organization's members to find their own answers to their own problems – a tricky task!

In our experience, many managers will readily accept the overall argument for a need to change organization structures and management styles for more effective performance. However, they feel that there is a lack of adequate guidance on how this transformation takes place. This reverts back to the desire for instantly applicable, off-the-shelf solutions to their problems. The real world, even from an organizational development perspective, is less clear cut. The concept of perpetual transition management, as an approach to implementing and sustaining organizational change, is an example of dealing with change as it is lived. To this end, it is the job of the effective change agent to get those involved with the change process to pay attention to how it is lived. It is only in this respect that the experience of change can be learned from, and applied effectively at a later date. The change agent to be effective needs to constantly work on the basis that he or she is eventually doing themselves out of a job, and that the client is big enough to be able to handle his or her own problems – a tricky task!

In Part 4 of this book we look at the practicalities. By examining case studies of change we ask the reader to look at real organizations, their experiences, and how they have applied both systems intervention and organization development models of change. By doing so, we ask you to place yourself in the role of change agent, examining the problems and attempting to attain solutions.

Part 4

Practical Cases in Change Management

10

Cases in Systems Intervention

INTRODUCTION

Throughout this text every effort has been made to illustrate the models and theories discussed by introducing, when appropriate, short cases and examples taken from a wide range of change management projects. The variety of examples employed in Chapters 3 and 5 allowed a number of different features and attributes associated with the Intervention Strategy Model (ISM) to be illustrated. In this chapter we will return to a few of the ISM-related examples and develop them into full change management cases, thus enabling the reader to follow a sample of ISM studies in their entirety.

Three cases taken from a range of diverse organizations have been selected. The first comes from the National Health Service and illustrates the use of the ISM on an externally imposed change. Caledonian Airmotive plc provide the second case, which involves a considerable reorganization of a manufacturing system; however, this organizational change was tackled successfully by employing a systems interventionist approach. This case exhibits many features associated with the Total Project Management Model (TPMM). The final case is taken from the ranks of the recently privatized industries and again involves an externally imposed change, with organizational implications, at British Gas (Scotland) plc.

The case format will meticulously follow the change management route taken by each problem owner and their associated team of change agents. At the end of each case there will be a brief review of the key points to be noted and the lessons learned.

CASE 1: THE ARGYLL AND CLYDE HEALTH BOARD

As of March 1991 the fifteen Scottish Health Boards, in response to the Government's White Paper entitled *Working for Patients*, had to be in a position which permitted completed returns of Scottish Morbidity Records (SMRs) to be made to the Common Services Agency (CSA) of the National Health Service (NHS) in Edinburgh, within two months of the end of any particular month. Prior to March 1991 the data within the completed and aggregated SMRs, which are the recording documents for the case histories of each patient treated in an NHS hospital, relating to a full year's returns did not have to be submitted to Edinburgh until the summer of the following year. The whole process of gathering, collating and validating SMRs had to be accelerated. The importance of these documents to each Health Board cannot be overstated. The CSA collates the data for all fifteen Boards in Scotland and funding is then allocated according to the numbers and types of patient treated.

Background information specific to the change

On admission to an NHS hospital an SMR document is initiated for each patient by a member of medical records staff. At this point the document contains basic patient information and demographic details. On discharge, clinical codes detailing diagnoses and any operating procedures carried out are assigned and recorded by coding staff of the Medical Records Department. The information required to complete this final section of the SMR is taken from the discharge letter, which must be completed for each patient by their medical consultant.

In Argyll and Clyde Health Board the use of a computerized patient administration system, by each of the major hospitals, obviates the need for paper SMR documents, all relevant data files being held on magnetic tape. The tapes from each hospital are submitted to a central computer centre at which the tapes are input to the SMR standard system. After a cyclical process, involving the production of error and query reports followed by data resubmission, the standard system produces aggregated and validated data for the Board. This output is then forwarded to the CSA to await further analysis after which funding allocations will be decided.

The problem owner and the definition phase

The problem, which as far as this case is concerned is limited to the acceleration of SMR processing speed, was assigned to a member of the Board's Information Services Division (ISD). ISD was ultimately responsible for data processing. The change situation had, on the appointment of the problem owner, been effectively entered. The problem owner then set about developing a number of diagrams to define the systems processes and environment under review.

It was at this point of systems specification that the Argyll and Clyde case was first visited. In Chapter 3, Figure 3.6 deals with the activity sequences associated with SMR production and Figure 3.7 describes the inputs and outputs from the SMR standard system.

The reader should now return to these figures in Chapter 3 prior to continuing. Review them carefully and then return to this case.

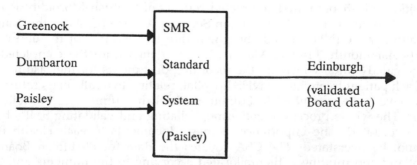

Figure 10.1 Geographic sources (computerized hospitals only).

In addition to the diagrams illustrated in Chapter 3 the problem owner also produced the input/output diagram, Figure 10.1, which detailed geographical information.

Having dealt with the definition of the systems information flow the next step was to consider the relationships which existed between system components. Prior to 1991, magnetic tapes were produced at hospital locations and ISD staff arranged collection by any member of staff who happened to be on site. Alternatively, tapes were entrusted to the internal transport system. The outputs of the SMR standard system were similarly treated. ISD's role was one of facilitation and co-ordination. Figure 10.2 depicts the relationship map used to identify all those who may be involved in the change.

The information flows and staff involved were well defined. As the objective, namely, 'to have the SMR data for month "n" validated, processed and submitted to Edinburgh by the end of month "$n+2$"', had come from on high and as such was not negotiable, attention was then turned to the factors which influence the achievement of this objective. Three factors were identified:

(1) The length of time after discharge before diagnoses details were available.
(2) The travel time of the magnetic tapes and error/query reports.
(3) The number of resubmissions of data before data were fully validated.

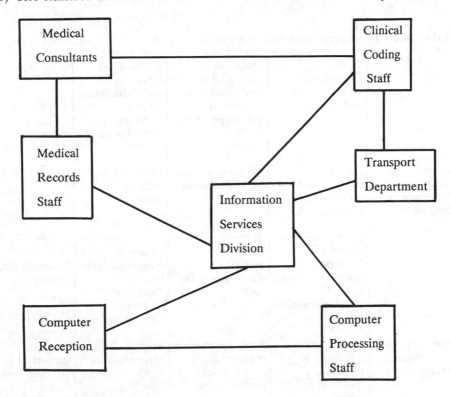

Figure 10.2 Relationship map.

The third factor was addressed by a separate study, undertaken at a national level, which dealt with the quality assurance issues associated with the integration of a new computerized coding system with the existing patient administration systems. Both studies knew of each other's existence and were working towards the same overall goal. The problem owner was therefore left with factors (1) and (2) to deal with in relation to the overall objective. Quantifiable time measures of success could be identified for both factors.

Evaluation phase

Up until this point the problem owner had essentially been working alone. On entering the design phase it was decided to involve representatives from those departments highlighted within the relationships map. A meeting was organized and structured around the two factors previously identified. After a brainstorming session and protracted discussions, a number of options were generated for each factor, against which they were then evaluated. Table 10.1 details both the options generated and the group's evaluation of them.

It was eventually decided that Option B, the interim discharge form, would be selected to influence Factor 1 and that Option F be selected for Factor 2.

Table 10.1 Option generation and evaluation

	Option A: Consultants code diagnoses and key in	*Option B:* Consultants write diagnoses on interim discharge form	*Option C:* Consultants write discharge letter immediately after discharge	
Factor 1 To minimise time from discharge to diagnostic coding	Lack of training and no access to the system	Additional work for consultants	Operationally difficult to achieve	
	Option D: Networking of hospital system to SMR standard system	*Option E:* Special van driver hired by ISD	*Option F:* Negotiate with Board Transport Department	*Option G:* Improve data quality
Factor 2 Speed up SMR processing (travel time)	Technically infeasible at present (possible in future)	Extra recurring cost, no leave cover, vehicle maintenance	Special arrangements needed	On-going subject of another study

Implementation

The problem owner tackled the implementation strategy as follows:

Factor 1:

An interim discharge form was designed by medical records staff and inserted in the patient's case notes. Consultants were requested to complete this at the time of discharge and return it to the clinical coding staff via the internal mail. The target was to have coding performed within three to five days of discharge.

Factor 2:

A meeting was held with the transport manager and it was agreed that a system known as 'Data In Transit' would be attempted. This involved making use of the existing transport runs but with the addition of the following three features:

(1) Specifically designed multiple-part forms to allow tracking of tapes and error and query reports.
(2) Specially purchased colour-coded transport bags for ease of identification.
(3) Special arrangements for pick up and delivery directly to and from the clinical coders at each hospital.

Items were then ordered and forms designed. The new scheme was explained to all staff concerned and there was no opposition. A consolidation period followed. ISD staff monitored the new system, lending support and encouragement when necessary.

Epilogue

The transport system as envisaged within Option F is fully operational and has considerably reduced SMR travel time. Factor 1, tackled by Option B, has improved slightly but the coding target of three to five days after discharge is not being met at all sites. At the time of writing the case this difficulty was being reviewed and an improvement imminent.

Case review

On the surface this case appears to be well suited to a systems investigation. The success of the new transport system bears testimony to the appropriateness of ISM. A well-structured and systematic solution was developed to answer a particularly hard problem. Throughout the case the problem owner followed the ISM approach, except in the definition phase, in which the need to formally address the issue of constraints appears to have been ignored. The financial constraint was an obvious one to those concerned and could be taken for granted; what appears to have been less obvious was the constraint placed on the solution by the medical consultants. This was an organizational constraint and should have been dealt with accordingly. The implementation strategy for Factor 1 did not fully address it. Involving a representative of the medical consultants in the design process did not guarantee acceptance of the implementation strategy.

An iteration was required to address this difficulty. The consultants probably do not recognize their important role within the process which ultimately decides their budgets. They must be tactfully educated and cajoled if they are to accept a change which appears to require a greater administrative load. The key lesson which may be taken from this case is simply that change creates multi-disciplinary problems, which often require a blend of the systems and organizational approaches to be applied, especially within the implementation phase.

CASE 2: CALEDONIAN AIRMOTIVE LTD

Caledonian Airmotive Ltd (CAL) participates in the highly competitive aero-engine overhaul business on a world-wide basis from their production facility at Prestwick Airport. The company is well established and has developed a reputation for excellence. An extremely dynamic internal environment has developed in response to the ever-increasing demands placed on the company from their customers, who operate in a highly volatile market where time is indeed money. The ability to readily adapt to changes, imposed in the main from external sources, is seen by the company and their market-place as a distinct competitive advantage. CAL's main customer grouping, the airlines, require two main classes of engineering support: (1) Provision of serviceable engines after a repair or overhaul in as short a time as possible. (2) Provision of a repair service with respect to line replaceable units (LRUs), which are removed at the operator's base and sent for repair independently of the engine.

There are a variety of engine components which can be classed as LRUs, and this diversity requires a flexible production response. Management is therefore faced with the problem of maintaining mainstream engine overhaul and repair production whilst dealing with the varied disturbances caused by processing LRUs. In a competitive environment in which the minimization of engine turnaround time is crucial, the single manufacturing system must favour the mainstream flow work associated with complete engine overhaul and repair. As a result LRU work, profitable though it is, must be fitted in to mainstream production schedules and therefore incur turnaround delays.

Background information specific to the change

The accessory shop which was responsible for LRU repair formed an integral part of the mainstream production process and was dependent on such services as the machine shop, provisioning, non-destructive testing (NDT) inspection and new part stores. As priorities always went to complete engine-related activities the LRUs suffered delays. The situation may be seen as a mismatch between customer requirements, namely, quick turnaround on both engine and LRU repairs, and the company's norms which seek efficient production flows. The company aims to be more capable than their competitors at identifying and correcting mismatches and by so doing maintain a competitive edge. The LRU problem was therefore treated seriously and formed the basis of an extensive change management exercise.

The change objective, or project brief, was clear:

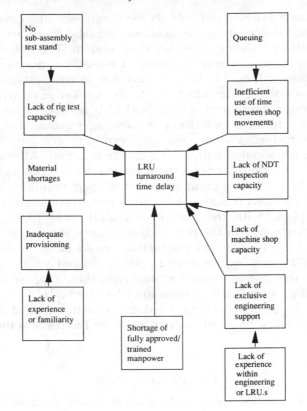

Figure 10.3 Multiple cause diagram for LRU delays.

to successfully intervene in the working process of the current accessory shop system with the aim of effectively changing that system from being one of dependency to one of self sufficiency, and to create a stable new environment which can support both shop engine and single item LRU requirements, to such an extent that a competitive edge is achieved with respect to turnaround time and customer satisfaction.

The problem owner and the definition phase

Senior management commissioned an analysis of system relationships, work-flow patterns and the causes of turnaround time delays. They also appointed a project manager with direct knowledge of the problem and the necessary skills and position to facilitate the change. In Chapter 3, Figures 3.10 and 3.15, the accessory shop relationship and influence maps were introduced.

The reader should now return to these figures in Chapter 3 prior to continuing. Review them carefully and then return to this case.

In addition to these figures a multiple cause diagram relating to LRU delays was also produced. It is shown in Figure 10.3.

The project manager's initial reaction was that there was one obvious solution: a truly autonomous accessory shop, operating as a satellite plant.

This conclusion was based not only on the diagrams so far covered but also on highly detailed flow diagrams detailing virtually every activity and link associated with the existing accessory shop system. The detailed, technical and, most importantly, sensitive nature of these flow diagrams precluded their publication within this text. In addition to the systems studies the project manager also spoke informally to the market place who were very keen on the provision of such a dedicated LRU service.

Indulging in a forward loop the project manager gathered representatives of finance, marketing, systems and engineering to evaluate the costs and general validity associated with such a course of action. After careful study it was decided that this was not a viable option due to both logistic and cost constraints. The assembled group then turned their attention to a derivative of the first suggestion. A semi-autonomous system could be created within the existing plant, with the control of critical areas passing over from mainstream production to the new LRU accessory shop. The only services to be shared with mainstream production would be of an administrative and functional nature, such as systems, personnel and quality. Analysis and evaluation of this option proved more favourable. Proposed expenditure could be justified against the increase in orders for both LRUs and engines, which would be gained through a reduction in turnaround time. Market research and detailed financial analysis were used to confirm the cost justification.

Evaluation phase

Armed with a validated solution the project manager set about the actual task of detailing the practical activity requirements associated with the solution. Several factors had to be addressed:

(1) Shop layout,
(2) Equipment requirements,
(3) Organizational structure,
(4) Training requirements,
(5) Disruption effects of change to the current production cycle.

The company and the project manager knew that the success of the change would rely on the willing support of all those concerned. Diagrammatic representations detailing the old and new systems, along with updated organizational charts, were produced in consultation with the key players involved. This material was then used to communicate the change to the rest of the organization. The project manager actively sold the concept first to senior management and then with their support to the other management levels and functions. Having gained widespread support and, through the delegation of responsibilities to change agents, addressed the factors raised above, the project then moved on to an implementation phase.

Implementation phase

A sequential implementation plan was initiated, which involved the parallel running of both the old and new systems, along with the involvement of the actual workgroups, who would be part of the semi-autonomous accessory shop in detailing their working environment. The plan was used to illustrate implementation issues within Chapter 5 and the reader should consult the relevant section for more detail.

The reader should now return to the section on the implementation phase, Chapter 5 (p. 77). Review the CAL example carefully and then return to this case.

The implementation phase has since been completed and the project is now going through a phase of consolidation.

Case review

The CAL project represented a major change-management exercise. In many ways the sheer scale of the project can be seen by the number of diagrams which could only be alluded to and the volume of planning and implementation detail which could only be dealt with superficially. The change was successfully managed by adopting both traditional systems-based and project management methodologies, while at the same time building into the project an element of involvement, education and understanding.

The project manager did not follow the ISM in a logical manner. The approach taken was far more like that advocated by the TPMM. The definition phase concentrated on developing an understanding of the systems environment and bringing on board the appropriate expertise to solve the problem. As the project had to be validated prior to commencing change activities there was no choice but to corrupt the ISM to facilitate the generation of a solution within the definition phase. Chapter 6 stressed the point that in project management the solution to the problem has generally been agreed prior to engaging in detailed planning. The CAL case was no exception to the rule. However, it may have been possible to avoid the initial evaluation of the totally autonomous solution had the constraints associated with the project been more fully defined. Given that the desired solution had been both found and validated prior to the formulation phase there was no need for evaluation of options. Instead the project team set about analysing and planning for the key factors associated with the project solution. Again this process reflects the second phase of the TPMM. Implementation involved the development of a sequential plan which in many ways may be considered similar to a network-based activity schedule.

The major lessons for the practitioner which may be drawn from this case concern the actual application of intervention strategies. Firstly, an optimal solution can still be achieved even when the format of the model has been corrupted to reflect an actual live environment. Secondly, care should be taken that the modifications adopted to the format do not result in the complete omission of key process steps. Intervention models contain the steps that they do because both researchers and practitioners have found them useful. The last point to note from this case concerns the TPMM. When dealing with projects it may be better to adopt the TPMM derivative of the ISM model, always of course remembering the importance of the softer organizational issues.

CASE 3: BRITISH GAS (SCOTLAND) PLC

There are twelve autonomous operating regions within the UK Gas Supply Division of British Gas. This case concerns the Scottish Region and in particular its central purchasing department. Each region serves a customer base which has its own unique appliance population. Regions hold local stocks of parts ordered on a regular basis and can therefore offer their customers an 'off-the-shelf' service. All other spare parts for which local stockholding cannot be justified, due to irregular demand, are known as 'one-time-buys' or OTBs for short. OTBs are ordered directly from the suppliers, usually the appliance manufacturer, and take, on average, about fifteen days to be delivered to the customer.

Background information specific to the case

As part of a drive to improve standards of customer service, British Gas, at corporate level, decided to set up their own stockholding facilities for OTBs. Two national stockholding centres, one at Manchester, the other in London, opened for business in March 1991 and provided the regions with approximately 80 per cent of their currently ordered OTBs. By centralizing the purchasing and holding of such stocks, economies of scale would be available to British Gas as a whole, and there would be no cost disadvantage for the regions trading with the new central resource. Regions were instructed that on the opening of the new facilities they should all be in a position to commence ordering immediately. Lead times for OTBs were expected to drop from fifteen days to a few, probably three or four, thus improving customer service.

The problem owner and the definition phase

The problem owner within the Scottish Region was the purchasing manager, who was given the following change brief: 'to change (or intervene in) the current system of ordering OTBs to enable the purchasing department to make optimal use of the additional national stockholding, thereby effecting an improved service to customers'.

Following the problem initialization the problem owner quickly involved the other key players, namely, the departmental systems development officer and the spares buyer. The steps taken by this group of change agents when defining the systems environment were detailed within the section of Chapter 5 dealing with the definition phase of ISM.

The reader should now return to the Definition Section of Chapter 5 (p. 69). Review the British Gas example carefully and then return to this case.

A number of diagrams are referred to within the British Gas example in Chapter 5. The figures here illustrate the diagrammatic output of the change agents. The first diagram deals with the OTB flow chart, Figure 10.4. It was produced to further the management group's understanding of the present system.

From the flow chart the group moved on to develop an activity sequence diagram, Figure 10.5, depicting the situation for both before and after the

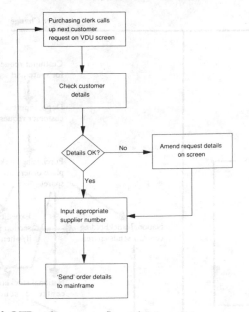

Figure 10.4 Original OTB sub-system flow chart.

change. This was a useful analysis exercise and a means of communicating the exact nature to the ordering clerks most directly affected. It was possible at this stage to define the process elements of the proposed change due to the detailed information which was provided along with the notification of the corporate policy system. In addition, the process activities were unlikely to alter drastically as the change essentially involved altering only the source of supplies.

The activity sequence diagram highlighted the need to consider all the parties involved as there were going to be additional external links after the change. Again, before- and after-relationship maps were produced and are shown in Figure 10.6.

The systems definition stage was completed by the construction of two systems maps as shown in Figure 10.7.

With the actual systems definitions completed to everyone's satisfaction the problem owner then turned the managing group's attention to the change forces at work within the change environment. A number of Force Field Analysis diagrams, see Figure 10.8, were produced which both evaluated and described the forces acting on those involved.

It was evident from a number of the diagrams produced that the workload of the expediting section would be reduced by the changes. They were therefore consulted about the intended changes. All concerned staff, ordering clerks and expediters, were given assurances that no one would lose their jobs as a result of the changes. Redeployments, both sensitively managed and to related disciplines, were to be used to overcome the problem of reduced workloads and operative resistance. Both the assurances and the potential redeployments were accepted by the staff.

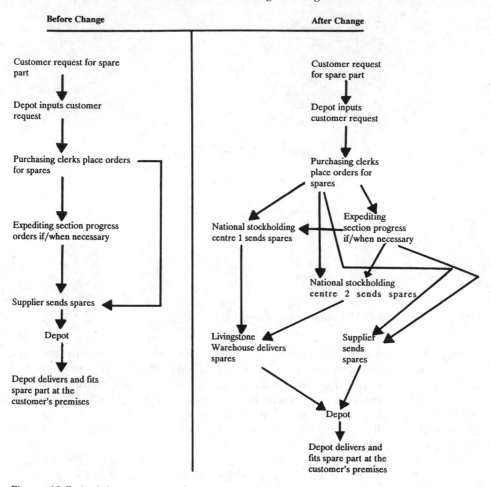

Figure 10.5 Activity sequence diagram.

The problem owner, confident of staff support, now turned his attention to the constraints acting upon the change situation. To this end an objectives tree was produced, Figure 10.9, in which priorities were included.

The performance indicators were identified from the objectives tree. They fell into two categories associated with the financial and human resource. Firstly, budgetary constraints would produce financial measures for training, systems programming and equipment.

Secondly, systems staff were in high demand and therefore their services were difficult to secure. In addition, there were performance targets associated directly with the change itself. A target date of March 1991 had been set, by which time 80 per cent of all OTBs had to be ordered from the new facilities. There was also an imposed delivery target of three to four days from receipt of the customer's order.

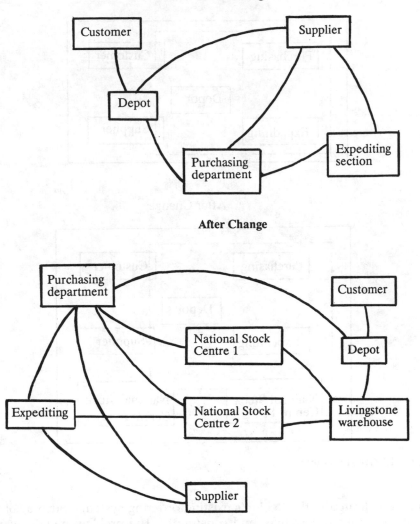

Figure 10.6 Relationship maps.

Evaluation phase

The actual process activities required for the new system had been previously detailed in the definition phase. The management team, along with the ordering clerks, now set about generating options for actually achieving the physical operations. This involved a detailed study of the existing computerized system which after much deliberation produced only one feasible solution. Each ordering clerk would require an additional visual display unit and terminal which would then in turn be linked into the new stock-holding centres' computerized systems. Existing kit could not deal with the additional load and still maintain an effective service. It would therefore

Before Change

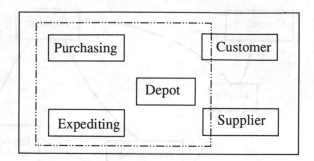

After Change

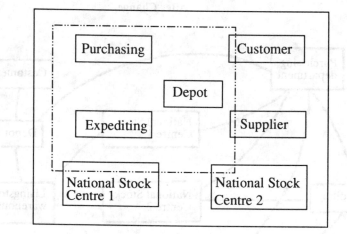

Figure 10.7 Systems maps.

remain dedicated to the Region's existing ordering systems. Such a solution satisfied the main objectives and constraints. The problem owner, wary of implementation difficulties, contacted the systems people and confirmed that their resources were indeed stretched, but they would do all they could to help.

Implementation phase

The implementation strategy comprised three stages. The first involved the acquisition and installation of equipment, which was immediately followed by the setting-up of communications links. During this time the operatives entered the second stage. They were given access to dummy screens to allow them to become familiar with screen layout and input requirements. The third stage, once the new system was operational, involved the running of ten pilot ordering runs. These tested the system and also satisfied the

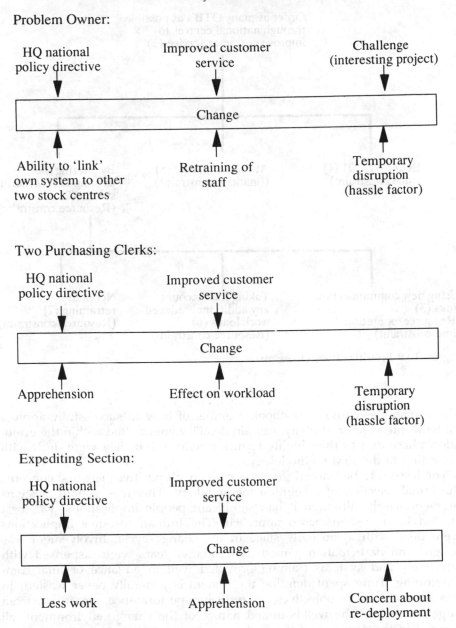

Figure 10.8 Force Field Analysis.

management team of the benefits associated with the new system and the efficiency of the central warehousing resource.

A number of minor iterations were made as a result of the operator-training phase and the pilot runs. These resulted in useful screen layout changes. Consolidation was never an internal issue and the national system appears to have achieved its objectives.

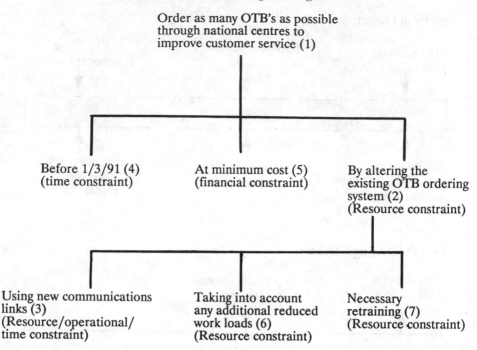

Figure 10.9 Prioritized objectives tree.

Case review

The British Gas case is a textbook example of how to successfully apply a systems intervention strategy. Certain details were omitted within the evaluation phase due to their highly technical nature, but they were dealt with according to the ISM methodology.

The lessons to be learned from this case are all positive. The first concerns the initial selection of a solution methodology. This was a 'hard' systems problem which, although it had significant people implications, was best tackled by a systems-based approach. The human resource implications were dealt with at an early stage in the change cycle. Involvement was sought and participation gained. Redundancy fears were dispensed with effectively and systems training provided well in advance of final commissioning. Time spent defining the system is generally never wasted. In this case the clear objectives, quantifiable performance measures, fixed target dates and the well-bounded nature of the change environment, all pointed in the direction of the ISM.

The second lesson concerns the forward loop from the formulation to the implementation phase. The need to be aware of the pressures facing the systems resource was built into the implementation strategy. Parallel implementation was achieved by ensuring that the operatives had access to dummy screens while the installation was going ahead. This both avoided potential implementation delays and allowed minor systems updates to be incorporated while the systems people were on site.

11
Organization Development Cases

INTRODUCTION

Cases 4, 5 and 6 concern organization development issues. Case 4, High Technology Change at VLSI, is set as an analysis of work organization change in a multinational enterprise (MNE). The company is described and the case study gone into, in some depth. You will then be set a number of discussion questions which act as the basis for studying the organization development process that this MNE undertook. Finally, we provide our own analysis of the changes that took place.

Case 5 looks at change from the perspective of those experiencing change at it is lived. MTC Ltd is an example of organization development as it impacts both internal and external environments.

Case 6, Group Performance Review, is much shorter and is aimed at getting you to reflect on how you would go about tackling a particular form of organization development intervention with the information provided.

These case studies have been designed both to satisfy the needs of the individual reader, and to act as group exercises in a more formalized setting. To the extent that they try to satisfy two needs at the same time there is a degree of compromise that has to be met. In the organization case studies, we have compromised in favour of the group learning approach rather than the individual. In our teaching on the management of change, we have found that a greater degree of thought and discussion is generated through group analysis of situations. Therefore, if you are considering these cases as an individual, it may be worth your while to think about working out a situation where they can be used in groups. Within your own organization, this could form part of an exercise prior to discussion of an actual change event that is likely to take place. You may also be considering some of the changes described in the cases. In this sense, they will act as a form of organization analysis. Look at what others did before considering how you wish to proceed.

CASE 4: HIGH TECHNOLOGY CHANGE AT VLSI

The use of semi- and fully autonomous workgroups in the electronics manufacturing industry in the UK and the USA has developed significantly over the 1980s and early 1990s (Buchanan, 1987; McCalman, 1988). The use of such groups and developments in socio-technical systems work have emanated from the large American base of subsidiary operations in the electronics sector based in the UK. The concepts and ideas may be largely similar to those propounded by the Tavistock Institute during the 1960s, but the applications and reasons behind these appear to be taking on a different set of criteria (Buchanan and McCalman, 1989).

This case describes the successful implementation of a 'high-performance workgroup' approach to integrated circuit manufacture in the very large-scale integrated circuits (VLSI) Division of Digital Equipment based at their manufacturing facility in Ayr, Scotland. It is argued here that this 'new' approach to work organization and management produces the manufacturing flexibility and product quality necessary to remain competitive in the highly volatile semiconductor business. This approach also contributes positively to personal skill and career development, and to the quality of working life. The case identifies the achievements and lessons from applying this approach in the VLSI Division, and offers practical advice on how this approach can be adapted for use in other environments. Similar approaches have been employed by other organizations with varying levels of success. However, what makes this particular case interesting is that it is set against a background of significant technological barriers to the humanization of work. The physical impediments to using workgroups as a form of work organization include: the use of cleanrooms to manufacture integrated circuits; the number of stages in the manufacturing operation separated by physical boundaries; and the restrictions placed on socialization with other employees because of articles of clothing, such as cleanroom masks. All these factors work to inhibit both the quality of working life and the ability to function effectively within a team-based environment. Simplistically, one would expect that physical barriers imposed by technological constraints would hamper the development of any form of group working.

The VLSI plant

The Digital plant at Ayr opened in 1976 with 25 people, as a pilot final assembly and test (FA&T) operation sourcing computer products for the British and European markets. This involved assembling components and testing systems imported from America. The plant has grown to over 365,000 square feet since then. The FA&T stage of the manufacturing process became obsolete in the early 1980s, and the plant bid successfully for a new small computer systems charter. In 1984, manufacture of the Micro PDP-11 was transferred to Ayr from Galway, giving the plant its first opportunity to develop a 'high-performance work systems' approach, and to begin developing the small systems business.

A commitment to high performance

The advantages of this approach in the Micro-11 business are reflected in product quality, production flexibility, responsiveness to customer demand, and growth in employee skills. Management across the site and its businesses recognize the competitive advantage of a flexible, committed, skilled, and highly motivated workforce. The plant's strategic planning manager explained:

High-performance work systems is a method of developing organizations in which all elements − people, technology, capital investment and so on – fit together. In these organizations, work teams are allocated an overall task and given control over work-related decisions. Additionally, every employee is trained in all the operations within their group, thus providing a high level of flexibility, both for the individual and the company, that cannot be achieved through traditional approaches.

The advantages achieved through high-performance working, management believe, would not have been possible with traditional ways of working, traditional ways of organizing, and traditional ways of managing.

Digital's Ayr plant is now a complex site with multiple businesses. It employs over 1,400 people, and the plant manufactures the full range of small system products, from personal computers, to MicroVAX and VAX-station products, as well as the complex and intricate semiconductor assembly and testing operation for VLSI circuits. For the first time, in the fiscal year 1989, Ayr shipped over $1 billion dollars worth of systems, a significant increase on the $800 million shipped the year before. Ayr is one of the corporation's most efficient plants and generates more than a third of Digital's European revenue. In 1989, Ayr became the first DEC plant outside America to launch a microcomputer system for world distribution that had been designed and developed in Scotland – the MicroVAX 3100. The plant also achieved the status of 'World Wide Manufacturing Reference Site' in 1989, becoming one of only eight of DEC's 35 manufacturing plants world-wide to hold this honour. In fiscal year 1987, the Ayr plant shipped around 17,000 systems which was expected to rise to between 40,000 and 50,000 by 1993.

Part of the growth at Ayr came from the expansion of the semiconductor business. The VLSI facility opened in 1985, representing an investment of $15 million, and housing one of the largest cleanroom facilities in Europe. This operation was so successful in its first twelve months that it was asked to provide full assembly and test capabilities for up to 80 per cent of the corporation's custom semiconductor needs. Also based on that success, a new advanced semiconductor wafer facility was built at South Queensferry, near Edinburgh, with an investment of $85 million. From 1989, the South Queensferry plant will supply Ayr, taking over from Hudson in America as Ayr's main silicon chip source.

This case tells the story of that VLSI success; how it was achieved, the benefits, the problems, and the lessons. The story is based on the experience of those who work in the VLSI assembly facility – production operators, support groups, and managers. The story describes the success and the achievements. However, when there is a willingness to change, to try out new ways of working, to break the mould of tradition, things do not always work out the way they were planned and expected. The high-performance work systems approach sets out to break a number of moulds. This account explores the problems too, and identifies the lessons for VLSI Ayr, and also for other organizations considering this ambitious and highly effective approach to work organization and management.

At the core of this new approach, as the manager explained above, is the autonomous team whose members are multi-skilled, allocate their own work, solve their own problems, and take many of their own decisions. This was the approach developed in the Micro-11 business in the mid-1980s, and has also been used effectively at Digital's plant at Enfield, Connecticut. This is not a system that can be developed and implemented quickly. The approach is still evolving, and those working with it are contributing to that evolution, and learning new lessons as it proceeds.

The VLSI facility began in 1983 as a small test operation, for chips made in America destined for the European market. In April 1984, the business employed 14 people when it tested and shipped its first product. At this time, the corporation was looking at ways to reduce dependence on expensive external subcontractors as a source of semiconductors. The corporation bought chips from major manufacturers such as Motorola, National SemiConductor, Texas Instruments, and Signetics. However, in the early 1980s, Digital decided to make its own sophisticated chips for newer products.

The VLSI charter

Management at Ayr developed a successful proposal to locate a volume assembly and test facility to achieve this goal at Ayr. The Ayr charter is to satisfy 80 per cent of the corporation's global demand for VLSI devices. The assembly and test operations are run separately. This functional division may be unnecessary and is now under review.

The assembly cleanroom was built in 1985, and from the end of 1985 until 1987 the ramp-up in output was dramatic. The number of units assembled and tested per week in December 1985 was 2,000. The number in December 1987 was 80,000 (not all of these passed through the Ayr assembly process). This was reflected in the growth in total employment in the VLSI business from 100 people at the end of 1985, to 450 at the end of 1987.

The manufacturing process has four stages:

Design: The chip is designed, a complex and sophisticated process which is still carried out in Hudson.

Fabrication: Chips are etched on to a wafer of silicon, typically 4 to 6 inches in diameter. Each wafer contains from 150 to 2,000 chips, depending on circuit size and complexity. Each circuit is tested electrically before shipment to assembly.

Packaging: Individual chips are cut from the wafer and are encapsulated in ceramic or plastic packages. Through metal pins in the packaging, the chips are electrically connected to the system for which they are intended when the package is soldered into the module (printed circuit board). This is explained in more detail later.

Test: Extensive testing is carried out on each device to ensure only good chips proceed to module (printed circuit board) manufacturing customers.

VLSI assembly in 1989 employed around 230 people, and occupied 40,000 square feet, including 10,000 square feet of specially designed cleanroom. The group manufactures about 35,000 units a week. The facility also includes an injection moulding room for plastic devices, a chemical plating shop, a repair and maintenance room and machine shop, and a failure analysis suite with a scanning electron microscope.

The VLSI assembly process at Ayr is complex. There are a number of interrelated stages in the assembly flow which affect final product quality and process yields, and which therefore demand constant attention to detail and to key manufacturing parameters.

The first step concerns the receipt and sorting of the wafers from the fabrication plants in Hudson, America, and now from South Queensferry in Scotland. The wafers are washed and loaded into manufacturing containers. Each die is then visually inspected to identify physical defects (a stage in the process which, it is hoped, will soon be conducted by the wafer fabrication plants themselves). The wafers are then prepared for further handling by mounting them on to a film frame.

The individual circuits or dies are then sawn from the wafer. The dies are then attached to their packages using either a silver-loaded epoxy glue (for 95 per cent of products) or a hot gold solder, depending on the product type. The positioning of the die relative to the package is critical.

Using automatic wire bonders, the contact pads on the die are then attached to corresponding posts on the package. Products vary from 40 to 250 wires. This is followed by another optical inspection, looking for unreliability and other defects, before the die is sealed. The product is then hermetically sealed using either a ceramic or glass lid (90 per cent use glass). The seals are placed manually. Gas content and conditions inside the product seal are also critical to quality.

The sealed product is then thermally stressed, and tests are made for leakages in the package sealing. The lead frames are then tin-plated, again using an automatic process. The product type, lot number, date of manufacture, and origin are then manually branded on the package. Some product is then manually loaded into an anti-static carrier, while others require trimming in a hydraulic press. Following a final inspection of all aspects of the package quality, the product is manually loaded into shipping tubes and transferred to the test group.

Assembly volumes were around 15,000 units a week, covering devices in five main product families. The devices processed are becoming more sophisticated all the time, making new demands on engineering and assembly skills, and on investment in appropriate test equipment.

The products in which these devices are used include systems such as the DEC 11/44s and 11/750s, Orion machines, and the Venus and MicroVax systems. Some of the new chips have the staggering number of 300 pins. Devices in the 250 to 400 pin range involve a different form of assembly process called tape automated bonding (TAB).

The business has a number of key support groups. The engineering group sustains existing processes and introduces new equipment. The technology group is also chartered to develop new processes and methods to improve production efficiency. The repair and maintenance group ensures that production equipment is fully functional. The business is supported by a materials group whose goal is to ensure supplies of raw materials and consumables; materials costs in the finished device amount to approximately 80 per cent of total production cost. The business has its own quality administration, finance and personnel functions.

The assembly facility includes a sophisticated cleanroom designed to protect products before they are sealed from contamination from air, static charge, people, liquids, equipment, chemicals, and other particles and items normally present in a manufacturing environment. The cleanroom floor, wall and ceiling materials are smooth and non-shedding, and air is ducted into the cleanroom through microfilters to scrub it clean of airborne contamination, particularly dust. The cleanroom pressure is higher than in the rest of the factory to improve cleanliness standards, and entry and exit are through double doors.

The special requirements of the cleanroom facility created problems of communications and interaction. Those working outside the cleanroom, in 'back of line' in particular, could have only limited contact with those inside the cleanroom. To move from one area to the other required a cumbersome and time-consuming change of clothes, into and out of a 'bunny suit'. Working inside the cleanroom, it was difficult to recognize someone from behind, as everyone in a 'bunny suit' looked the same from that angle. And conversations could be impeded by the suit hoods which covered the ears, and by face masks. These special conditions presented practical problems for the design and reorganization of work, problems which were being addressed and overcome.

VLSI business goals

Among the key goals of the VLSI business are: (1) high standards of product quality and reliability, (2) customer satisfaction, (3) deliveries on time.

The rapid ramp-up in production volumes in 1985 through 1987 left very little time for the consideration of organizational issues. The focus was on building up the volume, building up the physical facility, and building up the workforce. However, by 1988 the business had stabilized — comparatively. As the VLSI manager explained:

> We were all glad of a breather in financial year 1989 when build requirements levelled and even reduced for a brief period. We used this opportunity to concentrate on much needed training and skill development of our people. The programmes included specific training, general problem-solving techniques, manufacturing resource planning (MRP II), just-in-time (JIT), and supervisory and management development.

This was not the only change. Management also began to look at the overall organization of work in the assembly business. That organization had been successful in ramping up the business, so, as the old engineering proverb says, 'If it ain't broke, why fix it?' Management felt that, despite that past success, they could now achieve more with an improved organizational design. It was explained:

> Another key focus was in the area of organizational development. Work cell and team work strategies helped tremendously to utilize the skills acquired for the benefit of the business. We believe investment in people-development and manufacturing-excellence programmes have paid off handsomely in all aspects of the operation.

So, the business had a 'breathing space', a window of opportunity in which to take a critical view of operations, and a creative view of possible improvements. And those improvements were developed across a broad front – involving new systems as well as reorganization. The OD consultant to the VLSI business, explained this change in view in similar terms:

We had gone up a ramp and it had started to level off. And as it started to level off we started to look at the organization we had and we didn't like what we saw.

We had operators pushing buttons who weren't involved in any decision making. We were telling them how well they were doing. They hadn't a clue what was going on half the time.

So management got together to look at what we needed to do. We felt we could do better than this. So we looked at high-performance work systems and cell group principles again. And the JIT programme was starting to surface. We kicked off this whole programme on that basis. Gave us a focus for what we were trying to do.

Why was the organization not designed around teamwork or autonomous cells right from the start? Management looking back felt that this might not have been practicable, given the other pressures created by the rapid build-up of the business from scratch. As Alan Russell said:

I'm not sure how you would develop the high-performance-type operation that we're running today, from scratch in such a fierce ramp-up situation. So I don't criticize it although I didn't like how we were doing certain things. We had to deliver within the first six months, the machines were bolted to the floor, and we had to start to learn.

However, that traditional organization structure did have its problems. It had proved difficult to manage. A significant management hierarchy had built up around the business to co-ordinate and control it. A lot of engineering support and other decision makers were needed around the group to make it work. It was clumsy and inflexible.

So it was important that the management team had that breathing space, that time to review the organization, and also that they used that window of opportunity creatively. As was explained: 'It was really the assembly staff group, we really kicked off on the basis that, we've got time now, we've levelled out, we've got this mass of people milling around – let's start developing the thing for the future.'

The principles behind the organizational changes that were introduced involved: (1) dismantling the hierarchy, (2) giving decisions to those directly concerned, (3) creating self-managing teams, (4) creating opportunities for skills development.

The OD consultant explained this in the following way:

What we're trying to do as part of our stated goal is to get decision making at the lowest level and get some ownership for what's happening into the teams. Once you're successful in doing that, you can reduce the hierarchical structure and that's what we're doing right now.

But not reducing it by saying, right, you don't have a job any more. We can free you up now to do something else – what do you want? An example of that is me. I've been given the opportunity to step back from running the production operation and develop in another area. And I was asked what I wanted. There's opportunity there for a lot of people.

Traditional thinking

The traditional approach to the design of work says that you break the job down into simple steps, decide how each step has to be carried out, and then train people to do just that, and no more. Managers decide, production operators produce. Rewards are related to output. Meet the target, you get a bonus. Exceed the target, you get a higher bonus.

The traditional approach has a number of advantages. You do not have to put much time and money into training. You can move people from one simple operation to another without much difficulty. The link between effort and reward is easy to see. The whole operation is easier to supervise and control because everyone is doing their own small, clearly defined function. This is what we referred to in an earlier chapter as Taylor's scientific management.

The traditional approach also has its problems. People get bored with the routine, and start to get careless. Quality problems appear. Commitment is low, and absenteeism and staff turnover start to climb. And product and process changes happen slowly because people don't have the depth of skill and understanding required to absorb innovation and change quickly. This is called rigidity.

Most importantly, people working in this kind of environment never develop any real competence in the process – so they cannot solve problems, they cannot pick up problems before they arise, they cannot contribute effectively to improvements. And they do not get a chance to absorb skill and expertise that would contribute to their own career development as well as to the performance of the organization.

People who are bored with what they are doing and are developing no effective understanding of the business are not going to be highly motivated, receptive to change, or committed. The traditional approach to the design and management of work cannot encourage the levels of performance, the attention to detail and quality, the rapid problem-solving, and the flexibility required to survive, compete and grow in the modern competitive environment.

These issues have led to the development of other and more effective approaches to work organization.

The high-performance approach

This approach became popular in America in the 1980s. Companies like Procter and Gamble, General Motors, Zilog, Hewlett-Packard, Tektronix, Johnsonville Foods, Harley Davidson, Cummins Engines and Shenandoah Life Insurance have all introduced team-based approaches, as did the Digital storage systems plant at Enfield in the early 1980s. The benefits at all these companies have been staggering.

In practice, what this meant in the Micro-11 business in 1984 was the creation of teams with the following features:

(1) self-managing, self-organizing, self-regulating;
(2) front to back responsibility for the core process;
(3) multi-skilled, with no job titles;
(4) shared skills, knowledge and experience;
(5) shared problem-solving, within and between groups.

The Micro-11 business also designed the process layout to make communications easier, with support people located on the shop floor. They also designed a skills-based payment system to reward skills growth, and not simply production volume.

In practice, this approach has two other related dimensions:

The first of these is *trust*. Management and supervisors have to stand back from their traditional decision-making functions and let groups, teams, or cells work it out for themselves.

The second of these concerns *fit*. The way in which this approach is developed in one business has to suit the people, the history, the context, and the nature of that business. You cannot just copy what someone else has done, and hope it will work for you.

We can identify *why* an organization should want to move from a traditional style of work design and management. However, we have not indicated *how* this can be achieved. Is there a problem here? Yes, because in introducing these kinds of changes, many people find that their jobs change, that their skill and knowledge requirements change, and that their future career opportunities have changed too.

Change can be stimulating, refreshing, and challenging, as the future possibilities are often very positive. However, it is clear that some people are going to feel threatened, unsure, and anxious about how they will be affected. These issues have to be managed if change is to happen smoothly and effectively.

Let us look at the negative side first. From experience, we know what some of the main problems are likely to be.

Some of these problems are personal:

(1) some people just prefer traditional ways of working;
(2) it takes time and effort to change traditional thinking;
(3) the change process can expose personal feelings and emotions;
(4) once cell autonomy is established, those involved resist strongly any attempt to return to a traditional approach.

Some of the problems are managerial:

(1) the concepts have to be adapted to fit the circumstances;
(2) the boundaries of cell autonomy are often not clear;
(3) the supervisory role changes and can become ambiguous;
(4) management responsibilities and styles have to change too;
(5) 'regression under pressure', which means a return to traditional methods when the going gets tough;
(6) timing becomes an issue − who is going to be involved in what, and when?

These issues are almost bound to arise, regardless of how carefully change is planned. Knowing the main issues in advance, however, enables us to anticipate, recognize, and tackle them effectively. The kinds of organizational changes we are discussing are not 'one off'. We are dealing instead with a programme of transition, involving experimentation, trial and error, and continuous learning and change. Experience suggests that if this perpetual transition is to be effective and successful, four things are necessary (Buchanan and McCalman, 1989):

(1) Triggers: why are we doing this?

The reasons, or triggers, for change have to be clearly expressed and communicated. People accept radical change more readily if they understand why it is being introduced.

(2) Vision: where are we headed?

The 'ideal' future condition of the business should also be clearly expressed and communicated. The vision should be challenging, and stimulating. People accept radical change more readily in a climate of enthusiasm and anticipation.

(3) Conversion: how do we persuade other people?

People need to feel ownership of what is happening around them and the ideas that lie behind change. This is achieved through the formal structures of planning teams and steering groups. It is also achieved through the informal processes of encouragement and persuasion. People accept radical change more readily if they are genuinely involved in directing that change.

(4) Maintenance: how do we make the changes 'stick'?

Change and innovation can fade, as the original triggers disappear, and as the champions move on and are replaced by others with traditional views. To make these changes 'stick', resources have to be channelled into the maintenance and renewal of attitudes, values, and beliefs in the changed ways of working. This is again achieved through a combination of formal and informal processes.

One manager in the VLSI business explained the background to the changes that were made:

> The main problem has been the cultural change, getting people to realize they do have the ownership, they do have the capacity and the responsibility, not to feel insecure and feel they're doing themselves out of a job.
>
> But what they're doing is creating a new future and more development for themselves. It's getting that across to people that's the main problem. Most of the main issues have been people issues, not technical issues.

The changes have evolved through various stages, and continue to evolve. Any attempt to tell this story gets out of date as it is being written. However, the philosophy stays the same, the guiding principles stay the same, and the direction of change is consistent. So as you read this, remember that this is a snapshot of an organization at one point in time, and that most of the people have moved since the shot was taken. Change is a continuing process. As one VLSI manager explained:

Basically what happened is that we decided the objective was teamwork, and that we would give them the reasons why they should operate like that, then go and facilitate that happening on the shop floor. And our job is to facilitate, to nudge and nurture, and help and direct, and that was the process, and it's not complete by any means.

The changes had four main dimensions:

(1) The establishment of autonomous cells.
(2) The move from supervising to facilitating.
(3) The change in role for support groups.
(4) Changes in the management structure.

These changes were consistent with each other. Together they supported the goal of giving those with direct contact with assembly problems the ownership and responsibility for solving those problems. It would be difficult to say that any one of these dimensions was more important than the others. It would be difficult to drop one of these dimensions and run only with the other three. These changes were supported by an extensive training programme which covered the thinking behind the approach, JIT and total quality control (TQC), team building, and meeting and presentation skills. Cross-functional training was also critical to this programme of change, and this is still going on.

These kinds of organizational innovations come as a package deal, or they do not work effectively. The steps which the assembly staff group took to implement the high-performance system approach included:

(1) Identifying the need for reorganization
(2) Encouraging participation
(3) Organizing a suggestion system
(4) Categorizing and summarizing suggestions
(5) Producing a list of requirements, based on the suggestions
(6) Producing a list of opportunities
(7) Designing the organization to support the cells

Some of the requirements to be designed into the new organization were interesting because they illustrated the radical departure from traditional thinking that took place.

(1) No functional demarcation
(2) Reduce inertia in decision making
(3) Allow all team members to make full and equal contribution
(4) Minimize pain of transition
(5) Be flexible for future development
(6) Optimize people and organizational needs
(7) Improve ownership by teams

Autonomous cells

The VLSI assembly flow was managed on two production lines by twelve cells on each shift, each with four to six members. There were around 25 production operators on each line on each shift. Each cell was responsible for a key stage in the manufacturing process, and had its own area and equipment within the assembly area. The cell and its members were the 'first line of defence' in production problem-solving.

So, for example, at the front end of the process, there was a cell on line A which handled incoming visual inspection, second optical inspection, and saw. And there was a similar cell on line B. There were cells which handled the glass sealing and plating operations. Two cells, again one at the end of each line, dealt with tube loading, pin straightening, and other related final operations. The idea of the self-managing team or cell is the building block of the high-performance approach. A lot of other changes had to happen to support this teamwork approach, and these other dimensions were just as important. However, let us begin with the cells.

The first thing the assembly staff group decided to do was to break down the assembly flow into manageable sections. Each section would be allocated to a cell of six production operators. Initially, what management wanted to create was a 'team-forming skeleton', an environment which gave those involved space to work it out for themselves. There were two important aspects of those 'first steps', and about the way in which any business can be 'cut' into cells. First, the need to try out different approaches was recognized, to see how things would work, accepting that 'the first cut was not necessarily the correct one'.

Second, the physical and process barriers, created by equipment size, process interdependencies, and by the separation of the cleanroom by a brick wall, were appreciated.

There were some other difficulties to begin with. The management group did not have one defined end vision. They recognized that they were experimenting with different ideas and approaches. There were initially two vertically integrated and separately managed assembly lines, each specializing in a product family, and each with its own supervisors who ran their own areas and their own teams. The engineering group was split by process, and not by product, and individuals wanted to specialize in 'their' part of the process.

The product line division proved artificial, and it did not work. It was too inflexible. To achieve the goal of customer satisfaction, it was necessary to duplicate some facilities, up to a point, on each line, limited by the capital expenditure involved. And that duplication also gave each line more independence and autonomy.

An education programme was mounted, based on an American video-based training package called *New Age Thinking*. This was designed to make people more receptive to change, and to increase the level of confidence in the approach being developed. Not everyone appreciated this (it has an American evangelical flavour to it), but it was felt that the majority gained some benefit, and it helped to increase the visibility of the changes that were being proposed.

The list of cell tasks and responsibilities was wide and included:

(1) produce according to schedule,
(2) measure own performance,

(3) internal decision making,
(4) personal development,
(5) cell development,
(6) problem-solving,
(7) continuous development,
(8) training,
(9) preventive maintenance,
(10) documentation and recording,
(11) set-ups and change-overs.

Individuals were expected to bring a variety of skills to make up the complete team; one individual was not expected to cover all these. The assembly staff group also arranged a series of fortnightly lunch meetings. These were designed to allow cells to raise concerns and issues directly with operations and business management, without going through the supervisory structure.

Supervision of cell activities was done by one three-person 'shift team' for each of the two lines on each of the three shifts. Each shift team included a leading production operator, a quality auditor, and an equipment engineer. Each shift also had a senior supervisor or 'shift facilitator', with a supporting and not a directing role. Surely supervision is inconsistent with the idea of a self-managing cell? Yes, but we have to consider two issues here.

First, what were the functions of the supervisor, and how would these continue to be supported in a new organization structure? Second, in what ways could the job of the supervisor change, so that it was consistent with the idea of the autonomous team?

By late 1989, the VLSI assembly business had 7 supervisors for about 150 people. The average supervision norm for the company is 1 supervisor to 16 people, so the business 'should' have 9 supervisors. There were 11 at the end of 1988 when assembly employed almost 230 people. Why keep any at all? One reason was that, as the business was run across three shifts, there was a legal requirement that someone be nominated responsible for safety, and this requirement was unavoidable. A second reason was that operator appraisals were traditionally carried out by supervisors and it would be difficult to make any radical changes here. A third reason concerned management's level of trust in their people at the beginning of this approach. Supervision implied increased safety and reduced the risk of the approach 'going wrong'. For two years the business had been run in a very conventional hierarchical way, involving heavy recruitment of new staff, and the changes being suggested were seen as radical.

However, the final reason concerned the expectation that the role of the supervisor would change. As one manager explained:

For us to have changed radically the role of the supervisor to what we're aiming for now would have given several people heart attacks. We were taking the traditional supervisor out and allowing the cell to have the responsibility for a lot of things on a shift when there was nobody else around. That was really scary stuff. So the supervisors were built into the change mechanism.

But we're changing the job. Rather than be operationally responsible, somebody who is responsible for team building.

The first step in this part of the process was the appointment of the shift teams late in 1989. The job description of the shift facilitator included the following responsibilities:

(1) facilitation service for the shift team,
(2) salary appraisal for cell members,
(3) communication,
(4) advice to shift team,
(5) safety (by exception),
(6) discipline (by exception),
(7) development of shift team.

It was intended that the shift facilitator be a member of the line operations team, temporarily seconded on to the shift team, but with no operational authority on the shift. However, it was the shift facilitator who was responsible for appraising the performance of individual cell members. The shift facilitator was expected to be competent across a number of issues. They were expected to have experience in safety and discipline, leadership, reviews and appraisal, and in assembly operations. They were also expected to have interpersonal skills, team building capability, knowledge of personnel policies and procedures, communications skills, coaching and counselling skills, ability to command the respect of others, and motivational skills.

The responsibilities of the three-person shift teams are broadly similar, and overlap with both production operators and facilitators. These include cell development, personal and team development, shift decision making, cell co-ordination, the measurement of shift performance, shift problem-solving, training, documentation, communications, provision of support to the cells in the form of additional expertise, and interface with the test group.

Management had to change too

The VLSI assembly business was run by a four-man assembly business team which was cross-functional with no specific individual responsibilities. This team divided into two assembly operations teams, each with two members, who dealt with line operations, team member salary reviews, cross-business management, communications, team building, line co-ordination, and assembly performance measurement.

Successful application of the high-performance approach meant that management style, structure, and practice had to change too. When people work in multi-skilled, flexible, cross-functional teams, management has to become multi-skilled, flexible, and cross-functional too. Management in VLSI did this partly to set an example, and partly because this was the appropriate and effective way to develop.

Run the business with a management team that operates as a multi-skilled group with no specific job titles? And take out half the managers that used to run the business? And let them go and develop their skills in other areas?

Does that sound radical? That's what they did. One manager explained this in the following way:

What we've had in the past is functional groups managing their own bit. We've set the cells up as cross-functional teams. But the minute you get away from the operator level, it then becomes functional in that you've got the equipment engineering group managed by one person, quality group managed by someone else, the quality auditors are separate, you've got human resource people who are production supervisors who report to production managers.

So what's wrong with functional groupings, for a long time identified as essential in management textbooks? Another VLSI manager explained:

Things were a battle. You had this battle mentality. Whoever you worked with, you were in battle with on some issues, and I used to take a step back from it and think, why? If quality and engineering are in battle, why the hell is that? Quality have got the job of having good quality. Well, haven't engineering got that too? Why are they in battle? Why are production in battle with quality and engineering about quality?

The reason is that, to start off with, the objective and the goal is not the same for individual groups. Really the goal should be common, the goals and the ownership should be common, and the only way to do that is by team work.

With functional groups, there is a lot of bloodshed, stress, and bodies everywhere.

You can't change this just by introducing cells. Management structure had to change too, as another VLSI manager explained:

What we've done is take all that away in one fell swoop and we've just reorganized this week — the seven assembly managers, we only need four. So three of us are going to do something else with respect to development that needs doing in the business.

Four are going to run the business, but by the way, in that four, there's not a production manager and an equipment engineering manager — there's just a manager. Operations managers will have engineering, equipment, quality skills working for them. I use the term skills, not job functions. Essentially, the skills are set into teams, so we manage the group in multi-skilled teams.

We've just done that, showing by example how we've organized ourselves, and we're trying to get that to work down through the groups. There is insecurity in this, because we're asking people to reapply for their jobs. But it's not quite as drastic as that, because there's no question of anyone being left out. We're asking people what they want to do; do their skills match the profile to be a shift facilitator, or someone in engineering. Do you want to do that? We're trying to give people the opportunity to move around and be flexible within the organization.

The VLSI assembly business was run overall by an operations manager. The only functional split was the one between operations, run by two managers, and engineering, the responsibility of one other manager. However, engineering operations remained within the manufacturing teams, and the 'split' engineering function was concerned with technology development and design — longer-term and logistical issues rather than day-to-day problems.

This meant that there was still a management hierarchy, but it was flatter than before. What happened to those managers who were 'displaced' in this reorganization? Displaced is of course the wrong term. They moved into other support areas in relation to the business as a whole, to explore other issues and develop their skills and contributions in other ways and other areas — namely engineering, organizational development, and change facilitation.

Another manager explained this shift in the management role, and the change in opportunities that it involved, in this way:

> The objective is to get the responsibility devolved to the lowest level and at the same time to open up the channels for information to flow upwards and to be as freely available as possible.
>
> When I came into engineering at first, I used to tackle it from the point of view that if somebody phoned me up with a problem I would go and fix the problem, but also wonder why they weren't able to fix it themselves.
>
> My view of life, as an engineer, was that you had a responsibility to try and sort out the real cause of the problem, to try and get people to sort things out for themselves. Then you could take a step back and take another direction. I want to be able to help, but still be able to take a step back from it.

What did these organizational changes achieve? There are three parts to the full answer to this question. First, we will look at the performance metrics, and at the staggering improvements that have been made on a number of fronts. Second, we will look at the positive reactions of those employed in VLSI assembly, from an opinion survey carried out in late 1989, revealing widespread support for the changes in organizational design. Third, we will look at some of the problems and as yet unresolved issues that were also revealed in that opinion survey.

The main performance metrics, and how these have been affected, were:

(1) Assembly throughput from 500 to 35,000 items a week in two years, with frequent product changes,
(2) Assembly cycle time reduced, from 10 days to 2, with a processing time of 1.7 days,
(3) Process yield consistently on or above target, at around 98%, yield losses running at less than a fifth that of one year ago,
(4) Quality currently running at 3,000 measurable parts per million failures, with initial target of 1,000 and ultimate target of 500,
(5) Average inventory (work in progress) cut from 50,000 units to 10,000,
(6) Customer order slippage zero for July 1988 to June 1989,
(7) Product movement reduced by 35%,
(8) Working environment appearance improved, no clutter, less inventory, no fragmented assembly lines.

Yield is particularly important in the semiconductor business. Small percentage variations in yield can represent significant amounts of money — profits or losses. In relation to the quality measure, the Japanese work at the 40 to 50 ppm defective level. A high yield can still produce a high failure level — and all that this means is that the production problems are not being picked up.

Commenting on the significance of some of the improvements, one manager said, 'Other companies don't believe our cycle times!' Assembly cycle time is measured as the time taken from the point of pulling raw material into the process to the point at which it is checked off as finished product and shipped to the customer — which in this case is usually the test group. The aim was to have the shortest cycle time, and the fastest turnaround possible. With a total process time of 1.7 days, a cycle time of only 2 days was remarkable, because this meant a queue of work in progress on the shop floor amounting to only 0.3 day's work. So this reduction in cycle time has reduced the amount of inventory sitting on the shelves. This has saved space, and reduced the amount of cash tied up in working capital.

Reduced cycle times also increased flexibility, because it became easier to satisfy customer demands, and fluctuations in those demands. And in the semiconductor business, demand fluctuated very rapidly, and the assembly process had to be able to respond accordingly.

Inventory was reduced by reducing the shop floor storage. This in turn helped to expose other production problems which had been 'hidden' by the availability of buffer stocks. One manager explained:

> We simplified a lot of things. We took the racks out. We applied 'judoka'; when there was a problem, we stopped the line. You don't pile the inventory up. We applied it to set-up reductions because if you have a machine that takes four hours to change over, then you need to build four hours' worth of inventory for the machine further down the line, so that it doesn't stop as well.
>
> So the objective is to get the four hours down to four minutes so there was no inventory required to buffer that. We removed the 'just in case' part of the inventory because quite often we would have an unreliable machine so we would build inventory behind it just in case it broke down. So what we did was, we went and fixed the machine. We reduced the inventory and caused all sorts of havoc and heartache.
>
> It focused the problem on the machine, not masking it with inventory. It's paid off a lot faster than we expected.

The package of changes incorporating the cell working approach, just in time, and total quality management, led to these benefits. And on most of those performance metrics, there is more improvement to come. Those are not targets that have now been achieved, so they can be taken for granted. One of the targets behind these achievements is continuous improvement.

What has been the employee response to these organizational changes? We ran an opinion survey during the second half of 1989, with the help of cell representatives, to find out. The 144 people who completed the survey questionnaire included 103 production operators, 13 line process operators and facilitators, and 28 engineering and quality personnel.

The survey revealed four positive sets of opinions:

First, there was support for the cell-based approach to work organization. Feedback from cell representatives confirmed this finding from the survey data with comments such as: 'concept makes working life easier', 'cell concept is the only way to go', 'old-way thinking will have to be gradually phased out', 'JIT and TQC is only way to go'.

Second, it was confirmed that the approach generates high standards of performance. Once again, a number of comments from the cell briefing meetings confirmed this: 'large decrease in inventory, more flexibility', 'has improved business awareness', 'more aware of business metrics – yields, cycle times', 'quality has improved', 'makes company more profitable and improves job security', 'aware and striving for continuous improvement'. This approach developed business awareness and helped to ensure that operating problems were detected and resolved, quickly, at the point where they arose – if not before. It was through this growth in understanding that achievements in throughput and quality were obtained.

Third, job interest, variety, and people's ability to make their own decisions without supervision were rated positively. Comments from cell briefings which illustrate this include: 'job satisfaction has improved', 'much more scope for personal development', 'learning more skills', 'better awareness of business', 'more responsibility'.

This approach has significant advantages in terms of improving the quality of working life. That in turn can improve motivation and commitment, leading to the performance improvements mentioned above.

Fourth, attitudes towards colleagues, working conditions, and the company as employer were highly positive.

The survey also revealed four negative sets of opinions:

First, there was considerable dissatisfaction with the payment system, and with the conduct of pay and performance reviews. This was an anticipated response that was not unique to this case. Several other organizations have experienced issues associated with pay as a result of the movement from one organization design to another.

Second, there was dissatisfaction with what was seen to be a lack of adequate training to work effectively with this new approach. Those surveyed expressed reservations about the effectiveness of team information sharing, problem-solving, and decision making. Reinforcing the training issue, with respect to the changes in the supervisory role, one manager explained:

> I think the key thing is that we set up the cells without first developing the people who were to facilitate cells. So the supervisors were as much in the dark about the whole thing as the cells were. And I think that if we set up the supervisors with all the facilitation skills and enough time on their hands to develop the cells from the start, it would be even more successful.

Third, management style attracted criticism, with respect to lack of praise for good work, lack of information on which to base decisions, lack of consultation before introducing changes, and on interference with group decisions. One significant issue here concerns communications. One cell representative commented:

We still seem to be dependent on traditional management. Communications are poor. There is very little feedback to the ground level. For example, our performance on percentage yields; we are not told how well, or how badly we have done. The information may be there if you want to go and find it out, but it is not communicated to the floor.

Fourth, dissatisfaction was also expressed concerning use of abilities and career opportunities. The opportunities for career advancement were felt by the cell representatives to be good. However, many production operators were simply not aware of what was possible; 'maybe the operators are not seeing the opportunities', was one comment. Another cell representative said:

Abilities not being used − that's a general opinion. Management and supervisors are reassuring us that this would not happen, but it's not getting through. There's too much management input; we're not left to get on with it.

Holidays: the cells know whether and how they can cover for people who are off, but the LPOs are refusing people dates. And we don't understand why. The LPO is acting as chargehand, first line supervision. And that happens throughout, not just on one or two shifts. It's not clear whether the LPO is acting on its own initiative or on management instruction in making these decisions, and in overriding cell ability to make its own decisions. We don't know.

There is a feeling in the cells that they want to be left to manage on their own better.

The organization was introducing and developing a series of innovations in work design. In this learning process, it was inevitable that problem issues such as those identified here would arise in ways that could not easily have been anticipated. Rather than take these criticisms as damaging, the willingness to confront and address such issues is a symptom of a healthy organization. These issues need also to be seen in the context of the significant positive achievements of the cell-based approach in VLSI assembly.

Case 4: questions

We would ask you to examine Case 4 from the perspective of what Digital managed to achieve from the organization design changes implemented at VLSI, and how these benefits could be learned from by your own, and other, organizations. The questions are set to stimulate discussion rather than provide solutions. However, we have provided our own analysis of the resultant changes at VLSI and what benefits we believe have transpired. There is also an analysis of the lessons learned that could be applied elsewhere.

Question 1

What do you think were Digital's objectives in moving VLSI from what appeared to be a position in which it was operating successfully? What factors assisted this process of change?

Question 2

What do you think were the main implications of change for management of the VLSI assembly operation?

Question 3

What, in your opinion, were the major lessons learned from this case study in terms of managing organizational change? How could these be used and applied in your organization or elsewhere?

Case 4: answers

Question 1 − Objectives

During the course of the change process which took place at Digital's VLSI assembly operation, there were a number of objectives identified by management. The objectives of the organizational changes described in the case were:

(1) Improved productivity, output, quality, yield, and cycle time.
(2) Ownership of the process by the work-force, with decision making at the lowest level.
(3) Individual development and improved quality of work-force.
(4) Quality of work-life improvement through change from a mechanistic serial production process to a multi-skilled and flexible one.

These objectives can be associated with a change in organization design intended to develop the assembly operations from one steady state to another. In practice, this meant moving from a traditional style of manufacturing and managing operations to what could be termed a more 'enlightened' approach. What assisted VLSI during this process were a number of ingredients that were already in place and made transition that much easier to bear. The organizational changes in the assembly business had three main ingredients − stability, support, and self-management.

Stability: First, the business was experiencing *comparative stability* following a period of turbulence, production pressure, growth and rapid change. People had time to stand back, to look at what was happening, and to think through ways of doing it better.

Support: Second, there was considerable investment of expertise and other resources in *manufacturing support* in the form of MRP systems, JIT techniques, TQC, technology development, and reliability programmes. These other developments both supported and provided a focus for the series of radical organizational changes.

Self-Management: Third, there was the introduction of the *autonomous work cell* concept, teamwork, with group ownership of the quality issues, and group responsibility for operational decision making. This had been tried before in the Micro-11 business. However, each operation has to develop its own approach, not copying the details from somewhere else. The concept of self-managing cells in VLSI assembly had to be evolved on its own, learning from what had gone before and applying this to the uniqueness of VLSI.

The VLSI assembly business has started a process of organizational change and development which took time, patience, and effort to work through. The benefits are, however, significant and made this approach worthwhile. Not everyone is easily persuaded that this is the case, and there is a need to convert sceptics with hard evidence. It is worth noting the following comment: 'Having a fully autonomous work group was fine. How to get there was the issue. Some people are scared stiff of it because they don't know what it means. We need to mature before we can go to that.'

Many organizations, in Europe and America, are today moving away from the traditional methods of job and organizational design. Why? There seem to be two main reasons. First, the competitive environment has become tougher, organizations have to become more flexible and quality conscious and customer oriented, and conventional management systems are too slow and rigid to cope. Second, the levels of employee motivation, commitment and skills development required today to be competitive are not encouraged by our traditional approaches to management and organizational design. The world is changing, and organizations around the world are radically changing the ways in which they design work.

Question 2 — Management

The phrase, 'take a step back, and take another direction', sums up the change in the way in which management works in a high-performance system. There is time to escape from the crisis management and fire-fighting of conventional production and operations management, time to develop other skills and competences that contribute to the business in other — and often more meaningful — ways.

> The last person I thought it would have affected was me. And as soon as it started to affect me, I realized it was going to affect me more than anybody else. I wanted more responsible and capable people. I wanted to have that but it happened so quickly that it left me with what I am now — without a job.
>
> I actually am without a job, and that is why six months ago I saw this coming, and said 'Right, I'll go and fill in with other skills development until my career can develop elsewhere'.
>
> The job has changed incredibly from being involved with the engineering work to letting other people do it and therefore being facilitator, coach, counsellor, a mirror — a reflector — these sorts of things, and much less involvement with day-to-day nitty-gritty stuff.

What happened to the management of VLSI is of equal significance to what happened to operators in their teams. There are organizational development issues associated with Case study 1 which relate to how managers deal with changes in their own organization structure, functions, and responsibilities. What is important to recognize here is that there were implications for change on management's part as well as those of the workgroups or self-managing teams. Managers had to change from decision-takers to facilitators, and lost a lot of their day-to-day responsibility for fire-fighting on the shop floor. This could have serious implications in itself if managers are unaware of the likely changes taking place in their own jobs.

Question 3 — Lessons
From our analysis of Case 4, the key lessons from the VLSI experience with high-performance work systems can be identified.

Achievements: The benefits achieved from the high-performance work systems approach can be phenomenal, with respect to performance metrics, and also with respect to improved quality of work life and skills growth.

Timing: Good choice of implementation timing is important. VLSI had a period of comparative stability — a window of opportunity — that allowed people to stand back from the business and take a fresh look at how to improve it.

Triggers: Radical changes have to be justified by clearly identified business needs — for growth in volume, quality, and customer satisfaction. It does not work if people see all this as just another fad.

Vision: Management had a clear view of the guiding principles — ground-level decision making, dismantling the hierarchy, skills growth, and self-managing cells. Everybody needs to know where they are headed.

Experiment: You cannot copy what someone else has done. You have to develop an approach that fits the local circumstances. You need to try things out, encourage participation and involvement, and find out what works for you.

Package: High-performance systems need to be supported by a 'package deal' of supportive changes which back-up the change in organization design. In the VLSI assembly case, the changes taking place in organization development also included movements in total quality management, JIT inventory management, and materials requirements planning systems.

Support: This style of organization and management usually gets a high degree of support from the shop floor — and this creates demand for more information, more communication, more skills growth, more autonomy. If you ignore these aspirations, you create frustration.

Scepticism: However, not everyone welcomes this style. A lot of trust issues are exposed, as functional barriers are dismantled, and decision-making responsibility moves. The emotional issues raised here take time to work through. You need to have room for those who say, 'I just want to run my machine' (but keep working on them!).

Supervision: The role of the supervisor changes from the traditional planning, scheduling and directing one to a facilitating, coaching, team-building function. It takes time to evolve through this, new skills have to be acquired, and new perceptions have to be developed.

Engineering: Support groups change their contribution too. Production operators are given skills to handle their own equipment engineering problems — and this means that engineering can take a step back and do a real support job, not caught up in the day-to-day fixing.

Training: This has to be planned ahead of change; people need training in team skills and facilitation before the cell concept is implemented and the supervisory role can change. Continual training in new skills is also essential as cell members develop.

Rewards: The payment system and the conduct of reviews have to be designed and monitored with care. If there is one single main problem to point to in the whole approach, this is it. The whole basis of reward — for teamwork and skills growth — is so different from traditional payment systems. This takes time and effort to develop effectively in a way that fits local needs.

In a wider context, and relating back to Question 2, management are faced with a new challenge on two fronts with this approach.

First, as people are given more skills and more discretion to handle problems for themselves, management from first line supervision up has to stand back and let them get on with it. Experience shows that, while many managers find this refreshing and an obviously desirable development, some see this approach as damaging to their managerial rights and prerogatives. These views have to be respected, and they take time to work through.

Second, as the operational issues are handled directly by those involved, managers become less involved in these issues. The focus shifts to the broader issues — the logistics of the manufacturing process, vendor management, materials issues, European and corporate issues. The management view becomes broader, and there is more space and time to stand back from the business and take a fresh overview of what is happening, and how to improve it. This also means that managers develop cross-functional careers, as the old career ladders have been eroded — or dismantled altogether.

So, the two management challenges for the 1990s concern the ability to 'stand back and trust the system', and to develop broader cross-functional careers in organizations that lack the predictability and security of the hierarchical career ladder.

CASE 5: MTC LTD

Introduction

Change is a continuous process of confrontation, identification, evaluation and action. The overlap between systems thinking and organizational development emerges in Pugh (1978) and in Rickards (1985). Both approaches have a great deal in common and it appears the theories are converging, with both emphasizing the importance of the process of intervention and the need for any change strategy to have self-regulating loops.

In this particular case the problems are basically people oriented, and therefore tend towards the 'soft' end of the change continuum, resulting from changes made necessary through the rapid growth the company has experienced.

In applying the ODM, this case study has used, by way of illustration, the changes that were necessary as a result of the company expanding into another sector of the market, namely, the provision of a national training programme for accountants, the success of which was in part responsible for the significant growth experienced by the company.

Description of change

As stated, change is continuous and the volume of change is massive in organizations. It is perhaps because of this that political behaviour often emerges before and during organizational change efforts due to the fact that any reorganization is usually feared because it means disturbance of the status quo. This case study is no exception to this and due to very rapid growth displayed all the classic symptoms.

MTC Ltd were a substantial, diverse and financially sound organization operating throughout Scotland from 20 locations and employing around 150 people. They were primarily involved in providing a wide range of training programmes. In 1987, the company identified a market opportunity for a 'technician' level of accountant. The firm commissioned Coopers & Lybrand Management Consultants to conduct a market research survey to determine the likely level of demand throughout Scotland for such a training programme both for young people, through the establishment of a Government-subsidized Youth Training Programme, and for the adult population generally. Their findings indicated both that there was a very significant level of demand and that none of the company's main competitors were currently involved.

In order to capture the lion's share of the potential market the company had to move swiftly:

(1) To establish links with the Association of Accounting Technicians (AAT) who were the London-based body responsible for the award of the professional qualification which was recognized and indeed sponsored by all five major accountancy bodies in the UK.
(2) Similarly, to establish links with the Scottish sponsoring body, namely, The Institute of Chartered Accountants of Scotland (ICAS).
(3) To negotiate a contract for the provision of a national Youth Training Scheme programme with the Training Commission.
(4) Based on our market research, to quantify the resources that would be required in terms of additional premises, location of premises, equipment, timing, funding and manning.
(5) To deal with the scale of the operations meant that the company's administrative and personnel procedures had to be reviewed and up-graded with more formalized procedures being introduced.
(6) To deal with the organizational changes meant a reorganization was required which, with the anticipated increase in manning levels, etc., meant that certain roles had to be changed.

It is a paradox of organizational life that situations and problems which cry out most strongly for change are often the very ones which resist change most stubbornly and it was this resistance to change which was the major problem to overcome.

The organization development process

The philosophy of organizational development is one of long-term change, and organizational change efforts that are based on inconsistent strategies tend to run into predictable problems. An effective manager is one who anticipates, diagnoses and manages the change process over a period of time to ensure it is effective and in this case perhaps the use of a change facilitator or consultant would have been helpful in giving an unbiased 'helicopter' view of the organization. However, the organizational change was approached in the following way:

(1) At the planning stage consideration was given to the four principles and six rules given by Pugh (1978) as a guide to understanding organizational change together with the OD loop which emphasizes the recurrent nature of change.

In order to adequately explain the process that was employed, a series and sequence of questions and prompts were formulated as a guide (see Chapter 6, Figure 6.2).

(2) If the proposer or problem owner has sufficient power, the change can be pushed through but at the cost of conflict, resentment and reduced motivation. It was always anticipated that resistance to the change would be a major obstacle; the problem was to predict what form the resistance might take. The four most common reasons why people resist change are:
   (a) A desire not to lose something of value
   (b) A misunderstanding of the change and its implications
   (c) A belief that the change does not make sense for the organization
   (d) A low tolerance of change

Managers who initiate change often assume that they have all the relevant information required to conduct an adequate organization analysis, and that those who will be affected by the change have the same facts. Neither assumption is correct and again because of the messy nature of the problem it was decided to diagram the 'people problems' in order to overcome the fears and objections of the individuals involved in as systematic a fashion as possible. The diagrams are detailed in Figures 11.1 and 11.2.

On organizational grounds too, resistance to change can be understood when it is realized that from the behavioural viewpoint, organizations are coalitions of interest groups in tension and there is an interesting parallel here with the Cyert and March (1963) behavioural theory of the firm.

In overcoming people's resistance to having their job redesigned, there is a motivational opportunity to be gained. Internalized motivation is implicit in McGregor's (1960) Theory Y and is reinforced by Herzberg (1966) with his motivational factors which concentrate on the 'satisfiers' and this aspect was given considerable emphasis in order not only to overcome resistance to the change but also to maximize the benefit to be derived from it and help generate an ethnocentric culture within the organization.

(3) In summary the actual organization development process model used was as follows:
   (a) Confrontation with environmental changes, problems, opportunities. The decision to diversify into accountancy training meant that a considerable upheaval would be required as there was a high level of influencing factors both internal and external to the organization. Some of these factors are detailed as follows: external − AAT, ICAS, Training Commission, sponsor companies, competition, geographical

*   Why do people object to change?

*   How can you anticipate people problems associated with change?

*   How can you help people to accept change?

Helping People Accept Change

●   Involve them by:
        - discussing it with them
        - foster their ideas

●   Communicate by means of:
        - meetings and discussions
        - presentations
        - training

●   Recruit and transfer in good time

●   Avoid work peaks and consider convenience

●   Consider people's worries - think about:
        - individual's objections and how you will meet their fears
        - the benefits of change and how to sell them

Anticipating Problems of Change
"Force Field" Analysis

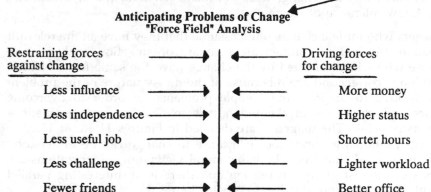

Restraining forces against change		Driving forces for change
Less influence		More money
Less independence		Higher status
Less useful job		Shorter hours
Less challenge		Lighter workload
Fewer friends		Better office

Change Process

●   Identify and remove restraining forces

●   Carry out change

●   Freeze the situation by reinforcing the new behaviour

Figure 11.1 Management of change; people problems.

        spread; internal — environment, resources, training, communication,
        motivation, funding, ethnocentricism.
    (b) Identification of implications for organization.
        The implications of these changes were far reaching but the most
        important element by far was how to overcome people's resistance

Change threatens   -   their present position ———————┐
                      -    their prospects ————┐   │
                                               │   │
Change requires   -   physical work   │   │
                      -    mental work   │   │
            ┌──────────────────────────────────┘   │
            ▼   ▼   ▼

How can change benefit their job?	How can change appear threatening?	What do people require from their jobs which change can threaten?
Enriching	Deskilling	Interest in their job
Broadening	Impoverishing	- using a skill - having mental challenge
Given discretion	Removing discretion	- using their discretion
Upgrading	Blocking promotion	Growth in their job
Increased responsibility	Removing jobs	- to more important work - to harder work
	Revising jobs	- to different work
Change of scene	Rejecting earlier work	A worthwhile job
Improved Reward	Rejecting ideas	- recognized by self
Improved status		- recognized by others
Training for job	Increased apparent difficulty	A secure job
Easier job	Appearing stupid	- ability to handle the job - fear of losing face
Permanence of job	Redundancy	- fear of losing job - fear of losing possesions
Better conditions	Degrading	

Figure 11.2 People's objections to change.

to change. This was dealt with by the process described in Figure
11.1.
(c) Education to obtain understanding of implications for organization.
It was evident that attention had to be focused at the individual
level and certain actions would have to be taken for those directly

affected; e.g. training, communication/involving, career planning, job enrichment, re-establishment of a degree of loyalty.

The fact that this process was interactive was recognized especially when, at the implementation stage, other factors were identified and the 'loop' would therefore continue.

(d) Obtaining involvement in the project.

It was felt that involving people in carefully planning the change and considering how it would affect them was the best way of overcoming resistance and would help develop a change philosophy.

(e) Identification of targets for change.

Having already gone through the first four processes this was self-evident.

(f) Change and development activities.

The process of change was accomplished by unfreezing, changing and refreezing. These terms can be explained as follows: Unfreezing – developing an awareness of the need for change and establishing the relationships needed for successful change; changing – defining problems, identifying solutions, implementing solutions; refreezing – stabilizing the situation, building relationships.

(g) Evaluation of project and programme in current environment and reinforcement.

The evaluation was carried out by determining both what the benefits were and what we had learnt from the process. Some of these are as follows:

> increased profitability,
> more accurate forecasting,
> increased motivation,
> increased propensity for change,
> clearer role perceptions,
> reduced inter-group confrontation.

Comments and conclusions

Few organizational change efforts tend to be complete failures but few tend to be entirely successful either. This was stated by Kotter and Schlesinger (1979) and reinforced by Pritchard (1984, p. 34), 'There is no right strategy; different combinations are likely to suit different company needs.'

In this particular case, whilst the changes had been successful, it was too early to evaluate precisely the 'bottom line' effect although there was ample objective evidence of significant success and the people who were directly affected felt that this style of management approach had been worthwhile.

In reality, if you operate in an aggressive expanding environment, change is continuous leaving little time for formal planning. Management of change has become a fashionable topic but in essence the processes described are merely the application of a logical and common sense approach when addressing a change situation and this has always been done by reasonably competent managers.

This approach to the organizational development process as illustrated was constructed using a 'logical' approach and yet it contains all aspects of the ODM.

In conclusion, it is important to look both conceptually and practically at managing change and particularly the interdependence of political, cultural and technical aspects of diagnosing, planning, implementing and evaluating strategic changes.

Case 5: questions

Question 1

What issues does this case study raise for the overall management of change within organizations?

Question 2

Using an example from your own organization, comment on the applicability of Figure 11.1 to the resolution of people problems during the management of change.

CASE 6: GROUP PERFORMANCE REVIEW

Introduction

There is no correct answer to this particular example. The number of ways of undertaking a group performance review are numerous, and so are the likely approaches. The difficulty that this case study provides you with is in your own approach to the OD process of change from entry to exit. Read through the case study problem as it is set, and design your own strategy.

During 1990, OILCo., a major oil company, established a number of empowerment workgroups (EWGs) throughout the organization. Six of these EWGs attended a training event during the latter part of 1990 on basic teamwork skills. EWGs are now approaching the end of their first year of operation and it would appear appropriate to undertake some form of review of their operation within OILCo. Experience of EWGs has led to questions being asked about their widespread adoption throughout the organization over the next few years.

As the internal change agent responsible for the initial training of the EWGs, you have been asked to outline a proposal based on examining the impact of EWGs, staff and management attitudes related to EWGs, a performance review of EWGs to look at more detailed issues, and an analysis of the likely implications of the move towards wider application.

The remit

The basic remit for this proposal is to establish what stage of development EWGs have reached within OILCo. There are four issues associated with this analysis.

First, there is a need to determine whether the EWGs that are already in existence have resulted in accomplishments that benefit the individual member, the EWGs themselves, and the organization as a whole. It is the intention here to characterize the EWG at work by showing levels of success and/or failure, and relating these to greater employee involvement within OILCo.

Second, there is also a need to examine where EWGs are developing to, and the levels of certainty within the groups that they have capability to develop. This issue is related to whether the EWGs are a temporary or permanent phenomenon within the organization, and whether those within the EWGs believe that they are worthwhile enough to be taken forward.

Third, what levels of skills and competencies do the EWGs contain? This issue relates to whether the groups feel confident amongst themselves that they have the necessary skills to be able to function as a coherent group and sustain accomplishments. A related issue here is the level of support that OILCo. itself can offer EWGs to optimize their effectiveness, and what form this should take.

Fourth, physical indicators to OILCo. of the value of workgroups. This issue is linked to the overall benefit of EWGs to the organization as a whole by improvements in the way work is undertaken.

Case 6: questions

Question 1

How do you intend approaching this problem? Draft a proposal outlining the way you intend carrying out the remit.

Question 2

Using the ODM, what are likely to be the major benefits that OILCo. can expect to gain from undertaking the proposal you put forward?

Analysis

Although there are no correct solutions to this case study, a proposal and project were carried out by the authors in conjunction with staff at OILCo. These can be seen as indicators of the ODM approach to managing change in organizations. The important learning points are associated with three specific criteria:

(1) Designing the process for involvement;
(2) Being able to acquire the necessary information to complete the project;
(3) Being able to provide both hard and soft data on the performance of EWGs.

A short summary of the proposal presented and accepted by the organization is outlined here.

The proposal

It is envisaged that the project will contain three stages.

Stage one: EWG workshops and opinion survey

The starting point for the project will be an opinion survey, designed by the author, and distributed among EWG members. The author will conduct the survey with EWG members through an informal workshop session to obtain feedback on their views related to development of the EWGs. Some form of formal data gathering will take place via the opinion survey but it is envisaged that more relevant information may be obtained by an informal discussion session held immediately after the survey has been completed.

The mechanism for data gathering will be for the author to visit each of the EWGs and managers that took part in the training events at their workplace. This would then be followed in the afternoon by a workshop to look at how the EWGs feel they are progressing. It is envisaged that each workshop will take a half-day to complete. The focus of the latter part of the workshop will be on evidence of success that EWGs can identify as benefiting OILCo. Each EWG will be asked to make a short presentation on where they have been able to make greater levels of contribution to OILCo. as an EWG, situations where the EWG has generated greater profits or cost savings that would not have occurred otherwise, and projected plans for the future with an indication of the costs and benefits linked to these plans.

This stage will provide a good source of both quantitative and qualitative feedback on how well EWGs are currently working. It will also highlight problem areas that need to be addressed. The survey data will be analysed by the author with feedback provided at stage three.

Stage two: managerial issues

Stage two involves a number of informal discussions with managers working within OILCo. who have EWGs within their own organization. It is envisaged that these interviews will act as a managerial perspective on EWGs and will provide ideas and guidelines on their effectiveness and the best way to move forward. This would involve a number of visits to the EWG workplaces and discussions with the relevant managers in these areas. This would be done on a confidential basis and selected (unattributed) commentary from these discussions will be incorporated into stage three.

Stage three: product delivery

Stage three is the production of a short (25–30 page) analysis of EWGs at OILCo. which will include:

A one page management summary,
The results from the opinion surveys,
Workshop feedback on critical performance measurements,
Managerial commentary,
A concluding assessment on overall group performance.

An example of the opinion survey is provided in Appendix 1. Opinion surveys are one of the key elements in organization development. They provide information on factors likely to influence the organization development change effort. They also have the benefit of allowing greater levels of contribution by those likely to be affected by change. However, a word of warning. Many organizations use the opinion survey as window dressing. That is, a large number of surveys take place but very little is done to action the results. Feedback of results from the opinion survey is an obvious mechanism for encouraging greater participation in the change effort. Participants have to be able to see, however, that the organization is taking their views seriously, is paying attention to the trends, and more importantly, is taking action based on these. Otherwise, the gathering of data in this way becomes an exercise in public relations that the public, those within the organization, view as phoney and, over time, worthless.

12
Epilogue

INTRODUCTION

We began this book by reference to a three-way conversation between the authors and one of our MBA students on the Management of Change course. In developing an epilogue that meets the criterion of providing an adequate conclusion, we go back to one of the consequences of that conversation.

In May 1991, one of our colleagues at the University of Glasgow asked to have a meeting with ourselves, the MBA Course Director and the Head of Department. The meeting was ostensibly to review the first year of the MBA. As a result, it emerged that a lot of the material we were covering in our course was being dealt with elsewhere. We were then placed in a quandary. Either we dropped the Management of Change course in its entirety because it was being dealt with elsewhere, or we removed the offending articles from our course to prevent duplication. Or, as it emerged from the course of the meeting, we recognized the cross-functional nature of a Management of Change course, and the fact that elements from subjects such as Operations Management, Organizational Behaviour and Financial Management were bound to be referred to in a course of this nature.

This did not take away the quandary, however. It was decided that there was a need for the MBA to be taught in a cross-functional manner, that what we currently did was to teach cross-functionally on an individual basis, and that to effectively manage change within our own organization, we had to recognize that here was a trigger for change that had to be dealt with.

The first year of the MBA programme has been revamped and redesigned using the Management of Change course as the basic model, and as the building block around which other subject areas are addressed. The first year is now presented using team teaching techniques. The individual disciplines are introduced in an integrated manner based on the content of the subject material to be discussed.

What we have done here is to identify the core management disciplines associated with the first year MBA programme, and examples are drawn from the varied subject areas of the presenters.

This means that students no longer categorize disciplines into subject areas but are able to delve into management in a systemic way. If you recall, in Chapter 7, Megson (1988) criticized the analytical and mechanistic approaches managers use to solve problems in organizations. We hope that in adopting this style, our approach allows us to achieve two objectives. First, the disciplines are presented on a cross-functional basis which removes a great deal of the duplication that used to take place. Second, they are introduced at a more practical level than would have been the case were the individual lecturer to deal with the theory and technique first before getting on to the practice.

The consequences of these changes are numerous. The reason why we tell this story is to illustrate three key points.

First, all organizations have to be able to effectively identify the triggers of change. Management, as it is now taught on MBA courses, *is* a multi-disciplinary subject. The functional barriers which used to separate finance from operations from marketing are now so 'fuzzy' as to warrant investigation. The investigation seeks to address the way the subjects themselves are taught. This is an opportunity (although many a lecturer will perceive this as a threat to his or her discipline). The opportunity, in this instance, lies with team teaching, with removal of duplication, and with the chance to get rid of what we term 'academic stove-piping'.

Second, organizations must recognize that once the triggers have been identified, the solutions that one proposes have to be investigated in a holistic manner. Thus, the first year of the MBA programme must be viewed as the system under study, not the individual courses. In Chapter 4, we stressed the need to view the change situation in terms of systems linkages and the environmental impact. The triggers and the consequences have knock-on effects for all. For example, one of the outcomes of the first-year review was that because of removal of duplication, we had more teaching time. If we take a holistic view of this, and align the need to teach more management skills rather than theory with more teaching time, we create another opportunity. In this case, we developed an outward bound pro-gramme to deliver one of the core management skills, team building.

Third, to be effective, change management needs to be supported from the top and be characterized by 'full-blown' participation. In this example, both the Director of the MBA programme and the Head of Department embraced the concepts from the outset. Rather than mere words, finances were made available to develop the changes. Senior management need to be seen to be making the time to be fully involved. There is also a need for this involvement to permeate throughout the organization, to gain commitment to the changes being made. In Chapters 3, 4 and 8, we investigated the use of diagrammatic techniques, structured analysis models, and the five-step process of planned change to effectively identify change agents and gain their commitment. It would be phoney to argue here that we adopted such an approach with the redesign of the first year. Because we knew of these approaches, we applied them subconsciously. By the end of the first meeting, the walls were festooned with lists, diagrams, and action plans for the next meeting. The problem owner, the MBA Director, had conducted the meeting in a structured manner. The problem was diagnosed and defined through a series of systems maps, relationship charts, and multiple cause diagrams. Solutions were generated via structured brainstorming sessions and evalu-ated against our predetermined objectives. Action plans were produced dealing with implementation and the change agents were despatched to deal with issues prior to the next meeting. This has to be seen in the light of *post-hoc* rationalization. As with most management departments, we talk a better game than we actually play!

Ten key factors in effective change management

The MBA story illustrates certain aspects of change management which are common to all transformation processes. We have identified ten factors which must be addressed and actioned if change is to be effectively managed. By ensuring that these factors have been considered, prior to initializing change, the problem owner and associated change agents will be in a position to confidently manage the process of transition from that which is inadequate to that which is desired.

(1) Change is all pervasive

Any process of change is likely to have an impact greater than the sum of its parts. A holistic view must be taken to ensure that the full environmental impact is understood. For example, in the case study of change in work organization at Digital's VLSI manufacturing operations, the movement towards high-performance work groups had 'knock-on' effects in terms of the changing role of the supervisor towards facilitator, the change in role for support groups, and changes in the style and structure of management within the VLSI setting.

When you consider making change in your organization, from buying a new coffee machine to introducing total quality management and gaining BS 5750 certification, look at change in terms of its impact on the organization as a whole. Forget the parts, look at the whole picture.

(2) Effective change needs active senior management support

Whether you believe in a top-down or bottom-up approach to change in organizations, one thing is vital, there is a need and desire for senior management to be *seen* to support the change process. This is self-evident. Without senior management support three things will be missing. First, the change will lack vision. Vision is supplied by those that can look forward. In most organizations, it is senior managers' responsibility to look forward, examine changes in the environment, and determine the future state of the business.

Second, you'll need effective allies. Senior management backing for the change process is crucial in recruiting the desired level of support to instigate change at all levels and different parts of the business. Coming from a production department, with a desire to change levels of customer satisfaction and awareness, you will need help from marketing. Senior management support for the change process will assist in gaining this help. It will allow you and/or the change project to cross the functional boundaries that often impede change.

Third, you'll lack power. When the visible problem owner or change agent talks, it is senior management that is really speaking out. Senior management support guarantees that the problem owner 'speaks quietly but carries a big stick', in a metaphorical sense. An example of this may be seen in the case study of Froud Consine Ltd. The contract managers, operating within their newly created function, gained the necessary resources and organizational support through the visible backing of the Babcock Industries' management change team.

Work on achieving senior management support from the outset. Talk out the ideas you have for change with your boss, or his or her boss. The sooner there is senior management awareness of the need and desirability, the sooner things will begin to change.

(3) Change is a multi-disciplinary activity

Most successful change projects accomplish their objectives via the project team. No one person is a change island. Recognition of the multi-disciplinary nature of change goes a long way in beginning the sequence of realizing the transformation. Problem owners are identified because of their association with the change. Change agents are recruited because of their expertise in facilitating change through its various stages. Their expertise may be based on people skills, technological know-how, or their experience of systems analysis. The British Gas case involved the redesign of a computerized ordering system, where the purchasing manager was seen as the problem owner and change facilitator. However, he had no direct knowledge of the particular ordering system in question. To provide him with support, he recruited a project team which consisted of the spares buyer and the departmental systems officer. This had the benefit of gaining both expertise in the technical field and knowledge of the organizational implications of the change.

When placed in charge of a change project, or when contemplating change in organizations, get yourself a team. The successful management of change, which is all-pervasive, will require a multi-disciplinary approach. None of us has the ability to deal with all the aspects of change management that are likely to occur over the lifetime of a project.

(4) Change is about people, pure and simple

In Chapter 7, we focused attention on the need to design organizations in a way that created effective performance. The key ingredient in this design was the human element. *Remember that people are the most important asset, people want and need to grow, and personal growth is the engine that drives organization performance.* Therefore, when contemplating change, involve the people in the process from the outset. Through active participation you accomplish two things. You gain commitment and ownership of the change process by all, and those experiencing the change will not need to be pushed, they begin to drive change themselves.

Change management is about people management. When managing change, you manage people. Remember the simple rules – openness, communication and involvement.

(5) Change is about success

Faced with competitive environments, which are growing in terms of both their magnitude and ferocity, organizations must be flexible enough to rise to the challenges of today and tomorrow. Creating an organizational culture, which is receptive to change, should provide a competitive edge that will last the test of time. Stand still and be complacent if you wish, but you can be sure that your competitors, both current and future, will be striving towards greater efficiency and effectiveness.

Make your change project a mission, a way of life. However, watch how you do it. Going boldly forth where no organization has gone before, discovering new planets, and seeking out new life-forms is all very well, but you need focus. The challenges created by looking too far ahead may be beyond the organization's current capabilities. On the other hand, dinosaur organizations become dinosaur organizations because they fail to adapt to their environment. Kanter (1989) argues that it is not necessary to be so far ahead that the outcomes are impossible to see. Set goals for success that can be accomplished and seen to be deliverable. Perhaps going on a five year mission is not the answer, a look round the corner may be all that is needed to guarantee success.

(6) Change is a perpetual process

How do we explain change that was successful? How do we explain change that never seemed to get going? How can we explain the change project that started off well but seemed to fade away after a couple of years? The answers seem to lie in the attention and resources devoted to managing change as a perpetual process.

We have cited throughout, the Buchanan and McCalman concept of perpetual transition management. Change is about identifying triggers, seeking vision, recruiting converts to the vision, and maintaining and renewing the need for change on an on-going basis. The effective management of change demands management action on all these fronts.

You have to be able to identify what is triggering change. This has to be expressed and clarified and communicated throughout the organization to gain understanding. There is also a need for some vision of how the triggers will affect the future of the organization. In this sense, there is a need to define what the future is, in terms of the challenges being faced and the future make-up of the organization. Having set a vision, there is a need to manage change through converting people to that vision. Most successful change programmes work on the basis of persuading people that this is the right way to go, by detailing the structure. The Digital VLSI case is a good example of this process being spread throughout the whole organization. Finally, watch the triggers. Change that fades away does so because circumstances change, those involved at the start move on, and the triggers become unclear in the minds of those left to carry on. The systems intervention model deals with a dynamic change environment by incorporating, in the design, iterative processes where you can step back and reappraise your position in light of environmental changes.

Perpetual change is what it says, you never get to the end, something else always comes along to impact the business in a new way.

(7) Effective change requires competent change agents

The change management project has a certain number of needs that must be satisfied. One of these needs relates to the required skills, knowledge and position of change agents. Analysis of the change situation will determine the appropriate management team in terms of their attributes. It will not, however, ensure that the change agents have the necessary competencies to effectively contribute to the process of change. To be fully effective, the change agent must have certain capabilities, over and above their functional skills and knowledge.

The competencies of the change agent were examined in Chapter 9. These relate to being able to communicate with, on behalf of, and through people involved in the change situation. The change agent therefore needs to feel comfortable in dealing with interpersonal relationships, coping with conflict and ambiguity, and the 1001 different emotions that humans can display as a result of the change process itself. People can get upset by change, they can also become overjoyed, over-enthusiastic or indeed shy away from it. The change agent has to be able to facilitate those involved through this process by taking their feelings and emotions into account, getting them to address how these emotions relate to change itself, and steering the organization forward.

As we commented in Chapter 9, many organizations have begun to address the management of change within their own organizations as a perpetual process. The competencies of the change agent are being directly dealt with by instigating training programmes to provide them with the necessary staff skilled in the techniques associated with organization development.

Technical skills, such as systems diagramming, network analysis, and charting in general, can be readily taught and acquired. In fact, many of the skills associated with project planning are now dealt with by sophisticated computerized packages. For example, Project Workbench and Pertmaster offer the analytical power to which the project manager provides the appropriate data input and interpretation of output.

However, people skills are the more important, and often the more difficult competencies to acquire. If you are Theory X, you are hardly likely to be able to develop good change management skills. You do not appreciate the enormity of the change. The basis of change management rests with the assumptions you make about people in organizations. Make the wrong assumptions and the management of change goes down the wrong path.

(8) In terms of methodology, there is no one best way

All we wish to say here is, do not take a singular approach. You must not be too blinkered about change management. In essence, there is no one best way. What works for one change situation may not be fully appropriate to another. For example, in take-over situations, the cultures of organizations involved may be seemingly incompatible and may require adjustment. The obvious approach is to adopt an organization development methodology. However, such an approach will take time and will not bring about immediate improvements in performance. It may be better to start the ball rolling by adopting an intervention strategy in the short term. This could provide a quick-win example, whilst over the medium-to-long term, an organization development cycle could be set in motion to accomplish the required objectives of change.

(9) Change is about ownership

We refer back here to people. What makes change happen? When it works beautifully, what causes this? The answers seem to rest with attaining ownership of the change process itself. In terms of the problem owner, change agents, and those being affected by change, there is a need to feel ownership.

The management team must feel that they are responsible for the successful implementation of the change. This responsibility is best discharged through a desire to succeed rather than survive. What we are concerned with here is a movement from control to commitment. When people are being coerced or manoeuvred into change situations by threat or crisis, the result is at best indifference and at worst resistance. When people feel ownership of the change process, and feel that it offers opportunity, they are committed to its satisfactory accomplishment.

Get ownership by getting involvement; get involvement by openness and communication; get people to live the change.

(10) Change is about fun, challenge, and opportunity

When faced with a challenge, most individuals respond positively. The psychologists would argue that it brings out the best in people. On the other hand, when faced with a crisis people can go one of two ways. They can emerge as strong individuals to meet that crisis, or they can become cowering wrecks under its enormity.

We have tried to make this book both interesting and easy to read. We work from the perspective that change management should be a challenging subject that offers the practitioner, the reader, and those associated with change, the *opportunity* to show their mettle. Change, as it implies, gives you the chance to move on. By providing opportunities you get to learn new and different things. Hopefully, you become a better person and contribute more to your organization. The *challenges* that you face through change management may be difficult, inspiring, and they may even make a better manager out of you. These challenges should be faced positively. Never shy away from the need for change. Sure, it's uncomfortable in some instances, but change can also be *fun*.

We use fun, in this instance, to denote an attitude of mind. Throughout the seriousness of it all — the drive for performance, the need to maintain a competitive edge, the desire for a better, more effective organization — there is also a need to show a human face. We teach change management because it fascinates us. The specific subject areas of systems and organization development are interesting, practical and challenging. However, if you have ever witnessed the way in which we teach them, you would also recognize that change management can be both gratifying and fun.

Make your management of the change project challenging. Provide those involved in it with the opportunity to develop themselves and the rest of the organization. At all points in time remember, no one ever said that achieving effective change and gaining organizational performance cannot be fun!

Appendix 1
Opinion Survey Questionnaire

We would like to ask you to fill in this short questionnaire, in confidence, as part of a study of new types of work organization and their effect on people at work.

*********** Thanks for your help ************

Jim McCalman

Centre for Technical and Organizational Change
Glasgow Business School
University of Glasgow
59 Southpark Avenue
Glasgow G12 8LF

PART 1

First, we would like to ask you for some personal background information. We appreciate that this may be difficult to give accurately, so please give us the best answer you can:

The number of years you have worked at this plant?
. . . .
How long have you worked in Phase?
. . . .
How long in your current position?
. . . .
Your current job title?
. . . .

We would like to ask you to rate your agreement or disagreement with a number of statements concerning what impact the change to Autonomous Work Teams has had on you, and a number of different aspects of your work.

You may find that in some cases you are not sure whether you agree or not, perhaps because circumstances change from time to time. In these cases, try to decide *overall* whether you agree or disagree with the statement — then if you are still not sure, circle the number 2.

Work through these items fairly quickly, and don't stop for too long to work out what we mean by the words we use here. We are interested in how you feel about your work, so how you use or understand these words is what counts.

We would like you to put a circle around the number which indicates how you feel about each of the 20 statements below:

on the whole, NO

well, it depends

on the whole, YES

The people in my group work effectively together to solve problems	1	2	3
People in my team encourage each other to work as a team	1	2	3
There is an opportunity here for people to grow	1	2	3
Team members help new people fit into the group	1	2	3
I look forward to coming to work each day	1	2	3
My team is able to respond when unusual work demands are placed on it	1	2	3
Good work is always recognized	1	2	3
My team makes good decisions and solves its problems well	1	2	3
I am treated fairly when I do something wrong	1	2	3
The people I work with are open and honest with each other	1	2	3
I support team self-management at?????	1	2	3
My team plans its work together and co-ordinates its efforts	1	2	3
People in my team maintain high standards of performance	1	2	3
People in my team share information and ideas	1	2	3
People likely to be affected by change are always asked for their ideas first	1	2	3
Managers don't interfere with the team much	1	2	3
Team members offer each other new ideas for solving job-related problems	1	2	3
The amount of work I have to do is about right	1	2	3
I have trust and confidence in the people in my team	1	2	3
Morale in our team is high	1	2	3

We would like to ask you to circle the number which best describes how you feel about the following statements:

worse than I would like it to be

as I like it to be

much better than I could hope for

the work itself

....

the interest of the work itself	1	2	3
the variety in my work	1	2	3
the way the work is organized	1	2	3

....

management

....

the way managers handle problems	1	2	3
the amount of praise given for doing a good job	1	2	3
the way suggestions and ideas are used	1	2	3
the overall management of the company	1	2	3

....

autonomy

....

freedom to work without too much supervision	1	2	3
the chance to rest or ease up when I feel like it	1	2	3
the chance to decide myself how to do my job	1	2	3

....

growth

....

the amount of training for the job	1	2	3
the way my abilities are used	1	2	3
the chances to get on	1	2	3

....

PART 2

Please answer the following six questions in your own words:

(1) What aspects of this work do you like most?
(2) What do you feel is the biggest problem or difficulty you face in your job at present?
(3) What do you think of the self-managing group concept of working?
(4) In what ways have your opinions altered since it was introduced?
(5) How has your experience of work in ???? affected your own personal development?
(6) Anything else you would like to add to the answers?

References

Argyris, C. (1970) *Intervention Theory and Method*, Addison-Wesley, Reading, Massachusetts.

Argyris, C. and Schon, D. (1978) *Organizational Learning: A Theory of Action Perspective*, Addison-Wesley, Reading, Massachusetts.

Beckhard, R. (1969) *Organization Development: Strategies and Models*, Addison-Wesley, Reading, Massachusetts.

Boddy, D. (1987) *The Technical Change Audit*, Manpower Services Commission, Sheffield.

Boddy, D. and Buchanan, D. A. (1986) *Managing New Technology*, Basil Blackwell, Oxford.

Brownlie, D. T., McCalman, J., Paton, R. A. and Southern, G. (1990) *The Glasgow Management Development Initiative: Selected Findings and Issues*, a commissioned research report for the Manpower Services Commission, University of Glasgow Business School.

Buchanan, D. A. (1979) *The Development of Job Design Theories*, Saxon House, Aldershot.

Buchanan, D. A. (1987) Job design is dead! Long live high performance work systems, *Personnel Management*, May, pp. 40–3.

Buchanan, D. A. and Huczynski, A. A. (1985) *Organizational Behaviour: An Introductory Text*, Prentice-Hall, Hemel Hempstead.

Buchanan, D. A. and McCalman, J. (1989) *High Performance Work Systems: The Digital Experience*. Routledge, London.

Burns, T. and Stalker, G. (1961) *The Management of Innovation*, Tavistock, London.

Cyert, R. M. and March, J. G. (1963) *A Behavioural Theory of the Firm*, Prentice-Hall, Hemel Hempstead.

Deal, T. and Kennedy, A. (1982) *Corporate Culture*, Addison-Wesley, Reading, Massachusetts.

Digital Equipment Corporation, Europe (1988) *Organization Development Training: Proposal for Skills Council Funding*. DEC, unpublished article.

Eglin, R. (1990–1) Interview with Richard Branson. Vol. 2, No. 1, *Best of Business International*.

French, W. L. (1969) Organization development: objectives, assumptions and strategies, *California Management Review*, Vol. 12, no. 2, pp. 23–34.

French, W. L. and Bell, C. H. Jr (1990) *Organization Development: Behavioural Science Interventions for Organization Improvement*, Prentice-Hall, New Jersey.

Galbraith, J. R. (1977) *Organization Design*, Addison-Wesley, Reading, Massachusetts.

Hackman, J. R. and Oldham, G. R. (1975) Development of the job diagnostic survey, *Journal of Applied Psychology*, Vol. 60, pp. 159–70.

Handy, C. (1989) *The Age of Unreason*, Business Books, London.

Herzberg, F. (1966) *Work and the Nature of Man*, Staples Press, New York.

Huczynski, A. A. H. and Buchanan, D. A. B. (1991) *Organizational Behaviour: An Introductory Text*, (2nd edn), Prentice-Hall, Hemel Hempstead.

Hunt, J. (1979) *Managing People at Work*, McGraw-Hill, Maidenhead.

Huse, E. F. (1975) *Organizational Development and Change*, West Publishing Company, St. Paul, Minnesota.

Kanter, R. M. (1989) *When Giants Learn to Dance: Mastering the Challenges of Strategy, Management and Careers in the 1990s*, Unwin Hyman, London.

Kotter, J. P. and Schlesinger, L. A. (1979) Choosing strategies for change, *Harvard Business Review*, Mar/Apr.

Lawler, E. E. III (1969) Job design and employee motivation, *Personnel Psychology*, Vol. 22, pp. 426–35.

Lawler, E. E. III (1986) *High Involvement Management: Participative Strategies for Improving Organizational Effectiveness*, Jossey Bass, San Francisco.

Lawrence, P. R. and Lorsch, J. W. (1967) *Organization and Environment: Managing Differentiation and Integration*, Harvard Business School, Boston.

Lawrence, P. R. and Lorsch, J. W. (1969) *Developing Organizations: Diagnosis and Action*, Addison-Wesley, Reading, Massachusetts.

Lewin, K. (1958) Group decision and social change in E. E. Maccoby, T. M. Newcomb and E. L. Hartley (eds). *Readings in Social Psychology*, Holt, Rinehart & Winston, New York.

Likert, R. (1967) *The Human Organization: Its Management and Value*, McGraw-Hill, New York.

Lippit, R. (1959) Dimensions of the consultant's job, *Journal of Social Issues*, Vol. 15, no. 2, pp. 5–11.

Lippit, R. and Lippit, G. (1975) Consulting process in action, *Training and Development Journal*, Vol. 29, no. 5, pp. 48–54; no. 6, pp. 38–44.

Lippit, R., Watson, J. and Westley, B. (1958) *The Dynamics of Planned Change*, Harcourt, Brace & Jovanovich, New York.

Lockyer, K. G. (1984) *Critical Path Analysis & Other Project Network Techniques*, Pitman, London.

McCalman, J. (1988) *The Electronics Industry in Britain: Coping with Change*, Routledge, London.

McGregor, D. (1960) *The Human Side of Enterprise*, McGraw-Hill, New York.

March, J. G and Simon, H. A. (1958) *Organizations*, John Wiley, New York.

Margerison, C. J. (1988) Consulting activities in organizational change, *Journal of Organizational Change Management*, Vol. 1, no. 1, pp. 60–7.

Margulies, N. and Raia, A. (1972) *Organizational Development: Values, Process and Technology*, McGraw-Hill, New York.

Margulies, N. and Raia, A. (1978) *Conceptual Foundations of Organizational Development*, McGraw-Hill, New York.

Margulies, N. and Raia, A. (1988) The significance of core values on the theory and practice of organizational development, *Journal of Organizational Change Management*, Vol. 1, no. 1, pp. 6–17.

Martin, P. and Nicholls, J. (1987) *Creating a Committed Workforce*, Institute of Personnel Management, London.

Matsushita, K. (1984) *Not for Bread Alone: A Business Ethos, A Management Ethic*. PHP Institute, Tokyo.

Matsushita, K. (1988) The secret is shared, *Manufacturing Engineering*, March, pp. 78–84.

Megson, L. V. C. (1988) Building organizations for performance, *Digital Equipment Corporation*, unpublished article.

Megson, L. V. C. (1991) People and technology: building organizations for performance, *Manufacturing Technology International*.

Paton, R. A., Southern, G. and Houghton, M. G. (1989) European strategy formulation: an analysis technique, *European Management Journal*, Vol. 7, no. 3, September, pp. 305–9.

Paton, R. A. and Southern, G. (1990) *Total Project Management*, University of Glasgow Business School Working Paper Series.

Peters, T. (1987) *Thriving on Chaos*, Alfred A. Knopf, New York.

Peters, T. J. and Waterman, R. H. Jr (1982) *In Search of Excellence*, Harper and Row, New York.

Pettigrew, A. (1985) *The Awakening Giant: Continuity and Change in Imperial Chemical Industries*, Basil Blackwell, Oxford.

Pritchard, W. (1984) What's new in organizational development?, *Personnel Management*, July, pp. 30–3.

Pugh, D. S. (1978) Understanding and managing organizational change, *London Business School Journal*, Vol. 3, no. 2, pp. 29–34.

Pugh, D. S. (1986) *Planning and Managing Change, Block 4: Organizational Development*, Open University Business School, Milton Keynes.

Pugh, D. S. and Hickson, D. J. (1989) *Writers on Organizations*, (4th edn), Penguin, London.

Rickards, T. (1985) Making new things happen, *Technovation*, Vol. 3, pp. 119–31.

Roethlisberger, F. J. and Dickson, W. J. (1939) *Management and the Worker*, Harvard University Press, Cambridge, Massachusetts.

Schein, E. H. (1988) *Process Consultation: Its Role in Organization Development*, Addison-Wesley, Reading, Massachusetts.

Schwartz, R. (1986) The Future, from the video series *The Business of Excellence*, Guild Sound and Vision Ltd, Peterborough.

Sherwood, J. J. (1988) Creating work cultures with competitive advantage, *Organizational Dynamics*, Winter 1988, American Management Association.

Simon, H. A. (1957) *Models of Man*, Wiley, New York.

Thorsurd, E. (1972) Job design in the wider context, in L. E. Davis and J. C. Taylor (eds.) *Design of Jobs*, Penguin, Harmondsworth.

Vroom, V. H. (1969) Industrial social psychology, in G. Lindsey and E. Aronson (eds.) *The Handbook of Social Psychology*, Addison-Wesley, Reading, Massachusetts.

Warner Burke, W. (1987) *Organization Development: A Normative View*, Addison-Wesley, Reading, Massachusetts.

Wille, E. (1989) *Triggers for Change*, Ashridge Management Research Group, Berkhamsted.

Wright, M. and Rhodes, D. (1985) *Managing IT: Exploring Information Systems for Effective Management*, Frances Pinter, London.

Index